Taxpayers' advocate William L. Raby is one of approximately seventy-five certified public accountants ever licensed to practice before the U.S. Tax Court as a result of passing its examination for admission to practice.

A partner in the national CPA firm of Laventhol, Krekstein, Horwath, & Horwath, Mr. Raby also teaches, lectures, is an editor of a professional journal, and writes a syndicated newspaper column, "The Reluctant Taxpayer," which is distributed all over the country by the Los Angeles Times Syndicate.

An earlier book received major critical acclaim and has been used as text material by more than forty of the nation's leading colleges and universities.

Carl Riblet, Jr., is a news professional who guided Mr. Raby's tax column from its infancy to national prominence with the Los Angeles Times Syndicate.

For many years, between assignments from major Eastern newspapers, Mr. Riblet wrote radio dramas, including Kraft Theater musicals and **The Voice of the Underground,** and was a TV newscaster on one of ABC's southwest outlets. He has traveled through Europe and South America, and covered the Israeli-Arab war from Tel Aviv in 1956. Currently he lectures on the subject of newspaper writing and editing and writes two nationally syndicated features for the Los Angeles Times Syndicate.

THE
RELUCTANT
TAXPAYER

THE
RELUCTANT
TAXPAYER

by William L. Raby
and
Carl Riblet, Jr.

COWLES BOOK COMPANY, INC.
NEW YORK

Copyright 1970 by William L. Raby and Carl Riblet, Jr.

SBN 402-12251-8

Library of Congress Catalog Card Number 76-90062

Cowles Book Company, Inc.
A subsidiary of Cowles Communications, Inc.

Published simultaneously in Canada by

General Publishing Company, Ltd., 30 Lesmill Road,
Don Mills, Toronto, Ontario

Printed in the United States of America

First Edition

To our friend
JACOB SMITH
who started it all

Contents

Preface

That honest taxpayers don't always get a square deal from the U.S. Treasury Department's tax collectors has been proved in the many thousands of quiet decisions made by the courts against actions and rulings of the Internal Revenue Service.

It is strange that this is so, because the service has an ever ready official answer to criticism. It goes like this: "The Internal Revenue Service does not want to collect one penny of tax to which it is not entitled."

The difference between what the tax collectors say and what they do may exist because most taxpayers don't fully understand their rights under the tax laws.

This book will help those who may wish to compel the IRS to do what it says it wants to do: keep its hands off money that is not legitimately owed to the government for taxes.

In these pages we do not attempt to expose IRS, and we do not lay on unduly with the whip of criticism. Our purpose is to show how a taxpayer can meet an IRS challenge of his income tax return. Anybody who examines the processes used to determine and collect tax deficiencies may emerge from the task with some conclusions on what can be done to improve those processes. We have set forth some ideas on the matter, and the reader will find them under the title of "Recommendations" in the last chapter.

Much of the basic text of this book had its origin in research for the nationally syndicated newspaper column by William L. Raby under the same title, The Reluctant Taxpayer.

Part of chapter 21 appeared in an article in *Taxes: The Tax Maga-*

zine of April, 1968, and is used herein with permission from the magazine and from Dr. Ralph Ireland, co-author with Mr. Raby of that article.

Names of all people and organizations involved in specific tax cases mentioned in this book have been changed to avoid embarrassment to many honest taxpayers.

Wherever necessary, in order to achieve clarity, we have taken small liberties with details of actual events. However, nothing essential to the tax points involved has been altered.

THE AUTHORS

Phoenix and Tucson, Arizona
June, 1969

CHAPTER ONE

The Taxpayer's Position

*The first great commandment is,
don't let them scare you.*

—Elmer Davis
in *But We Were Born Free*

If you have filed your federal income tax return and have truthfully reported all your income and taken only the deductions that Congress, when it wrote the tax law, intended you to take, then you do not need to fear the awful power of the U. S. Treasury Department's tax collection bureau, the Internal Revenue Service.

Once you have filed an honest return and paid the tax that you really owe, you have the strength of a grizzly bear. If an agent of the IRS calls you in for an audit and seems bent on clipping you for additional taxes, don't let him frighten you. Don't let him coerce you into signing papers that may work against your best interests as an honest taxpayer. Nobody in IRS has the legal right to make you sign anything but your tax return.

In dealing with revenue agents, always keep in mind the strength you possess because you are honest. You can resist any action of the tax bureau and its agents that may try to take additional tax dollars from you, provided you conduct your protest fight properly and legally. And, if you do make a legal protest, it may be because yours is one of those cases in which you have discovered that, while the official attitude toward taxpayers may be one thing—what the tax collectors call "fair treatment"—the treatment of specific taxpayers is frequently another thing.

In the vast majority of tax audits, IRS is possibly as fair as can be expected under the existing complex tax laws. Even so, the administrative structure of the tax collection bureau is such that often there is little the tax people at the lower levels can do to help you, even if they are so inclined. You may have to appeal the decision of the revenue agent, or the office auditor, to a higher level within IRS before its rules allow tax officials to use their own judgment in settling your case. Sometimes, taxpayers have only one recourse, and that is to go to court. When they do, it is wise to remember that the Internal Revenue Service may elect to go from one court to another in an attempt to secure a judgment in its favor in a particular tax controversy.

Forty years ago, back in the days when there were only sixteen major league baseball teams, a team in the National League had to fight the tax bureau on the issue of whether the ball club, in computing its corporate income tax, could charge off as an expense that year's cost of purchased player contracts. IRS argued that the contracts had value for years hence, and therefore all the cost could not be an expense of that one year.

The team managed to bring IRS to court, and there the baseball club contended that the value of a player contract for the years after its purchase was much too indefinite to justify spreading the cost. A player could not, it was true, continue in professional baseball except as the team's management might permit, but a player could quit baseball if he wished to go into some other venture. The IRS lost the case in the Tax Court, then lost again on appeal in the Circuit Court of Appeals.

The next year, the IRS went after a minor league club of the American Association. Again, the IRS lost in the Tax Court and on appeal. In 1935, IRS announced that it would allow baseball teams to deduct the cost of buying player contracts in the year in which the contracts were purchased.

Thirty-two years went by, and Congress reenacted the provisions of the tax law several times. The statute remained unchanged on the point covering baseball contracts.

Late in 1967, however, the tax bureau announced it would no longer follow the court decisions in these two cases, and henceforth the cost of purchasing a player contract must be charged to expenses over the useful life of the contract itself.

Why had the IRS changed its mind after all those years? Perhaps it had seen a possibility of upsetting the rule established by the two cases when, in a case involving the liquidation of a team in the Pacific Coast League, a Tax Court judge had said: "There may be some question regarding the practice of deducting in a single year the cost of the baseball player contracts, since the relevant contracts may have had a more than one-year useful life."

IRS often argues that it is interested only in the "right," and it says the reason it fights tax cases in the courts is to clarify the law. In the baseball case, though, the rule had been clearly established over a quarter century. What IRS, an administrative, not a legislative, agency was actually trying to do was to repeal the old rule and enact a new one without benefit of Congress.

As we have stated, taxpayers sometimes have to go to court to keep IRS in balance. The following pages will attempt to show them how to stand up to the Internal Revenue Service in an honest argument.

CHAPTER TWO

What's Sauce for the Goose

Anybody who says that our system of levying and collecting income taxes is painless has got to be an apologist on the Internal Revenue Service's executive staff or an astonished taxpayer who had something left after April 15th.

—"Isn't It the Truth!"
in the *Arizona Daily Star*

It is dishonest for a taxpayer to cheat the government out of taxes he really owes. No moral person would argue otherwise. It is equally dishonest for the Internal Revenue Service to try to collect taxes that are not really owed. Yet IRS often tries to force taxpayers to pay taxes they do not owe, and then buttresses its demands with unreasonable or unfair acts by its many agents.

In thousands of cases that have gone to court because the taxpayers involved didn't believe that the tax collectors had been fair, IRS has often been held to be acting contrary to law and precedent and has, accordingly, been the loser. And the cases that get to court are only a few of the many involving disagreement. In the category of deductions, for example, the tax people have made small taxpayers surrender millions of dollars they did not really owe.

This is one example of how such a miscarriage of the law can come about:

Prior to 1967, although IRS had been permitting taxpayers to deduct as medical expenses the premiums on medical insurance that covered doctor and hospital bills, it would not allow deductions for premiums on policies that provided, among other things, disability payments for loss of a leg or arm, or monthly payments while the insured taxpayer was recuperating from an accident.

The courts, on the other hand, had said many times that such accident and disability premiums were deductible as medical expenses.

IRS didn't like the court rulings and asked Congress to change the tax law. Congress did change the law in 1965 so that insured taxpayers could not deduct accident and disability premiums, as the courts had said they could. An important point to note here is that, by the very act of going to Congress, IRS was admitting that its interpretation of the law had been incorrect, that the disallowed deduction should, indeed, have been allowed.

Congress stipulated that the requested change take place for 1967 and subsequent years. However, from 1965 through 1966 and part of 1967, IRS continued to deny taxpayers their rights as stipulated by the courts. Premiums on disability and accident policies were disallowed as income tax deductions in those years until IRS was pressured by enough knowledgeable people to desist and admit that taxpayers had a right to such deductions and could, therefore, take them for the year 1966.

The public announcement of the new ruling was not made in time for millions of taxpayers to take account of it in their returns for 1966. It was made on May 17, 1967, one month after the filing deadline for 1966!

Some taxpayers, however, who had paid accident or disability premiums during 1966 and who, for one reason or another, had not succeeded in deducting them, succeeded in preventing IRS from getting away with such a fast shuffle. When they learned of the tardy announcement, they went to the nearest IRS office, asked for Form 843, and used it to file a claim for a refund of the tax money that IRS should *not* have collected in the first place—*plus interest at 6 percent.*

The IRS says it takes pride in the almost total acceptance by American taxpayers of the practice of paying taxes without having to stand up and fight against inequities and unfairness. A statement in the summer of 1967 by the then acting director for IRS in Arizona, Herbert B. Mosher, emphasized the tax men's pride in that accomplishment. He said: "IRS now has 97 percent taxpayer compliance."

The key word in that statement is "compliance." It can mean two things. If a person complies with a polite request in a polite manner, it can mean that he acts favorably. It also can mean that he does what he is told to do because he has no other recourse, or because he is afraid to resist even if the request is out of order or represents a wrongful use of power.

The commissioner of internal revenue himself encourages taxpayers to fight when they think they are right and IRS is wrong. In the letter that accompanied the mailing of 1967 tax return forms, the then commissioner, Sheldon S. Cohen, admitted that ". . . it is perhaps inevitable that in an organization of 60,000 people administering a complex law, occasional missteps will occur and some differences will arise. Our system contemplates this and has a number of built-in safeguards, including avenues of appeal for all taxpayers, large and small. I hope taxpayers will use these opportunities to resolve any controversies. . . . We welcome comments, suggestions, even criticisms. . . ."

Some IRS agents, contrary to the aforementioned quoted official policy, use many clever ways to induce "troublesome" taxpayers to comply. Their greatest power over the taxpayer lies in his lack of knowledge of his basic rights. The rules under which IRS operates are spelled out on the statute books, and the IRS interpretation of those rules can be appealed to the courts if it seems right and necessary to appeal. The taxpayer who has carried his fight with IRS into court can tell you that it doesn't do much good to fight with the tax collectors when you become emotional and don't know the procedures to follow.

Those who react to revenue agents by shouting, by refusing to cooperate when cooperation is clearly indicated, by failing to answer letters, by failing to argue effectively with IRS, are hurting only themselves. This is not to say that there aren't times when it pays to be loud and firm, but in such cases your behavior should be calculated—an anger that is designed to produce a result rather than a frustrated raging that shreds your own emotions without denting the armor of the IRS agent who is the target of your rage.

One way of coping with IRS is to hire a tax lawyer or tax accountant. Their fees range upward from a minimum of $20 an hour. However, you can handle your own tax dealings with IRS, without paying for advice, if you use reasonable intelligence and take the time and trouble to become acquainted with the procedures you must follow. Before hiring a lawyer, you should be reasonably certain that you cannot arrange a fair settlement on your own in the event you are called into the tax office for audit or consultation over tax returns. Many individuals who fall into the net of the questioning agents sign various pieces of papers handed them by the agents. Most of the time, the taxpayer is well advised to sign. Too often, however, he gives up too soon. Take this example:

When the Internal Revenue Service had finished auditing a Seattle store owner's tax return, the agent asked the merchant to sign a Form 870, consenting to the assessment of an additional $10,000 of income tax. He signed the form, but it later developed he hadn't fully understood what he was signing. The bookkeeper who had prepared the store owner's tax return had said that, although the owner didn't understand why the $10,000 deficiency was being proposed, the revenue agent probably knew what he was doing.

About two weeks later, while chatting with a customer who was a lawyer, the merchant mentioned his tax headache. So far as he could tell, he said, it had all come about because he cashed checks for his customers. Every Thursday, he would go down to the bank and draw out a substantial sum of cash to use in cashing checks on Friday. Every Saturday morning he would deposit into the bank that same amount in checks, plus his daily sales receipts. The revenue agent had charged that the bank deposits all represented sales, and the tax deficiency appeared to be based upon that fact.

The lawyer declared that the agent's interpretation was erroneous and unfair. When he telephoned the revenue agent, he was informed it was too late to do anything; the case was closed, a waiver had already been signed by the store owner, and the only recourse left him was to pay the tax when the bill came in, then bring a refund claim against the government. The lawyer immediately sent a notice, signed by the taxpayer, to the district director of internal revenue, notifying the director that the waiver was being withdrawn.

"That waiver form is ineffective until accepted by the government," the lawyer explained to the merchant. "Therefore, you can withdraw it at any time prior to acceptance."

However, the IRS people were stubborn. Ten days after the notice of withdrawal had been mailed, the taxpayer received a computation of the tax deficiency, accompanied by a statement that he had agreed to pay it and informing him that he would receive a bill in a few days.

The lawyer consulted with the people in the local IRS office and was told that the matter was out of their hands. He talked to officials in the district office, with the result that he sensed he was getting a runaround. He went to see the district director personally. After reviewing the dates of the waiver, the notice of withdrawal, and the final acceptance of the waiver, the district director agreed with the lawyer that the store owner should still have the right to contest the validity of the tax before having to pay it. This the store owner did. And he won.

Although the highest officials of IRS have often been quoted as insisting that agents do not use threats of taking cash and property away from embattled taxpayers if they won't sign waivers, that has not always been the way it works out in practice. Witness what happened to a newspaperman in Chicago who was told by a low-ranking tax collection agent that if he didn't sign a waiver of the statute of limitations IRS would take his property. The taxpayer, who had been fighting a tax claim for several years, reluctantly signed the waiver. He believed the agent could cause him to lose his property to the U.S. Treasury. His property was his home.

Meanwhile, the newspaperman had been making regular monthly payments of $75 on the claimed assessment. The agent, to whom the payments were addressed, promised to go along with the procedure. Then one day a lien was slapped on the taxpayer's salary. Enraged, he phoned the agent. "Why did you levy against my salary? I was paying IRS the sum agreed upon and you promised to go along with it."

This is the answer given over the telephone by the agent: "You said your wife was sick and living in your house in Arizona. I called your hotel here and they said you and your wife had checked out. I figured you were shacked up with a broad."

The newspaperman was appalled. "That was my wife! She was

visiting me in Chicago as she often does, whenever her health permits and we can afford it. Do you mean to tell me that I have to clear it with you to come and go as I please? And what if I were shacked up, as you call it? Is my sex life any business of yours?"

The agent had no reply that was intelligible.

The ending to that case is interesting. After eight years of fighting the assessment, after suffering indignity and insult from IRS agents, the newspaperman was directed by a certified public accountant to a former Justice Department tax lawyer. The lawyer wrote a number of letters to IRS, pointing out that no valid claim existed. IRS answered none of the letters. Finally, the lawyer wrote to IRS that the newspaperman was about to take the case to court. Soon after, the taxpayer received a full refund for the amount he had paid on the claim. On one cold day in December he received five checks from IRS totaling more than $5,000, including interest. The case was closed.

In the opinion of the tax advisers and the lawyer, IRS paid the refund in order to stay out of court. If the taxpayer had succeeded in getting the case before a judge, it is highly probable he would have won, and then many other taxpayers who had been similarly and wrongly assessed would demand and get refunds in their own cases.

When a taxpayer signs a paper of agreement with IRS, he usually is agreeing to pay a tax deficiency. If he really doesn't owe the money and will have to strap himself to pay it, a most grievous offense has been committed against him by a government bureau that is supposed to be serving him.

Unfortunately, if you should go to the trouble of taking IRS into court, nobody will help you unless you can afford to pay for it. And if you lose, you will pay the tax deficiency and your costs. If you win, you will still pay your costs.

Can anybody logically insist that such a system is fair?

Fair or not, you can oppose the IRS and go to court. Once there, you, as a taxpayer of the United States, are just as important in the eyes of the judge as are all of the huge and still growing tax collection offices put together.

CHAPTER THREE

The People Who Work for IRS

On the whole we have been taking our lumps stoically, knowing full well that this is the lot of the tax collector. Indeed, the Bible offers cases of tax collectors being stoned to death, so in this light we are not doing too badly.

—Sheldon S. Cohen
Commissioner of Internal Revenue in 1965

There are many different jobs in the Internal Revenue Service, but the IRS people the public sees most often are the auditing agents, who seek more taxes from you, and the collection agents, who rake it in, sometimes with difficulty.

The employees who handle the collection of taxes are not much different from bill collectors working for a collection agency, a small loan company, a large department store, or any company dealing with consumers who run up bills and are slow in paying or try not to pay at all. They are used to being lied to, they are expert at chasing taxpayers who change addresses, and they know how to handle people who conceal assets.

The agents in the IRS collection division approach taxpayers from the standpoint of getting the money, using whatever methods may be most effective, and sometimes they can be pretty nasty about it.

A man named Franks who owned a laundry-dry cleaning establishment in California is today utterly convinced that the IRS has a policy of tricking taxpayers. This is what happened to him:

At the time his unhappy experience began, he was making payments to the tax bureau of $300 a month on back taxes. He owed the money, he wanted to pay it, and he had high hopes of paying it off sooner than he had at first estimated because he had a bidding chance to get a laundry and dry cleaning contract with the local Air Force base. If he got the contract, he would be compelled to hire more workers and purchase more supplies. Before he entered his bid to the Air Force, he went to see the IRS collection people. He asked whether he could skip the $300 payment for one month if he got the contract, and then pay $600 the following month. The $300 "loan" would help him finance the contract. The IRS told him to go ahead and get the new business.

He bid on the contract and won it. At the end of the first month he sent a bill for $2,800 to the Air Force. He needed the money to pay his employees and his higher bills—including the $600 he had promised to pay the IRS. But the Air Force had no money for him.

The IRS had seized all of the $2,800 due him from the Air Force.

Franks's business went into receivership. Without operating capital, the receivers could not carry out the Air Force contract. The Air Force placed the work elsewhere. Then the IRS and the Air Force each sued the ex-laundryman—IRS in the bankruptcy court for the balance of back taxes owed, and the Air Force in the same court claiming "damages" caused the base by the default on the laundry and dry cleaning contract.

The ex-laundryman explained to the bankruptcy court that the IRS had assured him he could safely go ahead with the contract, only to put him out of business when he did so. He said the Air Force was now suing him for $5,000 damages that *he* was charged with causing the government when the fault all lay with another arm of the government—the IRS.

The judge was sympathetic but nevertheless ordered Franks to pay both IRS and the Air Force on the grounds that IRS agents and collection people cannot bind the government by what they agree to do and cannot be sued for what they do. In other words—"the King can do no wrong." And the word *king* is short for Internal Revenue Service.

The ordinarily meek and patient taxpayer who has never had a session with IRS may explode in greater outrage over the experience of Franks, the laundry operator, than do people who deal all the time with IRS procedures and fight IRS politicies. The uninformed often ask the question: "What right does the tax bureau have to lie to tax-payers, seize their property, garnishee their wages, and destroy their reputations?"

The answer is: almost unlimited right, according to the courts. An example is the case of a discotheque owner who was told by an IRS agent that his place of entertainment would be closed by IRS just before the lucrative Christmas and New Year's Day holiday period unless he turned over to the government some valuable securities as assurance that he would pay back taxes the tax collector said he owed. Accordingly, rather than sacrifice potential income during the Christmas season, he put up the securities as bond. Promptly after the holidays he sued the government for return of the securities on grounds that he gave them to IRS only as "the result of illegal threats and coercion."

The U. S. District Court judge disappointed the discotheque owner, explaining: "The activity asserted as coercion was the statement by the revenue agent that unless the tax was paid promptly the night club would be closed by IRS before the holiday. This proposed action may have been rather harsh treatment, but to have done it would not have been a violation of the law. It was not an illegal threat or an illegal act of coercion for the revenue agent to threaten to do what the law gave him a right to do."

The collection of taxes is not a process of punishment and tax delinquency is not a crime. When the IRS uses its good business sense, which it often does, tax collection is made easier and more beneficial to both the government and the honest but delinquent taxpayer.

A Pennsylvania couple in their fifties owed $20,000 in taxes as the by-product of a bad business deal. They were naturally worried about what IRS would do to them if they didn't pay up soon. Their only asset was some undeveloped real estate near a growing city.

The IRS filed a lien against the land and started proceedings to sell it. The couple estimated that a forced sale for cash would bring only $7,000. They would still owe $13,000 to IRS after the sale. But if the land could be sold in small chunks with low down payments, it might be possible to get $50,000 for it.

Would IRS go along with such a plan? If IRS did, it would have a chance to get all its money, and the couple would have a chance to salvage a cushion for their old age.

The couple's lawyer persuaded an IRS collection man to recommend a way that would protect the IRS and yet offer the couple a chance.

"My boss probably won't buy this," cautioned the agent. But after a number of phone calls and conferences, the plan was accepted.

The land went into trust and was listed for sale with a real estate broker. All the money received from sales went to the IRS. It took five years, but IRS ultimately got the $20,000 owed for taxes, plus interest. The trust company got paid, the real estate firm got paid, the lawyer's fee got paid, and the couple had an old age stake of $30,000.

We would call that creative collection. It takes something extra to get the collection job done while treating people decently and with good feeling and business sense, and to keep promises and *implied* promises made to taxpayers in trouble.

Promises that aren't made in writing are often forgotten in fact or on purpose. A taxpayer named Harrington, who was in deep trouble with the revenue bureau because he hadn't reported all of his income, learned that a taxpayer can't trust every statement made to him by agents of the IRS.

Harrington's lawyer had advised him to file amended tax returns and to pay as much as he could of the tax and interest that were due. This he had done. The balance he still owed was $15,000. The IRS filed a tax lien aaginst his property for that amount.

The lawyer then explained to the head of the IRS collection division that a forced sale of the taxpayer's property would produce only $6,000. However, if Harrington's bank could be assured that no fraud penalty would be asserted, it would lend him the $15,000 he needed to pay IRS.

"I'll check with Washington and let you know," said the collection supervisor.

A few weeks later, assured by IRS that word had come from Washington that no fraud penalty would be imposed, the lawyer negotiated a bank loan for Harrington, who then paid the $15,000 to IRS. The tax lien was removed.

Nearly four years later, IRS demanded a $15,000 fraud penalty from Harrington. "You can't do that," Harrington said. "We had an agreement."

Harrington, however, was no longer dealing with the collection division. The IRS lawyer now handling the case cared not a whit about any oral agreements that might have been made with somebody else. Harrington had to pay.

The moral here is obvious: what you say may be used against you by IRS, but what its agents say doesn't mean a thing unless they say it on paper.

At the other end of the spectrum from the collection people, there is the Internal Revenue agent who is an accountant, with a standing much like any other professional man in his community. He works somewhat independently. Normally, he audits only the returns of business firms and taxpayers who have substantial amounts of investment income. He prides himself on maintaining an objective attitude and in trying to work out controversies to a reasonable result.

The office auditors usually have less experience than the accountant auditor. They handle a heavy volume of tax returns of individual taxpayers, and they deal in small amounts of money. They don't go to you; you come to them. They are more or less unaware of the nuances of the tax law. In order to wade through the heavy volume of work assigned them, they are often arbitrary in their determinations of tax liabilities. Many of them, however, are quite as human as the two IRS office auditors who helped an honest Milwaukee milkman with five children who had entered his twelve-year-old nephew as a dependent on his income tax return.

It didn't matter whether the milkman's five dependent children earned a lot or a little in a year, since they were all under nineteen, but a dependent who is not a child of the taxpayer cannot, regardless of age, be taken as an exemption on a tax return if the child earns more than $600. The milkman's nephew had earned $607 that year.

The IRS office auditor kindly and thoughtfully spelled out the facts to the milkman. He suggested: "Couldn't we just change the figure and put down $595 as the boy's earnings?"

The nephew had kept a record of his earnings, which really totaled $607, the milkman said. Besides, how could he raise his kids to be honest if he set them an example by lying on his tax return? If the $600 exemption rule was the law, then he would pay the additional $90 of tax called for by the law.

The auditor called in a colleague. He, too, was thoughtful. His idea was to ease the law a bit. Perhaps the milkman had actually adopted the boy, in which case the nephew would be treated as a son for tax purposes and it wouldn't matter how much the boy earned. No, the milkman hadn't adopted him. The boy's father was alive, in a mental hospital.

The examiner asked if possibly the boy had had some expense in connection with his paper route. Tire repairs? Bike license? Anything? The milkman thought there had been some expenses that came to about $15. The IRS man thereupon altered the tax return to show the boy's earnings as $592, instead of $607. He shook hands with the Milwaukee milkman and wished him good fortune. Three men were happy, the milkman, the auditor, and the examiner, who said, "Anybody with five kids who takes in a sixth and tries to raise them on what that guy earns is entitled to a dependency deduction, even though the law has to be bent a little to do it."

Then there are the IRS *special agents,* the Dick Tracys of the service, whose job it is to investigate situations that may constitute fraud. And right here take this warning: If ever an IRS special agent is involved with you in a tax situation, you should be aware of the fact that you are under investigation for possible criminal prosecution. Conduct yourself accordingly. Oftentimes, the special agent will attempt to conceal his identity as an investigator of possible tax crime, or he may not inform the taxpayer of the implication that springs from his position as a special agent. A taxpayer in Nebraska learned, two years after he had bought 100 percent of the stock of an ice cream manufacturing company, how such agents sometimes operate.

One day two IRS employees came to his office. They said they were investigating the tax returns of the former owner. They didn't tell him they were special agents and that their sole job was to investigate tax fraud. They didn't tell him the most important fact—that they were investigating his own tax returns and trying to gather evidence of fraud against him.

When the Nebraskan finally learned what was going on, that he was suspect, he sent his lawyer to court to get an order prohibiting the IRS from using the evidence the agents had obtained by going over his books and records.

The judge held that the taxpayer had been wronged: "All evidence direct and indirect, written and verbal, relating to the tax matters of plaintiff obtained by defendants [the IRS employees] was obtained by an unlawful scheme of fraud and deception in violation of the Fourth Amendment of the Constitution of the United States; the evidence of such fraud is clear and unequivocal." The judge decreed that none of the evidence so obtained could be used against the taxpayer.

Now, those two IRS employees no doubt considered themselves to be decent and hardworking family men. Somehow, however, they had come to think they owed no duty to deal honestly with a taxpayer under suspicion of tax fraud.

The treatment of taxpayers is more sophisticated and sometimes more fair higher up the ladder in IRS, where you may run into supervisors, assistant district directors, district directors, and a host of other officials. Fortunately, some of the undesirable, arbitrary decisions that are made at the lower levels can be remedied if a complaint is made to the proper official at a higher level.

A Wichita woman whose employer was served with a notice that IRS was garnisheeing her wages discovered that it paid to go higher. The tax claim against her was already being checked into by her accountant, and it seemed quite possible that the IRS determination was in error.

The people in the IRS Collection Division, whose sole job it is to collect the tax that the piece of paper says is due, were indifferent to the woman's plea that she be given more time so she could have the case fully checked. Her accountant went to the assistant district director for the local district, explained the facts, and asked for help. The tax official agreed that the request for more time was valid. He had the garnishee order removed and the woman was again able to draw her paychecks freely.

The basic philosophy of coping with an IRS agent is to get done with whatever audit or question has been raised with as little inconvenience to yourself as possible, and also with as little additional tax to pay as possible. Of course, the ideal would be a situation where the revenue agent offered you a refund after he finished his examination. Actually, that does happen about seven percent of the time. In order to deal effectively with the revenue agent—and by revenue agent we mean anyone in the Internal Revenue Service who communicates with you, whether by mail or otherwise—you must understand the language he talks and his point of view.

The tax bureau deals heavily in averages. If your medical expenses exceed a "reasonable" amount for your level of income, there is a good chance that IRS will want to know why. The question may offend you, but you are only hurting yourself if you tell the revenue agent something like "it's none of your damn business what my medical problems are."

If you can explain the medical expenses with canceled checks and receipted bills, by all means do so. However, if you should be dealing with a revenue agent who does not accept reasonable explanations and is truculent in his demands for proof, then you must have some idea of when to stop talking to him and start being uncooperative.

Similarly, if you get notices generated by the IRS computer system, you will not help your case by tossing them in a wastebasket. By giving such cavalier treatment to one too many of those notices, you may find that the IRS has slapped a levy against your bank account or is trying to garnishee your salary check. Levies and garnishments are areas in which, under present law, there is little you can do to punish IRS for whatever embarrassment it may have caused you. As a result, it is unwise to take the position that you are not going to pay any attention to "silly" computer notices. Instead, try to understand what the question is and try to give a responsive answer. You can combat a computer best by adopting its own peculiar way of thinking, if one story that has swept across the country can be believed.

A taxpayer received several notices that said liens would be slapped against his property if he didn't pay the balance of his tax due. Each computer notice gave the amount due as $0.00. Letters and phone calls to the computer center didn't stop the notices from coming to the taxpayer. Then he was inspired. He made out a check in the amount of $0.00 and sent it to the Internal Revenue Service. Nothing was ever heard again from the computer.

Why do people become agents of the Internal Revenue Service? Why do they resign? While there is obviously no all-conclusive answer to these questions, there is an interesting story told by one former revenue agent—whom we can call Hector—about why he worked for IRS, and why he left the bureau.

When Hector was graduated from college with an accounting major, he was attracted by recruiting literature that described job opportunities in the IRS. His grades weren't quite good enough to get job offers from the large CPA firms, but the starting pay with IRS wasn't bad. So he went with the tax people, where he had good training and satisfying work.

He was polite to the people he encountered, and he enjoyed his associations with attorneys and accountants as well as with taxpayers generally. When he worked on a tax audit, he usually came up with deficiencies. On the average, these more than justified the time that he put in on the particular returns. He even developed an instinct for spotting returns that did not justify spending much time on. His supervisors thought of him as one of the most productive agents in his office. His future in IRS was bright.

One day, Hector visited a taxpayer whose return he was auditing and discussed with him the deficiency he was proposing to slap on him. The taxpayer was quite upset about the agent's proposal. If he had to pay the large amount being discussed, he would be bankrupted, and he protested that he had acted in the tax matter with the best legal and accounting advice available in the city. The agent said that their meeting was being held only to discuss the proposed deficiency, and that the taxpayer had many appeal rights if he disagreed. He arranged an appointment with the taxpayer for the following week.

The taxpayer failed to show up for the appointment. Hector telephoned his home. When he asked for the man, the request evoked sounds of grief from a woman, who told him that the taxpayer had been buried two days before. She was his widow.

"When did he die?" Hector asked.

The widow told him both the date and the time of death—the day of the agent's interview with the taxpayer, barely a few minutes after Hector had left his office.

A few weeks later, Hector had a conference with the taxpayer's attorney, who convinced him that the proposed deficiency was incorrect and should be reduced to a fraction of the amount the agent had proposed as reasonable to the now dead taxpayer.

About then, Hector's conscience began to bother him. Had he killed the man by making the stiff proposal for a huge tax deficiency? Then he began to consider the possible effect of other tax problems he had settled so efficiently with other taxpayers.

Six months later, Hector found himself under so much official criticism for wasting time and for a drop-off in his productivity, while also suffering grave doubts about his own role in the tax collectors' world, that he resigned from IRS and opened an office to help taxpayers.

Although most agents may be indifferent to the troubles and heartaches they all too often dispense to taxpayers, it's a horse of a different color when an IRS agent, himself also a taxpayer, chokes at paying taxes he doesn't think are legitimately owing.

One young agent named Will urgently wanted to be a better tax expert. He had gone to law school at night and in four years acquired a law degree. On his income tax return he deducted the expense of his law studies.

"Not deductible," ruled a brother agent who audited the return. "Not an ordinary expense, since most revenue agents—including me—don't go to law school. Not a necessary expense since a law degree was hardly required for you to maintain your position."

The new lawyer had the logical idea that the law course had sharpened the skills he needed as a revenue agent, that if he had intended to practice law he would have resigned from IRS to do so. He explained this to the auditing agent.

The brother agent was cold to the argument and demanded that he pay. But Will was tough. He carried the case into court, and there he won the deduction on the basis that his law studies were, of course, helpful to his work as a revenue agent.

Then, having won his first law case, Will, the lawyer-agent, resigned from IRS and went into practice as a tax lawyer. With his solid experience as a revenue agent, he ought to find a measure of prosperity as he tangles with the many IRS people who subscribe to the erroneous idea that, whenever one taxpayer pays a dollar less than the maximum amount IRS can extract from him, all the other taxpayers of the United States have been cheated out of that dollar.

In state property taxation, it does work out that way. If one taxpayer in a school district, for example, has the assessed valuation of his property set at a lower figure than it should be, all the other taxpayers in that district must pay more tax by the amount he has underpaid, because the tax rate is set by dividing the total amount of tax revenue to be raised by the total assessed valuation of all the property against which the tax is to be levied.

The national government does not set the federal income tax rates in order to raise a specific amount of revenue. Nor does anybody any longer seem to maintain seriously that the federal budget should be in balance. In fact, many reputable economists think that the national economy is benefited more when taxes are cut than when they are raised.

This being the case, every dollar of income the taxpayer can keep from having to send to Washington, and can spend on himself, will actually provide that much more spending power to be poured into the local economy, and that much more stimulus to local business growth and expansion.

Thus, contrary to the basic folklore of IRS economics, the taxpayer who pays the minimum amount of tax that he is required to pay under the law is probably helping the economic growth and progress of both the nation and his local community when he puts the money into local circulation. On the other hand, the revenue agent who unfairly, or illegally, deprives the taxpayer of dollars that the taxpayer would spend locally is acting as a drag or deterrent to economic growth and progress.

If IRS were to adopt the economic philosphy that governs most of the federal government's other fiscal activity these days, its people would be resolving doubts in *favor* of the taxpayer, not against him, with the objective not of collecting the maximum amount of tax, but of collecting the minimum amount consistent with a reasonable and orderly administration of the federal tax law.

CHAPTER FOUR

You and the IRS Agent

To suppose that tax officers can be encountered carelessly and addressed frankly is an elementary error, which may create hardship and expense for the unwary and the innocent.

—Oliver Stanley
in *The Sunday Times*, London, 1967

A mistake often made by a taxpayer in dealing with the Internal Revenue Service is to let down his guard and assume that a smiling revenue agent is his friend. You can be sure he isn't. What he feels about you most likely is that there is a better than even chance you owe more taxes than you have paid. His bosses have often reminded him at refresher workshops for agents that about 55 percent of tax returns audited turn up more taxes due—an average of $550 more tax per individual involved.

The agent wants something from you if your return is under audit—enough information to write a report that will make him look good. He is thinking first of himself, and then of you. He wants to be able to prove to his bosses in IRS that he did a good job, that he saw evidence covering the key items in your tax return.

If you are a salesman, the agent may ask you to bring in records of auto mileage, motel receipts, and a pocket diary he thinks you may have covering your meals and entertainment expense.

But what if you refuse to bring in your records? What will happen if you don't tell the tax collector anything at all? Some people do stand silent. These are the things the tax man can do: He can try to get the information elsewhere—from your bank, your employer, your business associates; he can arbitrarily determine a tax deficiency, which you will have to prove wrong; or he can issue a formal summons demanding that you appear at a certain time and place, and possibly with certain records, to answer his questions. If you don't obey the summons, then he can ask the U. S. District Court to order you to obey. If you don't obey the court's order, you can be fined or imprisoned for contempt of court.

One IRS agent so antagonized an Iowa farmer and his wife whose return he was auditing that, after several visits, they refused to give him any more of their records. The agent then issued a summons to their bank and obtained, along with other information, a record of the total deposits they had made for the years in question.

He next issued a summons to the two taxpayers. They appeared at the requested time and place, but again they refused to produce their records. The thoroughly incensed agent had no power to levy fines or send them to jail, so he taxed as additional income the total amount of the bank deposits the couple had made for the two years, plus a 5 percent negligence penalty, even though he knew that not all the deposits were, in fact, income. His thought must have been that, by proposing to tax everything deposited in the bank account as income, the farmer and his wife would be forced to produce the records he wanted in order to prove it wasn't all income.

The two Iowans didn't react the way most taxpayers do under similar circumstances. They didn't tell all, and show all, and do all, that the revenue agent demanded. Instead, they protested the arbitrary assessment, and the lawyers for the IRS agreed with them that the assessment was improper because it was arbitrary. The lawyers sent the case back to the agent for further auditing. The stubborn man then issued another summons ordering the farm couple to produce the same records he had originally sought. When they didn't produce the records, the IRS agent went to the U. S. District Court to obtain an order that they produce the records. But the court didn't look with much favor upon that tax collector.

Said the judge: "It is the opinion of this court that the conduct of the Internal Revenue Service with regard to this taxpayer for the years in question constitutes an attempt to abuse the processes of this court. . . ."

The Iowa husband and wife did not have to produce the records.

If you do as most people do, and tell an agent as much as you can of what he wants to know, he may want to get your signature on a piece of paper that says you agree you owe an added tax.

Don't sign it!

Do not sign it unless you are sure you really owe the tax and are prepared to pay it. The agent wants that little agreement because it helps him to get "brownie points" from the boss for obtaining what the powers at IRS call "taxpayer cooperation." He may suggest that if you sign the agreement you will save some interest on the added tax. If he does, he is giving you a snow job. The amount of interest you would save is peanuts compared to the tax the signed agreement can and perhaps will cost you. The agent is holding out on you if he doesn't tell you that the innocent-looking agreement cancels your right to argue over the added tax before paying it.

One victim of such a maneuver was a divorcee who believed the amounts she was receiving from her ex-husband were child support payments, not alimony, and thus were exempt from federal income tax. A revenue agent who audited her ex-husband's return discovered that she had filed no return. He asked the ex-wife to sign a Form 1040 income tax return, which he filled out for her, and also to sign a Form 870 waiver agreement.

The divorcee asked the agent if she should discuss this with her attorney or with a certified public accountant before signing it. The tax man advised her that signing the tax return form and the waiver were just perfunctory actions, and that when she got the notice from IRS she could take the matter up with her lawyer or her accountant.

What she got next from IRS was a statement of tax due that had to be paid within ten days.

When questioned by the woman's accountant—a *CPA*—the revenue agent said all he had told the ex-wife was that she could "still take the matter up," and by that he had meant she could file a refund claim and bring a court action if the claim was denied by IRS.

The amount was too small to warrant the expense of going to court, so the divorcee was effectively deprived of an opportunity to argue as to whether she owed the tax or not. The revenue agent had defended himself by describing the divorcee's confusion. Perhaps she was confused, but the point is that IRS personnel must always bear in mind that the average taxpayer possibly has only one experience in a lifetime with IRS procedure.

Agents should make sure the taxpayer understands the implications of everything he is asked to sign. Rather than discouraging taxpayers from seeking professional advice, IRS personnel ought to urge them to get it. However, when an agent is in a hurry to close a case and get on to the next one, it may well be that he doesn't take all the time he might in making clear just what is involved. In fact, it may be that sometimes it is easier to close a case with a signature if the taxpayer doesn't fully understand what he is triggering against himself with that signature.

If you ever decide to sign an agreement with IRS, get whatever you can in return. For example, if the agent will allow part of a deduction of, say, $2,000 that he had proposed to disallow, and if he will reduce the tax he has added to your year's tax bill from $600 to $350, tell him you will agree to the partial deduction or the $350. While the auditor-agent won't give you the reduction if there is no justification for it, you may be able to swing it if he is half convinced that maybe you deserve it. He probably will keep the agreement he makes with you, but not necessarily—so watch out.

An agent who had audited the returns of a veterinarian proposed to reduce the amount of deductions for business travel expense of the animal doctor. He also wanted to treat a real estate trust of the taxpayer's as having no tax reality, thus taxing all of its income to the taxpayer personally.

The veterinarian dickered with the agent, who then said that if the taxpayer would agree to the travel expense disallowance, he would agree that the realty trust income should not be taxed to the taxpayer. The vet signed an agreement to pay the added tax and supposed the matter was done with.

The agent didn't live up to his side of the bargain. A few months later, the IRS sent the veterinarian a bill for still more taxes on the basis that the income of the real estate trust was the income of the taxpayer.

"You can't do that," the vet said and went to court, where he argued that his compromise with the revenue agent was legally binding and that the IRS could not collect the tax deficiency from disallowing the travel expenses and also the deficiency resulting from taxing the real estate trust income to him. He said he would not have agreed to pay the travel expense deficiency if the IRS agent had not agreed to forgo taxing him on the trust income.

The court saw the question as being concerned with whether the revenue agent "had authority to make a binding agreement. Obviously if there was no contract there could be no breach." The judge concluded: "Any arrangement the taxpayer made with the revenue agent had no legal standing."

The point is all too obvious: regardless of what a revenue agent may do to loosen up taxpayers, he has no power to bind the IRS to an agreement.

However, even if a taxpayer cannot persuade the agent to make a deal that forgives or lowers a tax deficiency, all is not lost.

CHAPTER FIVE

Your Rights in a Tax Fight

Of all debts, men are least willing to pay the taxes. . . .

—Ralph Waldo Emerson

Assume that before you filled out your tax return you resigned yourself to the basic requirements for getting along with the Internal Revenue Service's know-it-all computers. You filled out your return *exactly* the way the form demanded. You gave your zip code number, crossed out no words, added when you should have, and subtracted when you could. You started out honest and intimidated, and you stayed that way right up to the minute you signed the return and mailed it.

About the worst thing that can happen to you afterward is that you will get a letter from IRS.

A letter from IRS might say that no remittance accompanied your tax return. (You have the canceled check to prove you paid.) It may take two or three or twenty letters, but some day you will convince the IRS computer that you paid on time. Or a letter might ask you to prove the amount of your medical expenses. (As if you couldn't.) You won't be worried when that kind of letter from IRS arrives at your door.

Not all of your contacts with IRS will be so painless. The tax bureau may audit your return.

Most audited taxpayers are subjected to what is called an *office* audit. In such a case you will get another kind of letter. It will ask you to bundle up and mail to the auditor the checks and bills and whatever else you may have at hand to help back up certain deductions. Or the letter may ask you to come in to his office for a discussion of one or more of the items on your return that he questions.

Be careful to have photocopies made of anything you send in the mail or leave at the IRS office. Make a detailed record—with names and dates—of every conversation you have at IRS. In the event you can't reach an agreement with the agent, such a diary-type record will help you when and if you talk to people higher up in the IRS pecking order.

Don't feel that the IRS agent who questions you is a sort of sacred cow. If he acts like a jackass, tell him so—in a nice way, if possible.

An Akron widow was worried sick for weeks because an IRS agent had told her to show him detailed figures on food, clothing, and household expenses to support the dependency deductions she had taken for her children. Outrage at last smothered her worry. She demanded to see the agent's supervisor. She asked him if it wasn't obvious that any idiot could see, from the size of her income and from what it cost to support children anywhere in the United States, that she must be providing at least two-thirds of her children's support. At that point she dumped a shoebox of cash register tapes, scribbled calculations, and department store charge tickets on the supervisor's desk. Then she stalked out. The next day the agent phoned to tell her that IRS would allow her dependency deductions.

Whether you are talking to an agent at his IRS office desk, or receiving him in what he calls a field audit at your place of business or your accountant's office, there is one cardinal rule to follow: never volunteer information.

Let the agent ask the questions. Answer them in good faith and truthfully, but volunteer no information whatsoever. A taxpayer trying to be helpful may blurt out information that isn't in question, but that may send the agent down another road of inquiry. If the agent wants to know about something, he'll ask. If he doesn't ask, don't make trouble for yourself.

Don't lie to the agent. If you don't know the truthful answer, say you don't. If you can't remember, say you can't. People go to jail for lying, but not for bad memories. And don't try to bribe the agent, even in the most subtle way. You may be a kindly appliance dealer, but offering to give the agent a portable color TV set for his sick daughter is going to be misunderstood. Don't even offer to arrange for him to buy it at wholesale.

Some revenue agents can act like con men. They will try to impress the little taxpayer, especially, with their importance, with the size of the organization they represent, with the damage they can do the taxpayer if he doesn't cooperate. They play on fear, greed, and ignorance. Each year hundreds of thousands of little taxpayers sign various types of papers, agree to pay deficiencies, and then strap themselves to pay taxes that many of them do not really owe. People have reportedly committed suicide because, when their bank accounts were seized for unpaid taxes, the only way they could see to provide for their families was to kill themselves so the families could have their life insurance.

If you are right, you can stand up to IRS and win your point.

IRS is trying to pluck the most feathers from the reluctant taxpaying goose while producing the fewest squawks. If you don't make any noise, you may sometimes get plucked for a bit more than is absolutely necessary. If you don't know your rights, the chances are much greater that you'll get plucked.

What are your rights?

First of all, you don't have to take any abuse from a revenue agent. Most agents are nice, decent people, trying to do a job. If you run into one of the other kind, request to see the agent's supervisor and ask him to assign another agent to audit your return.

You don't have to accept what the agent says you owe as added taxes. The IRS itself has provided several levels within its organization to which you can appeal what you consider a wrong decision by an IRS agent. Taxpayers who appeal decisions are usually quite surprised at how fairly they are treated by the IRS higher-ups.

TAXPAYER'S DECISION TABLE

Step	Appeal Level	Problem and Nature of Appeal	Alternatives
1	Revenue Agent	Proposes deficiency	(A) Sign waiver and pay bill
			(B) Sign and pay, then file for refund, or
			(C) Go to step 2

TAXPAYER'S DECISION TABLE (continued)

Step	Appeal Level	Problem and Nature of Appeal	Alternatives
2	IRS District Conference	Informal conference	(A) Reach agreement (B) Pay, then file for refund, or (C) Go to step 3
3	IRS Appellate Conference	Informal conference	(A) Reach agreement (B) Pay, then file for refund, or (C) File Tax Court petition and go to step 4
4	IRS Appellate Conferee plus IRS lawyer	Informal conference	(A) Reach agreement, or (B) Go to step 5
5	U.S. Tax Court	Formal trial	(A) Accept judge's decision, or (B) Appeal judge's decision (To U.S. Circuit Court of Appeals)

(See Appendix B)

If you can't reach some sort of an agreement with the revenue agent who audits your return, you can take your gripe to a district conference. Some 150,000 taxpayers do so each year. It works like this:

The revenue agent will tell you what his report will say. Some weeks later, you'll get a letter informing you that the agent has proposed an addition to your tax. A copy of the agent's report will be enclosed. The letter will state that you have the opportunity to ask for a district conference.

When the amount involved is under a few thousand dollars, and when the question is basically a factual one, taxpayers have found that a district conference gives them a fair shake. However, when the amount of the tax involved is more than $5,000, or there are questions of tax law, a district conference may not work as well. IRS often takes the position that is not 100 percent reflective of what the tax law actually is, but rather of what IRS would *like* the law to be.

If your tax deficiency involves less than $2,500 for each year, all you need do to get a district conference is to request one. If more than $2,500 is at stake, you need to request the district conference in writing.

The IRS district conference is informal. You and the conferee sit together at a desk or table. The district conferee works for IRS. Like the agent, he has to follow IRS policy. But normally he is more willing to give and take than is the agent. His job is to settle cases; the revenue agent's job is to make audits.

Suppose you are an insurance adjuster working for yourself and using your auto for your work. Your wife has a second car that the family uses for pleasure driving. You took 100 percent of the expenses of your business car as a deduction on your tax return. The examining agent allowed you 40 percent, reasoning that you drove fifteen miles each day back and forth to your office, or about four thousand miles a year. You actually drove that car an estimated thirteen thousand miles for the year. He figured nine thousand of that was for nonbusiness driving.

You explain to the district conferee that you seldom go straight to or from your office and your home. You stop to call at clients' homes and offices along the way, and you lay out your daily schedule and route to make as many calls as possible, so that the average distance from your house to your first or last call is only two miles. The business car is not suitable for social driving because it has the name of the agency painted on it.

After about half an hour of discussion, the IRS conferee may agree with you that the revenue agent went too far in his estimate. The conferee allows you 85 percent of the auto expense, instead of 40 percent, and the case is settled.

In an office audit situation, you can, of course, confer with the examiner's supervisor before going to district conference.

Your next step, if you can't get anywhere with the revenue agent, his supervisor, or the district conferee, is to get your case up to the Appellate Division of the IRS. Suppose you have had an unsuccessful session with the conferee at the district conference. Your best move is to tell him that you want the case referred to the Appellate Division of IRS.

However, if you have decided to skip a district conference and instead go right to the Appellate Division, you will have to file a written request to obtain a conference there. The request must be received by the IRS within thirty days of the date of the letter that proposed the tax deficiency you were unable to settle with the examining agent.

Note that the district conferee is so named because he reports his decisions, or his disagreements with a taxpayer, to the district director of IRS, as does the examining agent. The two are part of the district organization. Arizona is a district, for example, as are southern California and upstate New York.

The Appellate Division is a part of the IRS regional organization. All the western states comprise a region, and New England is a region. Even though an Appellate Division office is located within a district, the conferee reports to the regional office of IRS and not to the district director.

On the average, the thirty thousand taxpayers who take their complaints to the Appellate Division each year come out of it paying only about forty cents for every dollar the revenue agents originally wanted them to pay. The officials in the Appellate Division pride themselves on being independent and objective. They have the power to settle cases, without regard to announced IRS policy, on the basis of their estimate of your chances of winning the case if you go to court.

The conference with the Appellate Division conferee is just a matter of sitting down in an office with a well-trained and experienced man and explaining to him why you think you are right and the revenue agent is wrong. If he believes there is no merit to your position, he will tell you so, and offer specific reasons. If, in his judgment, there is a sound basis to your objection to paying the tax, he may ask what you would propose as a compromise settlement.

Providing all the facts have been thoroughly discussed between you and the applicable tax law has been reviewed, the fact that he acknowledges there is some merit to your position but cannot go all the way with you should be recognized as an invitation for you to suggest a compromise settlement.

Let's suppose you are the owner of a small contracting business and are in contention with IRS over the tax you declared you owed when you filed your return. These are the factors in the tax case:

You originally purchased a piece of land with the thought that you'd break it up into lots, build houses on the lots, and sell them one by one. Then you got in a bind for money and couldn't secure the necessary financing to build the house. As a result, you abandoned the idea of subdividing the land.

When a large contractor offered you a lump sum for the whole deal, you sold the land to him. On your income tax return, you reported your gain on the sale of the land as a long-term capital gain. The examining agent who audited your return regarded this gain as ordinary income because your primary aim in acquiring the land had been to hold it for sale to customers in the ordinary course of your business. You protested and asked for a district conference. The conferee stood firm with the examiner. Now you are at the Appellate Division of the IRS.

You discuss the matter with the Appellate Division conferee. He concedes there is a certain amount of merit to your argument, particularly in light of a Supreme Court decision defining what is and what is not a capital asset. However, he doesn't think your situation is close enough to the facts in the precedent case that you would be certain to win if you took your case to the Tax Court. At this point, you suggest, as a compromise, that 25 percent of the gain be treated as ordinary income and the balance as capital gain. This would reflect the relative strength of your position and of the IRS position, too.

You and the conferee talk about this at some length—it is bargaining, really—and soon you agree that a fair settlement would be to treat one-third of the total gain as ordinary income and the other two-thirds as capital gain. The case is thus disposed of without all the expense and uncertainty of going further in the appeals procedure.

But don't rush out to celebrate.

One taxpayer thought he had a compromise worked out with the

Appellate Division in a situation in which the tax law was unclear. He believed life was going to be sunny once more. Then one day the conferee telephoned to tell him that the IRS lawyers had decided to take the case to court in an attempt to clarify the law as it applied to the case. The settlement was off. It must be said, however, that such reneging by IRS is rare.

Whatever rights you as a taxpayer may have, you are still subject to the caprices of IRS people who may want to try a new approach, or prove a new theory, or who may be in a mood to act arbitrarily. It sometimes happens that the taxpayer is not viewed as an individual, but rather as a "situation." He is not a man with a name, but another travel expense case. Against such dehumanization, your only defense is to reach beyond the IRS and go to the Tax Court.

If you do go to court, you will find that your case will get individual treatment. While the Tax Court is not a court that applies principles of equity, its judges do apply common sense, as a Wisconsin high school teacher of Latin and French discovered.

During Christmas vacation she had flown to Europe and made connections for a two-week trip on a cruise ship through the Mediterranean. Only French was spoken on the ship. The ports of call were places significant in the history of France and ancient Rome. On side trips the teacher—Miss Latimer—had bought maps, books, and pictures that would be useful in classroom presentations back at school. After the cruise, she had flown home to Wisconsin and gone back to her classroom.

When it came time to file her federal income tax return, she had deducted $1,300—the cost of the trip—as an expense of maintaining and improving her employment skills as a teacher of Latin and French.

The IRS, as might be anticipated, had objected to the deduction. Eventually the schoolteacher presented the facts to the Tax Court.

The court clearly appreciated the IRS view that Miss Latimer might have experienced great personal pleasure out of the Mediterranean voyage. But the judge also observed that she had put herself in an environment where only French was spoken, that she had carefully scheduled visits to places that were related to the subjects she taught, and that she had made definite arrangements to bring back materials allowing her to share her experiences with students in years to come.

The court also commented that the school board had given Miss Latimer a great deal of cooperation in allowing her to fit the trip within the rather narrow confines of a two-and-a-half-week Christmas vacation.

The French teacher was allowed her deduction.

CHAPTER SIX

Where and How to Sue IRS

The period of 1818–1861 was a Golden Era in the history of the American Republic. There were no [federal] internal taxes of any kind. . . .

—Aubrey R. Marrs
in *Reflections of a Revenuer*

When you owe the government the amount of tax that is legally due, you pay it, of course. However, if you permit the government to extract more tax than you legally owe, you are giving it an opportunity to engage in a type of legalized robbery.

When Internal Revenue Service wants too much of your money, you have, as a good and upright citizen, a civic duty to put up an argument. If you fight a tax case, you will get an enlightening lesson in how our country's tax system operates, and the swing of your legal fist will help to keep IRS on its toes—even if you miss.

You can sue Internal Revenue Service in one of three courts—the Tax Court, the United States District Court, and the United States Court of Claims. In Tax Court, the judge is sent to your region from Washington. The U.S. District Court is local, and it is the only court where a tax case can be tried before a jury—a local jury. The Court of Claims sends a hearing commissioner from Washington when necessary.

You don't have to pay the additional tax charged against you until your case has been decided, if you pay the $10 filing fee and start suit in the Tax Court. But the procedure demands that you pay the tax and file a claim with IRS for refund before suing in either the District Court or the Court of Claims, and you must wait six months after filing the claim before you can bring suit in either court.

After the long wait, you start the suit by filing with the court a paper that recites your grievances and asks the court to make IRS pay back the mony it has collected. Then you wait until a trial day is set.

IRS may back down from facing you at trial in an impartial court. It often does. Sometimes, when IRS thinks the taxpayer has a fair chance of beating the government at the trial, it will work out a deal that gives him back part of what he is asking for.

That is what happened in the case of a concert pianist who was so angry his hands shook whenever he talked to IRS about the windstorm losses to the expensive landscaping around his house. He had paid $4,000 to remove broken trees, clean up mounds of debris, and move shrubs. An appraiser had estimated the value of the property after the windstorm at about $1,000 less than it had been before. The pianist had deducted $5,000 on his tax return—$4,000 for cleaning up and $1,000 for the drop in the market value of the residence.

IRS would allow him to deduct only $1,000. The pianist could have gone to Tax Court without first paying the tax, but he felt he'd rather explain his case to a local judge who would understand local values. After he had paid $1,300 additional tax, he filed a claim for refund with IRS. Six months later he filed suit in the U.S. District Court. Before trial, the United States attorney and the pianist's lawyer met and agreed on all the facts, so that the judge wouldn't have to listen to arguments as to what had happened, but only on how the case should be treated for tax purposes. Then the trial took place. Six weeks after the trial, the judge ordered IRS to refund the pianist $1,300 with interest.

It is difficult for a plaintiff to plead in either the District Court or the Court of Claims if he is not represented by a lawyer, though the situation is somewhat easier in the Tax Court and many people do get along without a lawyer.

If you do need a lawyer, you may find it difficult to justify going to either the District Court or the Court of Claims when the amount involved is less than $1,500. Even should you win your case, you will have legal and accounting bills to pay. The result is that most taxpayers don't sue the government in those courts. They go to the Tax Court.

Although you can be your own lawyer before the Tax Court, you would be smart to get help from somebody who has experience with that court if the amount involved is large or the issues complicated. When the amount is small, and especially if the case is mainly a question of fact rather than tax law, you can do a reasonably good job of representing yourself.

The advantage of taking a case to the U. S. District Court, so that it can be decided by a jury of local citizens, is shown in the trial of a Wisconsin worker who didn't belong to a union on strike but, nevertheless, did not go through the union's picket line.

The union paid strike benefits to him, although he had never paid dues. IRS said the benefits were income. The worker reasoned that a local jury would understand that the union had really made a gift to him and his family. So he sued for refund in the U. S. District Court. The jury's verdict in the case was that the strike benefits were a gift, and therefore not taxable.

The Court of Claims has a reputation for looking into taxpayers' claims carefully and fairly. Its decisions can be appealed only to the United States Supreme Court, which hears few tax cases. The decisions of the district court are appealable to the courts of appeal. If you win in the Court of Claims, your case can be considered completed. If you win in the district court or the Tax Court, you may have to fight the case all over again on appeal—and, perhaps, lose. IRS is a winner in about two-thirds of the cases it fights in the appeals courts. Most taxpayers seek redress in the Tax Court, as did the Texan who loaned $5,000 to his son to help him get started in business.

The business failed and the son couldn't repay the loan. The father charged the money off as a bad debt loss, taking a deduction on his federal income tax return.

An IRS agent-auditor tossed out the deduction on the basis that the loan was really a gift. The Texan argued without success. He decided to go to the Tax Court to protest the additional tax of $429.

He wrote to the Tax Court in Washington, D.C., and received from it a copy of its rules (see Appendix D). He drafted a letter specifying his complaint against the proposed extra tax and sent it to the Tax Court with four copies and his check for $10. Nine months later, the father was notified that his case was scheduled to be called in his own city at 9 A.M. on a certain Monday morning.

The judge listened to his story and asked some questions. He listened without comment to the sarcastic comments of an IRS attorney who suggested that no father would loan money to his son with expectation of repayment. After arguments were filed and read, the judge said he believed the taxpayer's testimony to be truthful, and therefore no additional tax was owed.

In another case, the IRS—always willing to believe the worst—reasoned that a New Yorker was a tax evader because, although he had become the owner of some valuable properties, his tax returns showed very small amounts of income. The IRS agents figured that he must be spending only about $2,000 a year for living expenses, unless he had substantial income that he wasn't reporting on his tax return.

The taxpayer explained to the Tax Court judge that he had come to the United States penniless, and had been forced to work long hours and save to get ahead. He described how he made his home in a basement and how his meals consisted mainly of beans and oatmeal. He said he never purchased newspapers or magazines, that he saved every penny he could and made profitable investments with the savings. The judge not only believed the New Yorker, he told the IRS people that he considered them a disgrace to the government and that allowing a case of this sort to reach court was un-American and persecution of an honest taxpayer.

Not all taxpayers who take their cases to the Tax Court win, but they do reasonably well. Of the six thousand or so individuals who each year ask the Tax Court to take a look at the added tax the government is demanding, approximately five thousand effect a settlement with IRS before trial. In the cases that get settled out of court, the taxpayers pay an average of about twenty-five cents for every dollar of added tax the revenue agents originally demanded. That doesn't necessarily mean that the government is giving seventy-five cents on the dollar, however.

It is usual for IRS to propose assessment of more tax than it really expects to collect. In some cases the IRS even attempts to collect the same tax from two people.

A husband may claim that the amount he pays to his divorced wife is alimony and is deductible on his tax return. She may claim that the money comes from a property settlement and is therefore not income taxable to her. The government might tell the husband that he cannot take his alimony deduction and then, in the same action, tell the wife she has to pay tax on the money because it is alimony.

If the two former spouses could get together and decide that the wife will report what she gets as alimony so the husband can take his deduction, IRS would be quite happy to collect the added tax from the wife only. Such a settlement would show up in the statistics as having been a case settled for fifty cents per dollar of added tax originally proposed by the IRS agent.

About seven hundred or so cases are actually tried every year before the Tax Court. What are the results of those trials? The taxpayer who goes to court pays on the average from 35 to 40 percent of the amount of tax originally proposed. But many taxpayers come out with no deficiency.

One Ohio taxpayer was the sole stockholder of a corporation that operated at a whopping loss. He thought the corporation had qualified for a special tax break that allowed the gains or losses of the corporation to be reported directly on the tax returns of the stockholders, so he reported the corporate losses on his personal return and thus reduced the amount of income tax he personally had to pay.

To qualify for that special tax treatment of the corporation, an election in writing had to be filed with the district director of the IRS. The agent who audited the stockholder's return said the district director's files didn't show any such election had been made by the taxpayer for the year involved.

The stockholder told IRS he remembered signing the papers. His accountant told the IRS agent that he remembered giving a draft of the papers to the stockholder's bookkeeper, and he remembered inspecting the typed copies after she had typed them, and he remembered handing them to the stockholder to be signed. The bookkeeper told the revenue agent she remembered placing the signed forms in an envelope addressed to the Director of Internal Revenue and depositing the envelope in a mailbox.

To all this, the revenue agent replied there was no record of the election ever having been received in the office of the district director. The stockholder wasn't willing to pay the tax. He went to Tax Court.

Said the Tax Court judge: "We accept as credible the testimony as given, and find as a fact that the election and the required consent were, in fact, mailed as contended by petitioner. This, in turn, gives rise to a strong presumption of delivery which is not rebutted by mere negative evidence of absence of any record of receipt."

The judge believed the stockholder, who therefore was not required to pay the tax IRS demanded.

Now and then some big guns are aimed at IRS over what seems to be a matter of little consequence. In such cases, however, it isn't the amount of money that counts, but the principle involved, such as the fight in which an Arizona certified public accountant and a Texas tax lawyer teamed up to save a retired army sergeant from having to pay $204 more income tax.

The IRS refused to allow the ex-sergeant to treat his army retirement pay as community income under the community property laws of Arizona, where he lived. If the income were treated as community income, then the sergeant and his wife were entitled to reduce their tax bill by $204 each—$408. Otherwise, the tax bill would be reduced by only one credit of $204.

Although the taxpayer could not pay a big enough fee to the lawyer and the accountant to cover all the time and effort they would have to spend on the case, the accountant took the case to the Tax Court, where he was licensed to practice. He felt that IRS was pushing the sergeant around simply because he was a little guy with not much in the way of resources to fight back.

After two years of battling the IRS over a principle, the government got its comeuppance—or so the accountant thought. The Tax Court judge decreed that since the sergeant had been an Arizona resident on the day he retired from the Army, his retirement pay was, in fact, community income and he could take an annual $408 tax credit instead of $204.

IRS hit back. It appealed the case. Perhaps the tax bureau figured that the sergeant couldn't afford the expense of a second and costlier court fight. It seemed to the accountant that all the resources of the federal government were focused on an improper and unfeeling attempt to collect $204 from a retired GI who had earned the right to some peace. It was then that the accountant enlisted the help of a very successful tax lawyer who practiced in Texas.

The lawyer traveled from Dallas to San Francisco in behalf of the GI, who couldn't even pay the out-of-pocket costs of the litigation. He argued the case and he won it.

Not every taxpayer can get that kind of help, but many accountants and lawyers do take small tax cases if they feel IRS is being unfair.

Some taxpayers who go to Tax Court don't deserve to win. There was the landlord who installed a listening device in the apartment of an unmarried woman tenant. When she discovered the bug, she threatened to sue the landlord. He paid her $5,000 to keep quiet and not sue. Then he deducted the hush money on his income tax return as part of the expenses of operating the apartment building.

When IRS said it wouldn't allow the deduction, the landlord went to the Tax Court. He told the judge that his reason for bugging the young lady's apartment had been to make certain she was not engaging in immoral conduct that might bring disgrace to the building. The judge didn't believe him. The landlord had to pay the added tax.

You can, if you wish, be your own lawyer before the Tax Court, and the judge will usually advise you on how to bring out the strong points in your case. He will give you the benefit of every reasonable doubt. Tax Court judges are patient and understanding, even when a taxpayer comes in with a silly case.

A single woman claimed she was entitled to compute her tax as a head of a household although she had no dependents. (The law was quite clear that to get the special tax break of head of a household the taxpayer must have children or dependents.)

The revenue agent had been brusque and impatient when he listened to her first arguments, and she was unable to make her point in conferences with the district conferee and, later, the Appellate Division conferee. The tax deficiency against her was $75. She paid the required filing fee of $10 and brought the matter before the Tax Court. There the judge decided she was wrong. She, however, had the feeling that she had received justice. She paid the added tax of $75 graciously and willingly.

Somehow, it doesn't hurt quite so much to pay additional tax when your arguments have been given serious consideration by a judge. Too often, you feel that you're just some holes punched in a card or a number stored in a file. For some people, fighting a tax case gives them an opportunity to be recognized as human beings.

CHAPTER SEVEN

Whose Income Is It?

Taxes should be proportioned to what may be annually spared by the individual.

—Thomas Jefferson

On occasion, the Internal Revenue Service has attempted to force a taxpayer to claim ownership of income that was, in fact, not his. It has been the taxpayer's good fortune that the courts haven't always let IRS get away with this, such as happened in the case of an Illinois father in the cattle-feeding business who put his three teenage children into the cattle business, too.

IRS said profits reported by the children were actually taxable to the father—Cornman—because he, not the children, was actually earning the money.

When Cornman had set the children up in business, he had them open individual checking accounts. To finance their cattle purchases, they borrowed money from a local bank. The children, as individuals, signed the notes due the bank and the father guaranteed payment. The money then was used to buy cattle.

The cattle were shipped to Cornman's stockyard and put in a pen that was separate from his cattle pens. Employees of the father fed the children's cattle under what is called a custom-feeding arrangement. The children paid the cost of the feed, plus a feeding charge of six cents per head per day. The father made a slight profit on the deal.

When the cattle reached prime weight, they were sold and the proceeds deposited in the children's bank accounts. The gain on the sale of the cattle went into their tax returns.

There is no law that prohibits members of a family from doing business with each other, lending money to each other, or managing each other's property. But IRS gets suspicious when the effect, as with this father and his children, is to shift income from a high-bracket taxpayer, which Cornman was, to a low tax-bracket taxpayer, which each of the children was. IRS said the income reported by the children was really the father's. He insisted it wasn't.

A tax judge had to decide just whose income it was, whether the children actually had earned the money from the sale of the cattle. To the judge, the big question was: Where did the money finally go? After it went into the children's bank accounts, what happened to it?

One of the Cornman youngsters testified that she used her money to do a lot of traveling. Another told the judge he used his money to finance his college education. The third youngster said he had bought a farm. None of the money went to the father.

The judge ruled that the money was not the father's, and he did not have to pay tax on the cattle profits.

A pretty Peace Corps worker from Pennsylvania, who owned stock in a family corporation and was due to receive about $100,000 in dividends when the corporation liquidated, decided the money should be given to charity. The corporation had already filed a notice of its intent to liquidate—both with IRS and the appropriate state officials. She gave the stock to the charity, and the charity, not the Peace Corps worker, received the $100,000 liquidating dividend.

The IRS didn't object to handing the money over to a charitable organization, but the tax people wanted the United States to get its share. The IRS reasoned that since the Peace Corps worker had a right to receive the $100,000, even though she transferred the right, she must be taxed on that income.

When the case couldn't be settled in conference and went to court, the IRS cited precedent cases in which taxpayers who were entitled to receive items had attempted to give them away, but had still had to pay the tax. In one such case, a New England taxpayer had given away an endowment insurance policy just prior to its maturity. The courts had said that since the taxpayer had a contractual right to receive the endowment proceeds, and because most of the increase in value over and above what he had invested in the policy had accrued prior to the time he made the donation, he must pay tax on that increase in value even though the policy proceeds went to charity.

The girl from the Peace Corps argued that there was a big difference between an endowment policy and a corporate liquidation, because the amount paid under an endowment policy was a matter of contract and the insurance company couldn't go back on its promise to pay. The corporate liquidation was different for the reason that, although the corporation had adopted a plan of liquidation and it was unlikely that this particular corporation would repudiate the plan, the fact remained that abandonment of the liquidation plan was entirely possible. The judge concluded that the Peace Corps worker had given stock to the charity *before* she had a right to receive the $100,000. Accordingly, she was not charged with income on the liquidating distribution that was made to the charity.

When tragedy strikes a family, the IRS still must consider the tax status of the survivors, despite the picture of hardness such tax checking may give.

Such was the case of a Virginia plumbing contractor—Pulaski—who, with his son-in-law, had operated a successful business for many years. When his wife, daughter, and son-in-law were killed in an accident, he sold the business.

Shaken as he was by the tragedy, his memory no longer as sharp as it might have been, Pulaski experienced great emotional difficulties in going through an IRS audit of both his business and personal affairs. When he was unable to give the agents satisfactory answers to their questions, they proceeded to find tax deficiencies against him. They didn't believe him when he said that he couldn't remember certain things and that most of the office work of the plumbing business had been directed by his son-in-law. IRS wanted names, dates, amounts, as well as invoices, canceled checks, and paid bills to back them up.

In one year, for instance, a customer of the contractor's had presented about $600 worth of roofing materials to the son-in-law without charge. The revenue agents held that the value of the material was $600 in income—which he had not reported—to the contractor himself. Pulaski protested. The roofing materials were of a new type, he told the Tax Court judge, and the roof that was installed for his son-in-law was, in fact, torn off six months later as unsuitable.

The judge declared he could see the son-in-law may have received some income from the transaction, but he couldn't figure out how the contractor had derived income. For the contractor to have income, the IRS would have had to show that the roofing people had given the roof to the contractor, not the son-in-law, and that the contractor had directed them to give his roof to his son-in-law. In fact, the contractor hadn't even known about the new roof until it had been installed.

Unfortunately for Pulaski, however, he wasn't able to show that IRS was so obviously wrong on other items, mainly travel and entertainment expenses, and so he had to pay a tax deficiency.

A major league catcher had learned his trade from his father. Neither his high school baseball coach nor his American Legion coach had anything to do with his training program, and he and his father had made a deal that his father would get half of any bonus that the youngster might receive when and if he signed up for big league baseball.

He got a bonus of $110,000 from a major league team, payable over five years. Each year for five years, the ballplayer and his father each received $11,000, which they reported on their federal income tax returns.

As IRS sized up the transactions, the player was the one who was earning the money by playing baseball, and it was on his income tax return that the annual bonus payment of $22,000 should be reported.

A Tax Court judge said IRS was right, the full $22,000 a year should have been reported on the player's income tax return, but there remained another question to be settled: Was he entitled to a deduction for the $11,000 a year that his father had received as earnings due?

The IRS agreed the father had earned something and thought $2,200 would be a reasonable amount to deduct. When the ballplayer complained, citing all the years his father had devoted to his development, the IRS countered that the expenses of acquiring new skills are non-deductible, that most of what he was paying his father was similar to the expenses of getting a medical degree, which are not deductible for income tax purposes.

The Tax Court judge didn't agree. He held that the share of the bonus the player had to pay to his father was an expense that was ordinary and necessary in order to get the bonus in the first place. So the Tax Court ruled that IRS had improperly found a tax deficiency, inasmuch as the amount paid to the father was a proper deduction in arriving at the amount of income that was to be subject to tax.

An income omission by a Charleston dentist nearly put him behind bars. The dentist had needed some kitchen cabinets in his house and had made a deal with a carpenter to swap the work of building the cabinets for several hundred dollars' worth of dental work. When each filed his income tax return for the year, neither reported income from the swap of services.

The revenue agent who audited the dentist's return picked at random a number of patients' names from the office appointment book. One was the name of the carpenter. The dentist's books didn't indicate that a bill had been sent to the carpenter. Nor did they show cash collections from the carpenter. The office nurse must have disliked the dentist, because she told the agent that the dentist often had received payment in services rather than cash. Service payments to a lawyer, a physician, an electrician, a plumber, and an accountant who prepared the dentist's tax return never went on the books. The nurse told all. She said she was glad to see it all come out in the open.

The carpenter's tax return then received the agent's attention. He was clean, as the investigators say. The dental work was the only income item he had failed to report. The agent was satisfied the carpenter hadn't realized that, in paying his dental bill by doing carpentry work, he should have reported the amount of the bill as income. IRS gave him a small bill for additional taxes.

The Charleston dentist was in trouble. A special agent investigated and recommended the dentist be prosecuted for tax fraud. After a number of conferences with regional tax officials and with Justice Department attorneys in Washington, a tax lawyer was able to free the dentist from the threat of prison, but he had to pay some stiff penalties and, presumably, stiff legal fees, because he hadn't obeyed the tax law.

The business agent of a meatcutters' union,—a man named O'Rourke —had unselfishly worked out a way to save the union a lot of money it had previously been paying for insurance commissions. He hadn't realized, however, how really unselfish he would have to be until after the IRS got through with him.

The union's welfare fund carried health and life insurance on its members. Since the welfare fund did all the paperwork on the policies, O'Rourke was unwilling to permit the insurance people to receive commissions for doing nothing. He obtained a license to sell insurance. Whereupon he told the trustees of the welfare fund that from now on they could buy insurance through him, and he would donate to the fund all the commissions he earned.

The business agent's motives were noble. He accounted to the welfare fund for every penny of commissions paid to him. The commissions, however, really were income that he should have reported on his income tax return. The IRS charged him with $4,000 of additional income each year for three years—resulting in tax deficiencies of $3,800.

O'Rourke told IRS that every cent in commissions had been turned over to the welfare fund. How in the world could IRS say that he had income from the commissions? The IRS pointed to the facts.

The first fact was that the business agent was entitled to receive, and did receive, commissions from insurance companies in the amount of $4,000 a year. The second fact was that commissions received from an insurance company are taxable income.

While it was true that the business agent had also donated that same $4,000 a year to the welfare fund, the welfare fund was not a charitable organization, and therefore the donations were not deductible as charitable contributions. The agent had income with no offsetting deduction.

In Tax Court, the judge saw eye to eye with IRS. The judge said he admired the business agent for his unselfishness, but he ruled that the agent owed $3,800 more tax because the letter of the law must be obeyed even though it had given him what seemed an unfair tax problem.

A western water company with five hundred stockholder-customers had no income tax problems. Each year, the income from its customers exactly equaled its operating expenses. But one day more than water came up through one of its wells—oil!

Oil royalties soon amounted to a hefty part of the company's annual budget. The owner-customers saw their duty. The water rates were reduced so that at the end of the year, even after receiving the oil royalties, the company treasury was empty, as the owners had intended it to be. If the total cost of operating the water company had been $200,000 and the oil royalties amounted to $120,000, water rates were set so as to take in only $80,000 from the customers.

The customers had no objection. They were getting the benefit of the oil royalties in the form of reduced water rates. But IRS wanted somebody to pay income tax on the royalties.

The water company reported its income as $80,000 from water charges and $120,000 from oil royalties—a total of $200,000. It also showed operating expenses of $200,000, leaving no net income subject to tax.

IRS decided that the expenses should be deductible only to the extent of the $80,000 water income. The $120,000 of oil royalty income would then be subject to income tax.

The Tax Court ruled that the water company must pay income tax on the $120,000.

The company appealed, arguing that the full $200,000 of expenses was ordinary and necessary expenses of a water company, that the law did not deny the deduction of expenses solely because the IRS felt denial would produce a better tax result.

The U. S. Court of Appeals agreed with the water company. The $120,000 of oil royalties entirely escaped taxation.

CHAPTER EIGHT

A Matter of Principle

It just cannot be that God, even in His omnipotence, can be aware that there are income taxes; but if He is aware of them He must want us to get all of our hell right here on earth.

—"Isn't It the Truth!"

in the *Arizona Daily Star*

Taxpayers reluctantly put up with interrogation by the Internal Revenue Service over what the agents say are either discrepancies in their income tax returns or outright omissions. They resent the time and effort that have to be invested to satisfy the agents' curiosity. As a result, if the additional amount of tax assessed by the revenue agent is within their means, most taxpayers pay up and go on their way with a feeling of relief.

A few hardy souls, however, get mad about the decisions made against them. No matter how small the amount of money involved, they decide to fight.

An astonishingly large number of cases involving matters of principle brought into Tax Court are decided against IRS. Perhaps, it is because there is nobody more stanchly righteous than an honest but stubborn taxpayer who knows he hasn't hidden a penny from the tax collector.

There was a practical nurse—Mrs. MacKinnon by name—who said she wouldn't pay IRS a nickel it wasn't entitled to. The tax man had argued with her about half the items on her return, and she had lost part or all of nearly every argument. For a filing fee of $10, she got her complaint brought before the Tax Court. At the trial, she was her own lawyer and she told the judge her story. He then set the amounts of tax he thought she should pay.

The IRS had allowed her $152 for charitable contributions. The

Tax Court judge allowed her $1 a week more—$52 more for the year.

The IRS had allowed her $97 for sales tax. Mrs. MacKinnon rather impractically had claimed a sales tax deduction that would have required her to spend twice her income on purchases subject to sales tax. This the Tax Court judge couldn't swallow, but he did allow her $43 more than the IRS—$140.

The Judge also allowed her $18.53 for medically prescribed shoes and $20 for taxicab and car fares to get medical treatments. The IRS had thrown out both those items.

Special clothing for the nurse's job had cost her $250 a year. The IRS could see only $100 of it as deductible. The judge allowed $150.

In his written opinion, the judge took a swipe at both the IRS and the taxpayer:

"This case typifies a situation with which this court is all too frequently faced, namely, where the IRS during the audit and pretrial process perhaps overemphasizes the necessity for documentation and the taxpayer adamantly insists on the full amount of claimed deductions despite his or her inability to produce minimal substantiation. The inevitable waste of time, effort and money is appalling. In such situations the court can do no more than make an estimate of what seems reasonable under the circumstances."

The moral in this case would seem to be that, while it is all right not to let the IRS push you around, don't be unwilling to compromise here and there.

Some principled taxpayers, although they don't win out in court, do have the satisfaction of learning that the judge, obligated to follow the law that has been used against them, sees their point and respects them for it.

Smithson, an elementary teacher in the Watts section of Los Angeles, provided his students with supplemental learning experience at his own expense. He had equipped a special room in the school and opened it to any student from kindergarten through sixth grade outside school hours. The experimental classroom had television sets, radios, encyclopedias, and other items mostly absent from the homes of the pupils. Smithson also paid all the expenses of various birthday parties and other social events, and he contributed money to buy items like pencils, pens, mouthwash, aspirin, and sprays.

He deducted the cost of these items in his income tax return as business expenses. When the deduction was challenged by the IRS, he argued that the expenses were necessary to his professional life as a teacher and to his goal of bringing a new educational experience to his culturally deprived students. The IRS refused to allow the deduction.

Smithson appealed from the IRS decision and argued his own case before the Tax Court. His major point was that the low motivation and performance levels of his students reflected the need for the types of programs he had instituted.

Yet the court said it could not allow the deduction: "Petitioner undertook the special classroom project on his own; his employer in no way asked or required him to do so." Thus, the court concluded that the expenses were not "ordinary and necessary" business expenses. "We applaud the efforts made by petitioner. We believe that he acted with compassion and generosity. However, . . . only those deductions which are provided for by Congress can be allowed for federal income tax purposes."

When honesty shines from the words and demeanor of a taxpayer who goes to court, the judge is very apt to become aware of it. A refugee from Hungary who liked to bet small amounts on dog and horse races had won almost $3,000 on a twin double at a dog race one night in Miami. He didn't report the winnings on his income tax return, even though the track had reported them to the IRS.

The refugee explained to a revenue agent who interrogated him that after winning the twin double he had bet heavily on races during the following months, and that his losses for the entire year were far in excess of his winnings. He and the agent had difficulty understanding each other, because the gambler was not fluent in English and the agent knew no Hungarian. The agent demanded that he pay $667 of additional income tax.

The refugee asked the Tax Court to review the IRS finding, and he appeared before the judge on his own behalf. He had no witnesses, and no evidence except his own testimony. The judge wrote this decision:

"He appears to be a person of only moderate means. We found him to be a sincere and truthful witness. Although there was some confusion in his testimony, due in part to apparent difficulties with the English language, we are satisfied that after winning the twin double he bet heavily on the races during the succeeding weeks or months, that he had repeated domestic quarrels with his wife as a result of his gambling activities and losses sustained therein, and that his net gambling losses for the year exceeded his winnings. We so find as a fact."

The refugee did not have to pay the $667 deficiency demanded by IRS.

It is always heartwarming to see widows and orphans turn the tables on villains, especially when the villain is the IRS. A college student in Massachusetts worked part-time, earning slightly less than $1,000 for the year. He also received just a shade less than $1,000 from the Veterans Administration under the War Orphans Educational Assistance Act of 1956. His widowed mother—Mrs. Scott—contributed about $1,500 to his support and listed him as a dependent on her tax return.

A revenue agent informed the widow and mother that she must pay $240 of tax, plus interest, because she was not providing more than half the support of her student son. The agent said, "The total amount spent for his support was $3,500 ($2,000 plus $1,500), and you only provide $1,500, which is less than half."

Mrs. Scott had a copy of the tax law with her. She took it out of her purse. "You're wrong," she said. "It says here that scholarships received by a student shall not be counted in determining the cost of his support. Therefore, the total cost of my son's support was $2,500, of which I furnished $1,500, which is more than half."

However, the IRS doesn't believe that payments under the War Orphans Act are scholarships. IRS reasons officially that they are "veterans' benefits." Mrs. Scott went before the Tax Court judge without legal aid and argued her case. The Tax Court judge decided that the word "scholarship" must be broadly construed, that it means almost any gratuitous payment for study at an educational institution. The mother did not have to pay an additional tax of $240.

A man named Cooper was particularly outraged at IRS over a matter of principle. He had given his intended wife a diamond engagement ring that had cost him $1,200. Years later, it was lost when he accidentally slammed a car door on Mrs. Cooper's hand. IRS had a strange opinion about her perfectly natural reaction to the pain she had suffered. That opinion and Cooper's outrage brought the case to the Tax Court.

What had occurred was this: When the car door slammed, the impact of the blow apparently was centered on the diamond ring. Mrs. Cooper was lucky—if she had not been wearing the ring, her fingers might have been smashed. As it was, she suffered great pain, and in the first moments after the blow she screamed and shook her hand in agony. The shaking of her injured hand probably was what caused the diamond to drop out of the sprung flanges of the ring.

The couple and their children even sifted the gravel in the driveway in their search for the stone. It was never found. It was not insured.

Cooper claimed the $1,200 as a casualty loss on his income tax return, but IRS wouldn't let him take the loss. An agent said that what had happened was no different than if one of the couple's sons had torn the knee out of some new slacks, or if the wife had dropped and broken some dishes as she cleaned off the kitchen table.

Cooper told the story to the judge. The IRS attorneys, in addition to arguing that what had happened was not a casualty loss because it wasn't similar to such common casualties as a fire or storm, also contended that the diamond hadn't been lost as a result of the car door slamming on the wife's hand, but as a result of the wife shaking her injured hand.

The judge decided the shaking of the hand had been the natural reaction to the pain that had suddenly been inflicted, and that such an accident was indeed a "casualty" within the meaning of the tax law.

The fact that revenue agents are often needlessly arbitrary is a major cause for the common dislike many taxpayers have for them. For example, Frank Lutz, a Cleveland plastics engineer, carried on a job placement service, matching up the needs of corporations with the engineers available in his field. The employment agency's office was in his residence, where he also did some consultant work on engineering problems.

The residence was a ten-room house on a half acre of land. The front room served as the office. Areas of certain other rooms in the house were used for storage. The engineer paid his three sons—aged eleven, ten, and seven—each $10 a week for working as part-time office boys. On his federal income tax return he deducted the amounts paid to the boys.

The IRS audited Lutz's income tax return and disallowed the deduction, which totaled $1,560 for the year. The revenue agent ruled that, because of the ages of the boys, it was obvious to him they could not perform valuable or worthwhile services to a business and that, therefore, the so-called wages were in fact weekly personal allowances, ostensibly paid to the sons but actually put into bank accounts for their future use.

The father said the sons ran errands, washed windows, took down and cleaned screens, shoveled snow, mowed grass, tended shrubs, assembled papers for him, picked up mail, stuffed, stamped, and labeled envelopes, and generally made themselves useful around the house and in connection with his business.

He appealed the revenue agent's decision that no amounts paid to the boys be allowed as deductions. His appeal eventually was granted, and he was allowed to deduct $185 of the $1,560 in wages paid the boys that he had claimed on his tax return.

Study of tax problems and tax court decisions throws some light on what may happen, taxwise, to those who come out winners in Monday night poker games.

A Jersey City merchant named Lipkin played poker every Monday night with a group of seven or eight businessmen he had known since they were all boys. The games rotated from one house to another. Each host in turn supplied beverages and food. A player would win or lose up to about $100 in any one evening, and the winner one week might well be a loser the next.

Each player provided his stakes by bringing cash to the party or by cashing checks during the game. In a single evening, a player might write several checks, he might rake in other checks from a winning pot, and he might cash checks for others with money he had won.

Lipkin always deposited his poker game checks in his personal bank account. When IRS audited his income tax returns, it investigated all his bank deposits. The poker money had not been reported as income. When Lipkin said the poker game checks were of course not income, the IRS agent said he didn't believe him. He estimated that Lipkin had probably won, in addition to the bank deposits, another $4,000, and he arbitrarily added that amount to the man's income for the year, for a total of $7,500 in winnings.

Fortunately, the poker game buddies came to Lipkin's rescue when he took the argument with IRS to the Tax Court. The friends described from the witness chair the way the Monday night group conducted the games. The judge concluded that the net winnings of Lipkin could not have been more than $1,200 for the year. Had Lipkin kept a record of his winnings and losses, he might have had to pay even less.

Another taxpayer got mad before he tangled with IRS. He was the owner of a Georgia barbershop whose electric service had been turned off due to an error by a clerk for the local power company. As a result, the barber started a fight that he hoped would shake up the company's top management.

First, he purchased one hundred shares of the power company stock for $2,500. That made him a stockholder in good standing. Next, he wrote to approximately three thousand stockholders, asking that they let him vote their stock at the corporation's next annual meeting. He obtained enough proxies to get one-half of one percent of the votes for directors, while the management's slate of directors got the rest.

The corporation battle waged by the little man against the big tycoons had set the barber back a total of $675 in expenses. He deducted the $675 on his federal income tax return, describing it as "proxy fight expense in connection with stock investments." He got his claimed refund check in due time, but eventually was called in to the IRS office to explain.

The IRS examiner, privately tickled over the barber's attempts to grab control of the power company, allowed the deduction. His supervisor overruled him. The examiner explained to the barber what the supervisor had ordered, and suggested that he protest the ruling before a district conferee.

"A stockholder's effort to change policy might be deductible," the district conferee said to him later, "while just an attempt to get himself elected to the board of directors would not be."

The Georgia barber argued back that the only reason he had wanted to get elected was to change policy, not to get a $1,200 director's fee every year.

The IRS conferee offered to allow $300 of the $675 as a deduction. The barber accepted. A few months later, he sold the stock for which he had paid $2,500. It had climbed to $3,250. Profit on the stock—$750. Expense of fighting the utility—$675. Net profit—$75.

CHAPTER NINE

Unique Tax Arguments

Where there is an income tax, the just man will pay more and the unjust less on the same amount of income.

—Plato

Some of the arguments used by beleaguered taxpayers to squirm out of the clutches of the tax men are highly imaginative. That such creative activities by stubborn men and women are often rewarded by success is revealed in a host of interesting court decisions.

For instance:

How old does a horse have to be before she is too old for breeding?

IRS has ruled that the useful life of a horse held for breeding purposes is ten years. Ed Buford, a Pennsylvania breeder of Arabian horses, reasoned that the ten-year useful life of a horse should be measured from the time the horse was foaled. Therefore, when Buford acquired a seven-year-old mare, he deducted one-third of her cost each year for three years, and when he acquired a nine-year-old horse, he figured the useful life remaining was only one more year and deducted his cost in that year.

"That makes no sense at all," stated the city-bred revenue agent who audited the tax return. "Even though our own IRS depreciation guidelines say a breeding horse's useful life is ten years, when you bought a nine-year-old horse you must have expected more than one year more of service from her." A recalculated depreciation showed that the taxpayer had taken a deduction for $600 too much.

But in Tax Court the judge held: "The IRS has issued guidelines intended to assist taxpayers lacking a more specific basis for determining the lives of their own assets, and these guidelines adopt a depreciable life of ten years for breeding horses. Therefore, we hold that the useful life of each horse for breeding purposes ceased at the age of ten years."

Although a gambler can offset his losses against his gains, if any, he cannot deduct a net loss when making out his income tax return. Unfortunately for many taxpayers, their gambling winnings are much more obvious to the IRS than are their losses.

A Las Vegas casino dealer, appropriately nicknamed Blackjack, wanted to establish that he had gambling winnings so he could cut his income taxes. At first thought, the idea seems ridiculous. How can a taxpayer cut his taxes by showing that he has gambling winnings?

Blackjack worked all the casino games at various times. In the game of blackjack, he dealt cards, supervised betting, paid the winners, and collected from the losers. In roulette, he spun the wheel. At the crap table, he supervised the bets as made, and paid off or raked in as the dice came up.

In the casinos it is said to be common practice for patrons to make bets for their dealer at blackjack, roulette, craps, or any other game. When such a bet is made for him, the dealer's attention is called to the bet by the player making it. If the bet wins, the dealer gets the proceeds, but before pocketing the money the dealer notifies his immediate superior that the winning money was the result of a bet made for him by a patron. The proceeds of all such winnings are called "side money."

During one year, Blackjack got about $700 in so-called side money. He also did some gambling on his own time. He could prove that he had lost $1,800 during the same year. When Blackjack made out his income tax return, he figured he could offset the side money against his gambling losses and not have to report any of that $700 as income.

A revenue agent who called him in for an audit of his tax return insisted that the side money was not a return from gambling, but instead was an accumulation of tips from his customers—somewhat in the nature of tips a waitress would receive. IRS was ruled correct in court. The dealer had to report and pay tax on the full $700. Had he been able to treat it as gambling winnings, he would have had no tax at all to pay on it because of the offsetting gambling losses.

An almost winner in another category was Natalie, a divorcée who came up with an unusual argument for getting a deduction. The case was related to the regulation that you can deduct state income taxes on your federal income tax return, but you cannot deduct federal income tax payments on your federal income tax return.

While still married, the woman had filed a joint return with her husband. They were divorced the following year. The property settlement specifically obligated the husband to pay any additional income taxes for the last year of marriage, or for any other year during which joint returns were filed. Under state law, she also had a right to receive from her ex-husband half of any tax deficiency she might pay on the joint return, even if the property settlement agreement did not provide that he should pay the entire amount.

IRS audited the last joint return and decided that another $8,000 of tax was due. The ex-husband had left the United States, so IRS slapped a lien against Natalie's house. Despite her protest that he, not she, owed the tax, she had to pay the full $8,000.

Under terms of the property settlement agreement, her former husband now owed Natalie $8,000. There was no way to collect from him in a foreign country. The divorcée reasoned, "What that man owes me is a debt, and since it can't be collected, it is a bad debt." She claimed an $8,000 bad debt deduction on her tax return.

The revenue agent who audited her return thought he could allow the deduction for a bad debt, but his supervisor objected, saying, "She is personally liable for the whole tax on a joint return, so it is her tax that she paid and not his. If you allow her a deduction for $8,000 you will really be allowing her a deduction for paying her own federal tax."

Death can cause tax problems that may have to be settled in court if IRS gets hard-nosed. When the $30,000-a-year president of a brewing company died, the company paid his widow—Mrs. Witz—the salary that he would have earned for the balance of the year. She reasoned that this was a gift to her and didn't report it as taxable income. The IRS disagreed and sent her a notice saying it proposed to assess an additional tax against her for the year in question amounting to $6,600. The bereaved woman didn't want to get involved in an argument at that time, so she mailed the IRS her check.

The check was mailed in January. The statute of limitations on the tax year involved was due to run out in April. In May IRS got around to billing Mrs. Witz for the $6,600 assessment she had already paid. Her tax accountant looked at the dates and said to her, "You ought to try to get that money back." She had by then regained her emotional balance and didn't mind bringing suit against IRS in the U.S. District Court.

Her lawyer argued in court: "She is entitled to the money because the tax wasn't assessed until after the statute of limitations had run out. The IRS contention that the deceased's salary was not a gift is not relevant."

The IRS took exception: "She paid the tax before the statute ran out. Therefore, it doesn't matter when the formal assessment took place."

The judge quoted an old United States Supreme Court decision holding that the payment of a tax before it was assessed was a deposit and not a payment. Being a deposit, it became a payment only when a valid assessment was made to which it could be applied.

As a result, Mrs. Witz was held to be entitled to a refund of $6,600, and the court didn't have to wrestle with the fuzzier question of whether the salary payments sent to her in memory of her dead husband were gifts or taxable income.

Oklahoma has a so-called dead-man statute that the IRS lawyers—in court to contest a plea by the executor of a deceased taxpayer's estate to have a penalty assessment removed—contended did not apply in the case being argued. They wanted an IRS agent to recount on the witness stand a conversation he had had with a taxpayer now deceased.

"No," said the lawyer for the deceased's estate. "Our state's dead-man statute says you can't offer evidence of your conversations with a dead person."

"Yes," said the IRS lawyer. "For two reasons. First, the revenue agent isn't personally involved in the case, so the statute doesn't apply to him. Second, in any tax case, you are suing us, and therefore the dead-man statute doesn't apply. It doesn't affect testimony offered by someone who is being sued by the dead man—only someone who is suing him."

The judge had no problem with the first objection. An IRS agent is a government employee and, therefore, would be covered by the dead-man statute if the government were suing the taxpayer. The second argument presented more of a problem. On the surface, at least, it looked as if the IRS were right. The dead man, through his executor, had filed suit against the government claiming he didn't owe a penalty the IRS had collected. If the government were really defending a suit against IRS, then the dead-man statute would not prevent the IRS agent from testifying.

The judge must have asked himself: What really is involved in a tax case? Is the taxpayer really suing the government as one person would sue another person?

He decided that the tax law presumes the government is correct in everything it does so that it can collect its "lifeblood" without interruption. The only way a taxpayer can stop the IRS from doing anything it wishes is by suing the IRS. Yet it is really the IRS claim against the taxpayer that is the subject of the suit, and not some claim the taxpayer has made against the IRS.

The judge concluded that, although the dead taxpayer might technically be suing the government, the government was not really defending against a claim of the taxpayer, but was the party that had asserted a claim against that taxpayer—or his estate. Looked at in that way, the dead-man statute did apply, the IRS agent's testimony could not be heard, and the tax penalty must be refunded to the dead man's estate.

A New Jersey court put IRS in its place when the tax people traded legal punches with the government of Jersey City.

A numbers racket boss was in prison when, one July 3, workmen uncovered almost $2.5 million in United States currency, and boxes of gambling material, in a garage belonging to the convict. The money was turned over to federal authorities and, on July 5, the district director of the IRS assessed almost $3.33 million of back interest and taxes against the imprisoned gambler.

The next day, July 6, local police forcibly entered another garage owned by the gambling czar and seized $170,000 in currency. On July 9, the IRS district director demanded that the $170,000 be turned over to him, citing as his authority a tax law provision that automatically imposes a lien against a taxpayer's property interests existing at the same time as an assessment is made against the property. On July 6, when the money was seized, the IRS had already made an assessment against the gambler—its assessment of July 5.

"Not so," argued the Jersey City attorneys. "Under our state laws that $170,000 was confiscated as contraband and, therefore, did not belong to the gambler at the time your assessment was made."

The city then brought an action in the state courts to determine whose $170,000 it was. The judge concluded: "The money was taken from the garage by local law enforcement officials and confiscated as gambling contraband. On the said date, July 6 [the gambling czar] was in official custody and incarcerated in the state prison. The court concludes that the requirements of the state statutes had been fulfilled and that the subject currency was seized in connection with an arrest for violation of the gambling laws of this state."

The IRS then contended that the state court had no jurisdiction to consider the matter. But state judges don't like to be told that the IRS is a law unto itself or that the federal courts are to decide all matters. The state court judge concluded that the basic issue in the suit involved whether the gambler, under state law, owned the $170,000 on the date it was seized, or whether all money used by him in his illegal activity had been forfeited months before, when he was convicted of gambling. The judge decided the city could keep the $170,000.

A proxy fight for control of a southern corporation made the point that selfish motives can be good motives deserving tax consideration.

Fred Chilton, the 60-year-old president of a company, had been pushed out of his job. A group of stockholders loyal to Chilton then formed a committee in an attempt to kick out the new management group that had fired him, restore him to office, and seat themselves as members of the board of directors.

The proxy battle waged by the loyalist committee was fiercely fought. It included suits, countersuits, postponed meetings, and vacated meetings. The committee spent nearly $100,000. It succeeded in throwing out the new management and so found itself in power. As a result, it made arrangements for the corporation to reimburse it for all expenses incurred during the struggle.

"You can't deduct that $100,000 as a business expense," the IRS told the corporation's newest management. "Your fight was personally motivated. It had nothing to do with your business."

In Tax Court, the judge said he well understood that the members of the Chilton committee "were inspired to a substantial extent by personal or selfish motives. To conclude otherwise would be to assume a purity of purpose that is contrary to human experience and to exhibit a naïveté that is not required of any court.

"But their campaign was nevertheless as much in the interest of the corporation itself as was the counteroffensive mounted by existing management, which was also obviously motivated by personal or selfish considerations in seeking to perpetuate its control over the corporation.

"Any assumption that management is never motivated by personal considerations and that the insurgents' motivations are always personal —a view suggested, if not explicitly so stated by the IRS—has little relation to the real world."

The court finally allowed the corporation to deduct both the $100,000 it had reimbursed the loyalist committee for its proxy fight expenses and the corporate costs of carrying on that fight.

Taxpayers who aren't aware of the many fierce arguments and battles that are waged over tax problems tend to think a tax man's job is uninteresting. Just the opposite is true. Tax work, in and out of IRS, is quite intriguing. It goes from one problem to another; from a multi-million-dollar stock proxy fight to the case of the Hollywood bachelor with the pretty housemate.

Jack Lothar, the bachelor, had decided that life would be much pleasanter if a certain divorcée he was dating came to live in his apartment. She thereupon moved in. She prepared the meals, did the laundry, got Lothar off to work in the morning, and generally cared for other day-to-day living needs. He supplied the money for this comfortable existence.

At tax time, Lothar saw the line on the tax form that said "dependents." He studied the instructions, then decided his housekeeper qualified as "an individual who, for the taxable year of the taxpayer, has as his (her) principal place of abode the home of the taxpayer and is a member of the taxpayer's household."

She certainly was a member of the household. He listed the friendly divorcée on his tax return as a dependent not his wife, and thereby gained, as head of a household, a lower tax rate than he would have had as a bachelor.

The IRS is always interested in checking on taxpayers who claim as dependents people who are not relatives. A revenue agent talked to the bachelor.

"You'd be all right taxwise if you married her," the agent said.

"It's none of the government's business how I live my personal life," Lothar replied. "I'll fight you in court."

The Tax Court judge thought it was, indeed, the government's business. To the judge, it seemed that to claim a dependent "the support must be gratuitous and given to the recipient for motives of charity, affection or moral obligation without thought of receiving in return a quid pro quo."

Whether the bachelor was receiving merely housekeeping services or something more was really not at issue, the judge said. "If you hire a housekeeper, and her pay is the support you furnish her, she is not your dependent, but your employee. You get no dependency deduction for a housekeeper or a mistress. And if you are not furnishing the cost of maintaining a household for a dependent, you do not qualify for the special tax treatment given the head of a household."

The Hollywood bachelor was unable to cut his tax bill and was, therefore, obligated to pay the deficiency demanded by IRS.

Different departments of the United States government sometimes tangle with each other, and it is fun for some of us to stand by and watch. We may think of the government as speaking with one voice, but its various parts often converse in different tongues as they pursue their aims.

When a Comanche Indian woman died, the area director of the Bureau of Indian Affairs prepared and filed her federal estate tax return, as he was required to do. She had owned real estate that was being held in trust for her by the federal government, since she was a ward of the United States. Some of the income from oil and gas royalties on the land was held in a trust fund for her by the United States. Both the state of Oklahoma and the federal government had collected income taxes on the oil royalties, and the area director of the Bureau of Indian Affairs sued for refund of those taxes—totaling well over $200,000.

In addition, she had also owned property in her own name. This was not held in trust. The property—valued at $17,000—was worth far less than the $60,000 minimum value that is required to make property liable for federal estate tax. The Indian Affairs area director therefore filed an estate tax return showing there was no estate tax due. IRS conceded that it couldn't levy an estate tax on the land that was held in trust by the United States, but it asserted that all of the Indian woman's other assets, including the claimed income tax refunds of more than $200,000, were subject to federal estate tax. The IRS wanted $82,000 tax out of the estate.

The area administrator paid the assessment and then sued IRS to get the estate taxes refunded. The U. S. District Court judge who heard the case held that no estate tax was due and ordered IRS to refund every penny it had collected, plus interest.

The Bureau of Indian Affairs, which traditionally has done quite well in handling the tax problems of its American Indian wards, succeeded in getting back for her estate more than $200,000 in income taxes and $82,000 in estate taxes—improperly collected by IRS.

But IRS doesn't lose them all, not by any means, as a bright young man who had traveled in Japan, Okinawa, Formosa, the Philippines, France, Belgium, Germany, Spain, Morocco, and Switzerland discovered. When asked by the curious how he made his living, Frank Owens said he had learned to manipulate the slot machines made by one particular manufacturer and that he taught his system to United States servicemen at military bases where the one-armed bandits were in use at servicemen's clubs. For teaching a GI how to disarm the bandits, Owens charged a percentage of the jackpots that resulted.

In his federal income tax return, Owens reported his own winnings as income, but he treated as tax-exempt the much larger amount he claimed he earned for teaching his method of manipulation to others. In one year, he showed his income as $6,300. The tax-exempt teaching income, he claimed, was $20,000.

The basis for his argument was that the $20,000 was compensation for personal services rendered while a bona fide foreign resident. If the compensation had been for personal services, and if the young traveler had, indeed, been a bona fide foreign resident, then his tax treatment of the $20,000 would have been correct.

Confronted by an IRS agent, the bright young man argued, "I taught soldiers two things: to beat the game of gambling itself, hence breaking addiction to it generally, and to beat the element of chance by making a profit for themselves by their skill and knowledge. The money I earned is qualified under Section 911(b) Code of 1954 as 'other amounts received as compensation for personal services actually rendered.'"

The IRS rejected his contention and, later on, so did the Tax Court. As far as the Tax Court could see, even if Owens was a bona fide foreign resident, which was doubtful, he was not receiving compensation for personal services, but rather was engaging in a joint business venture with the soldiers who utilized his knowledge and their money to beat the slot machines for his and their profit.

There are two ways in which you, as a taxpayer, can be exempt from United States income tax on the first $20,000 earned in a year while employed in a foreign country. The simplest way, in terms of proving that you are entitled to it, is to be physically present in a foreign country for at least 510 days (seventeen months) during a period of eighteen months. The other way is to show that you were a resident of the foreign country for the entire year.

One couple, the Petersons, couldn't qualify under the seventeen-months test, so they tried to show that during one year they were actually residents of the Bahamas, where they had worked for a company under contract to the U. S. Air Force to maintain a downrange missile tracking station.

Mrs. Peterson was a typist; her husband was a supply supervisor. They had lived more than a year in the Bahamas and together earned about $12,000. On their income tax returns they claimed they were entitled to exclude from income the $12,000 they had earned.

IRS challenged the claim of foreign residence, declaring the couple must pay $2,000 of income tax on $12,000 reported as earned. IRS also spelled out that the couple could never become residents of the Bahamas for tax purposes, whether they stayed one year or twenty, and gave as its reason the terms of a deal in which the United States had transferred some destroyers to Great Britain and in return had received leases allowing United States use of bases in the Bahamas.

The missile base on which the couple worked had been set up under that treaty and was, for all legal purposes, a part of the United States. Although they were physically present on the island, the Petersons could never be a real part of the local community. Therefore, they weren't subject to its laws and had to pay income tax to the United States.

A Florida pathologist in a high tax bracket wanted to avoid paying taxes on part of his income from a hospital. He lost the argument with IRS, and the result was that nearly every schoolteacher in the United States was helped thereby.

The doctor had instructed the hospital to pay to an insurance company, instead of directly to him, the entire amount of $800 due him each month from the hospital. In turn, the insurance company paid the money into an annuity he had set up. The doctor then reported as his taxable income only the amounts actually paid directly to him by the hospital. The $9,600 per year ($800 times twelve) paid on the annuity was not listed on his income tax return in any category.

IRS auditors wouldn't accept the maneuver. They told the pathologist to pay income tax on the $9,600, even though it had gone to the insurance company and not directly into his pockets.

He decided to fight. His ammunition was a ruling IRS had issued a few years before. It provided that when a nonprofit organization bought an annuity for an employee, the amount it put into the annuity did not count as income to the employee until he started to collect on the annuity.

IRS said that particular ruling didn't apply to the pathologist because the hospital hadn't actually bought an annuity for him. Rather, he had bought the annuity, just as though the hospital had first paid the money into his pockets before he wrote his own check to the insurance company. The fact that he had the hospital make the payment for him had nothing to do with it.

While the case was working its way toward trial, IRS went to Congress to get the law clarified. It was fearful that if the pathologist won his case in Tax Court, many other similar cases would crop up all over the country.

Congress did change the tax law, but not exactly the way IRS wanted it changed. The revised law said that employees of nonprofit organizations could direct the organizations for which they worked to take part of their pay and buy annuities with it. If they did so, this part of the pay would not be income to them. But Congress also put an upper limit on how much pay could be kept nontaxable.

As a result, any employee of a nonprofit organization, including just about every schoolteacher in the United States, today can set aside part of his current earnings for future retirement without having to pay tax on the part set aside.

Curiously enough, when the case came to trial, the pathologist lost. The court decreed he had earned the income and had to pay tax on it, and whether the hospital paid the income to him or to an insurance company made no difference. But the law by then had been "clarified."

Even preachers of the gospel aren't free from the temptation to maneuver around the tax collector. The tax law helps clergymen by exempting from tax the rental allowance paid a minister as part of his salary to the extent that it is used by him to rent or provide a home.

The Reverend Mr. Knight, a tax-conscious minister, persuaded his church trustees in an Indiana town to designate his entire annual income of $13,500 as housing allowance and not as salary. The minister then claimed on his return that he had no income to be taxed.

IRS thought that was going too far with a good thing. Under the tax law, only so much of the housing allowance as was used to provide a home could be treated as nontaxable. Certainly, IRS said, the Reverend Mr. Knight didn't spend his entire income on housing.

The minister replied that he had purchased a new home during the year for $16,000, trading in his old home, plus $1,000 cash, for the new one. "Here are the papers to prove it," he said. "I spent $16,000 to provide a home for my family."

The revenue agent who was auditing the tax return had never run across a problem like this one. He had audited a few returns of ministers who were making mortgage payments, and he knew that those payments were considered part of the cost of providing a home, even though the ministers were also building up equity with every mortgage payment made. The ministers would ultimately have no mortgage payments to make and so would have to report almost all of their housing allowance as income.

Since it would balance out to the same thing in the long run, the agent decided to allow the Reverend Mr. Knight to treat the $13,500 as nontaxable.

"How did he pay for the house he traded?" the revenue agent's supervisor asked when checking the case.

After the agent had inquired and then informed his boss that the traded house had been purchased through housing allowances over many years, the supervisor wouldn't allow the exclusion. He said, "The minister excluded from income the housing allowances he used to buy the old house, so he shouldn't get a second exclusion on the same dollars now by treating the trade of the old house as though he were spending that much cash out of this year's income."

The clergyman had to pay tax on $12,500 of the $13,500 housing allowance he had received. The $1,000 cash he paid out on the new house was the only sum he could hold out in figuring his income tax.

A Chicago-based prizefighter was less subtle than the preacher in the hocus-pocus he tried to work on IRS. He went to court, but didn't prepare for the battle with the same devotion that had marked his training for championship fights.

The boxer was earning big money. He saw about 70 percent of his purses, and his income from television and advertising testimonials, disappear in taxes. He quite naturally feared for a day in the future when most of his money might be gone in taxes and high living. He didn't want to end up as Joe Louis had—forever indebted to the United States Treasury. He sought to forestall such a tragedy by forming a corporation that was supposed to change the 70 percent tax rate, wherein he paid $700 tax for each $1,000 earned, to a 22 percent rate.

IRS stopped the deceptive footwork. It demanded an additional

$10,000 in taxes for a year on the basis that the boxer's corporation did not exist in actual practice. It ruled that since the boxer really earned the income, it was the boxer and not his paper corporation that ought to be taxed.

In Tax Court, IRS told the judge the boxer had never given the corporation a contract for his services, that sometimes he took all the money received from television, and that he took money out of the corporate bank account willy-nilly, just as if it were his personal bank account and not subject to audit.

The Tax Court rang the bell on the fight by giving the decision to IRS. It ruled that the boxer's corporation was a transparent and poorly prepared attempt to escape taxes and that the fighter had not operated the corporation as a corporation should be operated. He was ordered to pay the additional tax of $10,000 plus interest.

One business firm that was profiting through the sale of stationery, pins, emblems, and other supplies to collegiate and honorary sororities and fraternities wanted still larger profits. Its management, located in New York, originated a scheme to organize its own sorority, with membership limited only to those who could afford the initiation fee.

Fraternities and sororities are, of course, tax-exempt. If the new sorority could accumulate money that was tax-free, the company then could build up a reserve on which it would have to pay taxes only as, if, and when it actually drew on the funds for bonuses or an emergency. But the company's executives underestimated IRS, which knew all about Greek letter organizations.

The sorority was established on a national basis. The thing was organized, as its constitution put it, "for the mutual pursuit of culture and friendly social contact among mature women." The average chapter had fifteen members drawn into the sorority by the supply company's paid organizer. The local group paid $300 to the company for a chapter charter. The national initiation fee was $50 per member, the annual national dues $25. All the money thus paid in went to the so-called reserve fund deposited to the national sorority's account at the bank of its choice in its home city. Local dues remained in the coffers of the chapter.

"No," said IRS when it saw the claimed tax exemption on the sorority tax returns. The whole thing looked very pretty on the ledger sheets, but the beauty of it was too flamboyant for IRS, an organization known to take a negative approach to tax schemes. The company, of course, was told to pay taxes for that year on every cent of income from its captive sorority promotion.

Taxpayers get good results from original reasoning when the basis for their reasoning is important to business or land operations. A Texas rancher reasoned that, if a truck fleet owner could write off as an annual expense on his income tax return a part of the cost of his trucks on the theory that they will last only so many years, then a ranch operator could write off each year part of the cost of his land, on the theory that the water that gives it life will last only so many years. And that is exactly what the rancher did.

He had an appraiser estimate what his land would be worth if the water beneath it were to disappear. The difference between what the land had cost him with water and the value the appraiser put on the land without water, he figured as the cost of water. Then he had a geologist estimate how many years it would be before the water table dropped to a level where it wouldn't be economical to pump any more water. The geologist estimated forty years. The Texan divided the cost of the water by forty and deducted that amount on his annual return.

"You can't do that!" said the IRS.

"Why not?" countered the rancher.

The IRS explained that the law permits depletion allowances for oil, copper, sand, gravel—for anything that is a fixed quantity and obviously will be used up—but not on water. Every time it rained, some of the rainfall soaked back into the water table under the rancher's land, IRS pointed out.

"Rain doesn't increase the water table enough," the rancher said. "Every year, the level drops. The geologist has studied it, and he says all the water will be gone in forty years."

There was no precedent for allowing a deduction for water depletion, so IRS told the rancher he could not take his deduction for one-fortieth of the cost of the water.

A judge heard the appraiser testify as to what the Texan's land would be worth without water. He heard the geologist testify that the water would be gone in forty years. The judge allowed the rancher his claimed tax deduction. He said that the rancher had bought water, that the water was being used up as a part of his business, and that the rancher was entitled to deduct each year a reasonable percentage of the original cost of that water to allow for what was used up that year.

When Mike Moriarity, a horse owner, put his money on a very fast thoroughbred, he wound up with a $300,000 tax problem. Flip-Over, which had originally cost Moriarity $20,000, won $275,000 in less than two years of competition. When an injury to a leg ended his racing, the owner put Flip-Over out to stud. The racing success of his colts put the big stallion so much in demand that he brought stud fees of up to $15,000 each, making him a very profitable piece of property.

Since IRS was taking 70 percent of the profit, Moriarity looked around for some way he could get a larger share—but at a smaller tax cost—without selling Flip-Over outright.

"Sell *pieces* of him," his tax adviser suggested. "The people who control General Motors don't own General Motors. They own shares. Why not sell shares in Flip-Over, and continue to be his manager?"

Flip-Over could be bred about 35 times per year, so Moriarity decided to divide the horse up into 35 pieces—on paper. He kept eighteen of the shares for himself and sold seventeen for $40,000 each, for a total of $680,000. On that sum Moriarity paid a capital gains tax of $170,000.

The IRS agents could not accept the tax avoidance project. They wanted to treat the entire $680,000 as ordinary income, taxable at 70 percent. Moriarity had paid $170,000 of tax, and they wanted an additional $300,000, arguing that all Moriarity had done was to collect stud fees in advance, since ownership of a share of Flip-Over entitled the shareowner to breed one mare per year to Flip-Over.

The Tax Court agreed with IRS that if Moriarity had been collecting breeding fees in advance, the fees then should be taxed at the 70 percent rate. The purchasers of the seventeen shares in Flip-Over had, however, really acquired an interest in all gains or losses from the horse, not just the right to breed a mare with him.

The judge decided that the sale of interests in Flip-Over was a bona fide sale of "pieces" of the horse, and so Moriarity was entitled to treat his income as capital gains taxable at 25 percent.

If a physicist from Tucson went seventy miles south on a work assignment, he would be in Mexico. He would not have to pay United States income tax on the first $20,000 of his earned income if he were present in Mexico for 510 full days (seventeen months) out of a period of eighteen consecutive months.

If that same physicist went thousands of miles south—all the way to Antarctica—earned $7,000 a year, and was in Antarctica more than 510 days out of a period of eighteen consecutive months, could he escape United States income tax on his earnings?

It would seem logical that he could. A physicist to whom this case applied thought so. His lawyer agreed with him. But IRS objected and demanded that the physicist come up with $1,300 of income tax.

On what basis? On the basis that Antarctica is not a foreign country! The law says that a taxpayer must be in a foreign country to avoid taxes.

"If I am not in the United States, I must be in a foreign country," argued the physicist. He said he knew the United States had challenged claims of other countries to certain parts of the Antarctic, but he argued that the United States itself had never asserted claims of sovereignty over any part of it.

The IRS answer quoted the tax law as saying that the term "foreign country" means territory under the sovereignty of a government other than that of the United States; since Antarctica is not recognized by the United States as being under the sovereignty of anyone, it is not a foreign country.

"It's unfair," said the physicist.

"Our job is the law and not its fairness," replied the IRS. "Besides, it's no more unfair than the fishing boat captain who had a room in Peru and who fished within two hundred miles of the Peruvian coastline. Peru says that it owns those waters, but the United States doesn't recognize that Peru owns the waters more than three miles out. We convinced the Tax Court that the captain was not in a foreign country when he was more than three miles off the coast of Peru—and he had to pay tax on all his income. Your case is weaker than this, since no nation claimed ownership of the part of Antarctica where you were."

The physicist had to pay.

In a few years there is likely to be a question about the tax status of a man who works on the moon.

CHAPTER TEN

When Gifts Are Income

I don't suppose we will ever get to the point where people are pleased to pay taxes.

—Lyndon B. Johnson

When a taxpayer claims that a gift of money or valuable property is not income, he is in effect stating, "Here is cash, or value, that the U. S. Treasury Department cannot touch. It is mine and mine alone." It is quite natural that the Internal Revenue Service takes sharpshooting aim at such a claim.

There are some gifts about which there can be no argument: If your father gives you $3,000 every year, it is a gift. Other forms of gifts can't easily be tagged in a category. When IRS says, "It isn't really a gift; the burden of proof is on you," you can pay the tax or fight. Lots of taxpayers take up the challenge.

A young woman named Julie was, at twenty-four, both irresistible and unresisting to fifty-five-year-old Peter of Phoenix. He bought her a condominium apartment, paid her living expenses, and thrilled her with expensive gifts. In return, she gave him companionship without the complications of marriage. No prying neighbors interfered, no private detectives invaded their love nest. It was a lovely time for both until IRS stuck its nose into the arrangement. Julie had failed to file income tax returns. A revenue agent wanted to know why.

"But I have no income," she answered.

"Where did this apartment and these furs come from?" the agent asked.

"I have a friend," replied Julie. "He likes to give me things."

"It looks like compensation for personal services to me," remarked the agent. He added that she would have to pay taxes and a penalty on what she had received.

"You've got to fight them," Peter told her. "It's not just the money. They're trying to tarnish our relationship."

When Julie appealed the tax ruling, IRS tried to make the point in Tax Court that she was really a one-man call girl. The gifts were her fees for practicing the oldest profession. Peter testified that his motives for what he gave Julie were his affection for her and his desire to continue their warm friendship.

"Not really any different than my motives when I give my wife presents," decided the judge. He ruled that Julie had no income and hence owed no tax, that absence of a marriage license did not automatically convert gifts to taxable income.

If you have received a gift that you and the giver are convinced is indeed a gift—no matter how it looks to the IRS agent—then you can, and may have to, go from the auditing agent's desk right up to a judge, as Julie did, and as a young couple in Los Angeles decided to do after a fruitless argument with IRS.

An elderly aunt had given $10,000 to an electronics engineer and his bride—Charles and Ida Bergstrom—after they signed a contract with her guaranteeing that she could live with them the rest of her life. The IRS went after the Bergstroms. They had failed to report the $10,000 "gift" as income on their annual tax return. Meanwhile, the aunt had died after living with them for a year or so.

"You could treat the $10,000 as a gift and not have to report it as income if it were, indeed, a gift," the IRS said. "A gift, however, is the exact opposite of a payment for services to be rendered. You received the $10,000 for services, and therefore it is taxable."

The young engineer tried to explain to IRS the full story of his aunt's unselfish motives in giving them $10,000. He had been reared by her, and they had always been as close as mother and son. The aunt knew, he said, that she would always have a home with them. She had wanted them to have the $10,000 during her lifetime so she could take pleasure in observing their greater security in a hard world.

At the time the gift was to be made, the family lawyer had worried over the possibility of grumbling by other relatives. He feared that after the aunt died some of them might challenge the gift and try to take a portion of it away from her favorites. It was he who had suggested a contract stipulating that the $10,000 was a gift made in return for the young couple's promise to provide a home for the aunt for the remainder of her life. The lawyer had reasoned that no one could then reasonably stake a claim on the money. The lawyer, however, had forgotten about the tax collector.

The IRS contended the contract was the best evidence possible that the sum of $10,000 had been paid for services and was not a gift. The revenue people gave no credence to the stories told by the Bergstroms and their lawyer. The couple paid the $3,000 additional tax bill that resulted from the IRS ruling. They then sued for a refund and finally were able to tell their story to a jury—the same story they had told the IRS. The difference was that the jury believed them. The young engineer and his wife won their case against IRS, and their tax money was repaid with interest.

It has been demonstrated innumerable times in contests with IRS that whenever a gift is related to services rendered, the tax problem is intensified.

A Philadelphia city fireman who had worked on his days off as gardener for a wealthy man is a case in point. When the rich man was unable to get his driver's license renewed because of his age, the fireman began to serve as his chauffeur, and was paid each day for the work of that day.

Sometimes the employer made cash gifts to the fireman—one of them for $2,000—in addition to wages, of course. He was fond of the fireman's wife and three children and frequently invited the family to visit in his beautiful home on the Main Line. In one year, the fireman received extra checks totaling $1,225; in the next year, $7,840, and in the year the employer and benefactor died, $6,850.

In an audit of the estate, IRS discovered the canceled checks made out to the fireman. On each check was the one-word notation—"gift."

"These are for extra pay," stated IRS, and asked the fireman to pay $3,800 more on his income tax, plus interest.

Although the employer had said the checks of large amount were gifts, a revenue agent ruled that anything paid by an employer to his employee was additional compensation and taxable. The fireman took his problem to court.

The Tax Court judge ruled that the picture of the relationship had to be viewed as a whole. The sum of approximately $2,000 the fireman had earned every year for his part-time services seemed to the judge to be reasonable pay for those services. Furthermore, an amount such as $7,840 would appear to be more than additional pay. When the fireman and his wife described the friendly relationship between the rich Main Liner and their family, the judge said it was clear that none of the extra checks had been intended by the benefactor to be additional pay. The fireman therefore didn't have to pay the added tax.

Then, of course, there are transactions claimed as gifts that by their very nature give rise to suspicion they are in reality something else—a gift that would not have been made except for reasons of competition in business.

A New York investment adviser who published a weekly newsletter received a gift of 2,000 shares of a certain corporation's stock. The stock had a value of $36,000. IRS said the investment counselor must pay tax on the value of the stock because it was not a gift but, in fact, a fee paid to help drum up investor interest in the company and push up the price of the stock.

The investment man was able to upset the IRS contention, but he had to pay the tax bill anyway.

IRS had good reason to think the stock was payment to him for touting the company because, during the years before he was given the stock, his newsletter had rarely mentioned the company. After the gift was made, the small publication had mentioned the company and its activities more than sixty times in two years. The IRS agent had counted them. He wouldn't swallow the story of a big company giving away $36,000 worth of stock for nothing in return.

The investment counselor appealed to the Tax Court to rule that he, the taxpayer, did not, in fact, owe a tax on $36,000 worth of stock. The trial revealed that the investment man had acted for the company in the beginning as a middleman in lining up a big contract. Everything had been set, but the company had backed out at the last minute. So the investment man did not receive a promised commission of about

$40,000 for setting up the deal. His disappointment must have been cured, however, when he received one day by registered mail an envelope containing the stock certificates in question.

The Tax Court found no evidence that the stock had been received as payment for mentioning the company in the newsletter. The judge ruled that the $36,000 in question was taxable, however, since the stock gift obviously was a consolation payment for the lost commission.

The president of a small-town bank in North Dakota was charged with contributing to the delinquency of a girl employed by the bank. After a trial he was acquitted. Tongues in the town continued to wag, however, so the banker sued the girl and her family for slander. He won a judgment in court for $5,000, but he was unable to collect it because the girl and her family didn't have $5,000. The banker's expenses in pushing the suit into court had amounted to $8,000. The officers of the bank agreed the bank should reimburse its president for the expenses.

When he didn't report the $8,000 as income on his tax return an IRS agent asked him, "Why not? It was decent of the bank to pay the bill, but such expenses are personal and not deductible. Therefore, it is just so much additional salary for you. You must pay tax on it."

The banker informed the tax agent, who was a big-city dweller and only temporarily assigned to the small town, that it was apparent he didn't understand small towns and small-town banking. He spelled out to the agent that, so far as the community was concerned, he, the president, *was* the bank. In a small town, a bank is like a church or a school. It is an institution more than a business. People don't deal with it because it makes larger interest payments than some other institution, but because they trust it or because it has moral character. The bank's deposits had actually dropped five percent in the months after the case involving the female employee, and had climbed back up to normal only after the banker won the suit for slander.

The revenue agent remained unconvinced. So far as he could see, all the bank had to do if its president was an embarrassment was to boot him out and promote one of the vice-presidents to his job.

The banker was willing to go to Tax Court if he really had to, but he had his fill of courts. He said to the agent, "I won't accept your ruling as final. Where can I go higher up in Internal Revenue Service to explain my case to someone who might have a better understanding of it, someone who is better qualified to judge that this was a gift and not a salary payment?"

The agent told him that a district conference at IRS was available to all taxpayers who were not satisfied with the decision of the agent who was first assigned to their cases. The banker said that was exactly what he wanted.

He went to the conference alone. The conferee assigned to the case was broad-minded. He had been a small-town boy himself, he said. He understood why the bank was just as much involved in the morals case as was its president. He reversed the revenue agent's decision and ruled that the bank president owed no tax on the $8,000, that even though the court actions named only the president, and not the bank, nevertheless the bank's success and profitability were as directly involved as was the bank president's reputation. The $8,000 given by the bank was, indeed, a gift.

Sometimes, however, neither IRS nor the Tax Court defines a gift as legitimate even when it obviously is to almost everyone else. If you plan to present an expensive gift to an athletic star or a coach, be sure not to give it to him because of the games he has won. Instead, reward him for his contribution to the community or for his educational achievement, for the literary style of his locker room exhortations or the artistic value of the pinup girls pasted on the inside of his locker door.

Because a certain pro backfield star was the outstanding player in the 1961 National Football League championship game, a sports magazine awarded him a plaque and an expensive automobile. IRS demanded that the big-time athlete pay income tax on the value of the car.

The tax law says that gifts are not taxable income. The question then was whether the car was a gift from the magazine to the player. IRS thought it was not, that the magazine's motive was not inspired by generosity but by a desire for advertising and promotional benefits.

IRS conceded that the gift of the auto fell into the category of a prize or an award, but whether the car was taxable to the player depended upon whether he could show it was given him "in recognition of scientific, educational, artistic, literary, or civic achievement." When the Nobel Prize, for example, is awarded for literary or scientific achievement, the recipient doesn't have to report it as income. IRS didn't think the award of a car for playing football was in the same category as the award of a Nobel Prize for promoting peace or writing a novel.

Is football educational, artistic, or scientific? The question has plagued lawmakers and college administrators for decades, ever since the University of Chicago dropped football on the basis of a decision that it was not educational.

The football player decided to fight. He took the case to the Tax Court, where he argued that football was educational, artistic, and scientific. It was educational because it was taught in leading colleges and universities as a part of certain physical education courses. It was artistic because the grace and skill of a running back were comparable to those of a prima ballerina. It was scientific because a football player had to be a mathematician in order to unravel the diagrams of plays.

The judge said he also thought that football was a terrific game, that it was fun to watch and a leading American industry. He ruled, however, that the player had to pay income tax on the value of the car because it was not a gift in the true tax meaning of the word.

Marietta, the telephone operator at a country club outside Minneapolis, found herself in tax trouble because she thought that a Christmas present she had received from the club was a gift in the real meaning of the word, rather than income on which she was required to pay income tax.

The tax-exempt club provided eating, dancing, and sports facilities for its members and their guests. "No tipping to the club employees" was the rule. So, each holiday season the members were invited to contribute to an employee bonus fund. Each club employee received a distribution—described as a "Christmas gift from members"—based on the length of his employment, his salary, the quality of his work, and the amount distributed to him the previous year.

For many years Marietta had not reported the cash Christmas gifts in making out her income tax return. The club had not reported the gifts on the withholding statements it furnished employees and had not deducted income tax from the gifts. In fact, lawyer members had informed the club's board of directors that the gifts were not taxable income to the employees since they were made directly by the members.

The IRS took its cue, not from the opinion of the club's lawyers, but from the Supreme Court definition of what constitutes a gift for tax purposes which holds that for something to be considered a gift, and therefore not subject to income tax, it must be based upon detached and disinterested generosity, out of affection, respect, admiration, or charity. IRS said the Christmas gifts from the members to the employees were intended as compensation for the services rendered by the employees during the year. Marietta, the telephone operator, therefore had to pay income tax on $400 she had thought was a Christmas present.

In another Christmas case, a greeting card manufacturer decided to discontinue its annual Christmas party and instead give each employee a $25 gift certificate as a Christmas present. The employee could then redeem the certificate in any store that handled the company's products —but only for merchandise.

The company had considered the certificates as gifts to its workers, and so it did not withhold tax on the amounts involved.

The IRS ordered the company to pay the withholding tax that would have been due if the certificates had been additional pay. The company went to court and charged IRS with violating one of its own published rulings, to the effect that the value of a turkey, a ham, or similar item distributed to an employee at Christmas as a means of promoting goodwill did not, in view of the small amounts involved, constitute wages subject to withholding. The IRS countered with the argument that the gift certificates were readily convertible into cash, and therefore the ruling, by its terms, did not apply to them.

However, on the back of each certificate was this statement that the store redeeming it was required to endorse: "We have honored this bond in payment for merchandise selected in our store." The judge said such an endorsement made it quite clear the certificate could not be turned into cash.

IRS argued further that the ruling didn't apply because the certificates were not of "relatively small value." The judge disagreed, declaring that a certificate for $25 was certainly of "relatively small value" in terms of current price levels, and concluded that the Christmas gifts did not have to be reported by the employees as taxable income.

The problems of politicians who have received campaign contributions that were then spent for personal rather than political purposes have been detailed many times, even in the U. S. Senate in the case of Senator Thomas J. Dodd, Connecticut Democrat.

Typical of many such cases was one involving a Wisconsin sheriff who was $12,000 better off two years after he took office than he had been on election day, and who was currently living in a fashion that required a fairly large income—more than the job paid.

Since the income reported on the sheriff's tax return was so much less than the amount he was spending plus the amount by which his net worth was increasing, IRS concluded that something crooked was taking place. It charged the sheriff with tax fraud.

The sheriff had an easy explanation for his affluence. He said many people had donated many political gifts to him. One had been from a former patrolman in the sheriff's department prior to the sheriff's election. After the election, the patrolman had made a gift of $1,000 to the sheriff. Soon afterward, he had been promoted over some corporals and sergeants to the position of lieutenant. A businessman who was in the habit of giving the sheriff $500 every year as a contribution to his campaign fund was the supplier of gas and oil for the sheriff patrol's automobiles.

The sheriff insisted the gifts did not constitute taxable income to him and, even if they did, he certainly was not guilty of tax fraud. He had relied on the advice of his lawyer in not reporting the gifts on his tax return. The lawyer had, in fact, written a letter to the sheriff stating he had checked the law and had found that gifts to assist in the sheriff's political campaign were not taxable income.

But gifts used to pay personal expenses or deposited in personal bank accounts could hardly be said to be used in political campaigns. The sheriff was found guilty of tax fraud and sentenced to eighteen months in prison.

The pay you get for working is taxable income, but what about the pay you may get for not working? State-paid unemployment compensation is exempt from federal income tax, for example. Strike benefits are another matter. The following two cases involved strikers in different labor disputes. One received benefits on which he didn't have to pay federal income tax. The other's strike benefits were subject to tax.

The first striker—Kowalski—worked for a plumbing equipment manufacturer. Although he wasn't a member of the union, he joined the others and walked off the job when the union called a strike. Then he went to the union's headquarters and asked for help, and the union gave him food vouchers and paid his house rent.

It was the policy of the union to grant assistance to strikers on the basis of need, whether or not they were union members. Benefits were not cut off if a man didn't participate in the picketing. After receiving help from the union for several months, Kowalski joined the union.

The IRS classified the strike benefits by Kowalski as taxable income. The case eventually reached the Supreme Court, which held that those particular payments were not subject to income tax, but rather were gifts to the striker.

The striker in the second case—Canebreaker—a truck driver, could hardly argue that the benefits he received constituted a gift. When his local went out on strike against the trucking company, both the international and the local started paying him strike benefits. The IRS treated the strike benefits as income and asked Canebreaker to pay more tax. The union, however, had a different idea and helped the trucker appeal to the courts against the IRS levy.

The Tax Court judge noted the benefits had been authorized before the strike vote was taken, and he commented that this fact undoubtedly had some influence on the willingness of the truckers to vote for the strike. Accordingly, he stated, "It is not without significance that benefits were payable only to striking members." Canebreaker was ordered to pay tax on the benefits he had received.

In none of the gift cases discussed so far in this chapter did the donors or recipients argue over the value of the gifts. They could not, because in every case the gift, or payment claimed as a gift, was in hard cash. A dollar is a dollar. What happens, then, when a taxpayer receives something like a mink coat and later discovers the luxury wrap wasn't worth what the giver said it was? This letter from a contestant on a television program poses such a question:

A year ago I won a full-length mink coat on a TV show. The TV producer gave me an information return (Form 1099) which listed the value of the coat as $3,195. I reported this amount as income on my tax return, even though two competing furriers to whom I took the coat for appraisal each informed me that he could not sell the coat at retail for more than $1,800. Is there anything I can do about this tax I have overpaid?—LL.

While TV producers normally report the manufacturer's suggested retail price as the value of the prizes they give away, such valuation is not the last word. If the lady could show that there existed a retail market for the mink coat in which it would have sold for $1,800 at the time she received it, she might be able to get back the excess tax she paid. However, the burden of proving that the value was only $1,800 was on her. It was not the job of the IRS to prove that it was worth $3,195, or any other specific figure.

CHAPTER ELEVEN

Medical Expenses

The first nine pages of the Internal Revenue Code define income; the remaining 1,100 pages spin the web of exceptions and preferences.

—Senator Warren G. Magnuson, 1966

Whether or not many items of medical expenses are deductible from tax returns is a matter that has produced many head-to-head discussions between taxpayers and agents of the Internal Revenue Service. Some of those cases have gone to court, but one that did not get that far was outlined by a young advertising copywriter in a telephone call to the tax people.

"I'd like to know," she inquired, "the answer to a question that may be very important to women who are not married. In making out my income tax return, can I deduct the cost of birth control pills? I am not married."

The answer she got was reasonable: "You can deduct the cost of birth control pills, subject to the percentage limitation on income, if either your physician or your psychiatrist prescribes them. Otherwise, the pills would be nondeductible personal expense, like toothpaste or deodorant."

Some agents, however, are unyielding about it. They sometimes state that IRS is willing to let anybody deduct the cost of all kinds of pills from federal income tax as a medical expense, provided the pills are prescribed for the prevention of disease or the relief of pain, but that The Pill is another matter.

What if the woman taking The Pill is married and already a mother? Pat McGinnis, a used car dealer in New Jersey, found the answer when he deducted from his tax return the cost to his wife of taking The Pill.

The couple had two children. They wanted no more because the second child had been born by cesarean section and the mother had been close to death for several days afterward. Their physician had later prescribed birth control pills. When the husband and father made out his income tax return for that year, he included the cost of the pills in the family's list of medical expenses.

It so happened that the return was selected by IRS for audit because the other medical expenses and other deductions were high for the husband's level of income. The IRS assigned a woman auditor to talk with the husband. Rather embarrassedly, she pointed out to him that such "personal expenses" were nondeductible. She said she would disallow the $40 item (the cost of the pills) and stated firmly she would not discuss the matter further.

The used car dealer was embarrassed, too. He asked to speak to her supervisor. In the meeting that followed, the supervisor, also a father, agreed that perhaps birth control pills ought to be deductible under some circumstances. He was unwilling, however, to take responsibility for authorizing such a deduction. In due time, the Washington office of IRS ruled that "the cost of oral contraceptives prescribed to prevent childbirth may be deducted as a medical expense when, in the opinion of the physician, the possibility of childbirth is a serious threat to the life of a wife."

That ruling was reasonable, but IRS has sometimes demonstrated a peculiar kind of blindness when it has ruled on misfortunes due to sickness.

Consider the case of a little girl in Los Angeles who had been born with cystic fibrosis, a chronic hereditary disease of the pancreas and lungs for which there is as yet no known cure. The most her parents could do to make her comfortable was to battle the mounting course of the disease by installing an air conditioner in her bedroom. The rest of the house remained dependent on the random fluctuations of the weather for comfort.

To be incurably ill, to be unable to play with other children, is bad enough for a child. To be in isolation in a single room compounds it into a tragedy. The emotional impact on the child and her family was so severe that their doctor recommended that the entire house be air-conditioned. Then the girl could have a nearly normal existence inside the home.

Her life became better at once. The cost of the central air conditioning was $2,500. Because the installation was estimated to have increased the value of the house by $1,000, the parents deducted the balance of $1,500 as a medical expense on their federal income tax return for the year.

The IRS agent who audited the return didn't look at the house, nor did he visit the sick girl. His job was not to explore, but to deal with pieces of paper and faceless names. He didn't approve of the way the tax return covered the family's problem. He said the single-room air conditioner was, in his opinion, sufficient to delay the deadly progress of the cystic fibrosis, air conditioning of the entire house was a luxury, and the cost, therefore, was not deductible because all the members of the family benefited.

The Tax Court's vision was broader. Its judge said he understood the problems the family had solved so well with complete air conditioning for the house. He was aware, too, he said, of the psychological problems of an ill child, especially the problems of a child who was saddled with an incurable disease. The judge ruled that since the central air conditioning had been installed in the house on the recommendation of the attending physician, the parents were entitled to a medical expense deduction for the cost of putting in the unit to the extent that it didn't increase the value of their house—$1,500 worth.

The Tax Court displayed a similar outpouring of common sense and a measure of compassion in the case of a Louisville waitress. She had a difficult time with the tax men when she wanted to deduct the cost of meals and motels for a trip to the Mayo Clinic in Rochester, Minnesota, where she had undergone successful surgery for a complicated condition of varicose veins.

IRS said it would not allow the entire deduction, although it would allow five cents a mile for the expense of driving her auto from Louisville to Minnesota and return.

The IRS argument was simplicity itself. The law allows a deduction "for transportation primarily for and essential to medical care." Driving the car from Kentucky to Minnesota and back was transportation, all right, but food and overnight hotel or motel accommodations were something else again in the IRS official's mind, the idea seeming to be that the waitress didn't need to eat or sleep on the three-day auto trip.

"If we were to hold otherwise," IRS officials contended "it would open the door to all sorts of shenanigans. Taxpayers would take trips to obtain medical treatment, but would go by roundabout routes with stopovers at resort facilities."

"So what has that to do with me?" asked the waitress when the case reached the Tax Court. "I took no roundabout routes, and no stopovers except to sleep."

"You are right," ruled the Tax Court. "We can deal with such abuse situations as they arise and sift out those expenses which are not required to bring the patient to the place of medication." The waitress was allowed to take the deduction for the costs of the meals and motel accommodations.

Problems involving deductions for children's medical expenses are not all related to physical health. A Delaware teen-ager, whom we shall call Don, was good-looking, healthy, and appeared to be happy. But he was six years behind his age group in school. Although his intelligence was rated as above average, he wasn't learning anything. Psychiatrists had diagnosed the trouble as a neurotic block against learning—part of severe emotional problems that led to excessive flights of fantasy, day-dreaming, self-deprecation, and an inability to sit still or concentrate except for limited periods of time.

His psychiatrist was convinced Don needed a therapeutic-educational program that would allow him to experience some academic success and thus break his lifelong pattern of failure. The psychiatrist recommended a particular academy where students were taught individually, at their own level and at their own pace. The headmaster provided psychotherapy for those boys needing it.

Although the cost amounted to $11,000 a year, as compared to $3,500 for twelve months at a regular boarding school, the academy proved well worth the price. In less than two years, Don managed to finish work that was equivalent to the normal high school curriculum. He later attended college and then served with success in the army.

When Don's father filed a tax return, he deducted as a medical expense the $11,000 he had paid the academy. IRS refused to allow the deduction, insisting that the $11,000 spent was "the cost of ordinary education."

The father went to the Tax Court and appealed the IRS decision. In the course of the trial, the IRS lawyers became aware that the judge was impressed by the evidence, so they took time out to explain to him that IRS was reluctant to allow such a deduction because to do so would "encourage parents to obtain a recommendation from a psychiatrist before sending their children to private schools" in order to get a medical expense deduction.

The judge said he didn't believe the IRS had anything to fear in making a precedent of the case because "courts dealing with such deductions would require strong proof." He said that Don's father had proved his right to a deduction and should receive it. However, he added that the deduction should not include what would otherwise have been "ordinary education expense." Accordingly, he allowed a deduction for the amount by which the academy's charge of $11,000 exceeded the $3,500 that would normally have been paid to a private boarding school.

As we have stated, or implied, by citing the record in many pages of this book, IRS often attempts to rewrite the tax law, and IRS usually rewrites the law *against* the taxpayer. Here is another example dealing with a case the court put down in quick time:

When a corporation pays personal living expenses of a stockholder, an argument with the federal tax people is bound to arise. But when a corporation pays the medical expenses of one of its stockholders, the payments may sometimes be allowed.

Each of two men—Brown and Andros—owned 50 percent of the stock of a garment bag manufacturer. Both worked full-time for the corporation, which had agreed in writing to pay all their medical expenses and all the medical expenses of their dependents. The expense amounted to $5,000 one year—$2,200 and $2,800 respectively.

IRS objected. The corporation, said IRS, could not deduct the $5,000 as an expense. In addition, Brown and Andros each had to report his portion of the $5,000 in expenses for medical care as dividend income. The corporation's accountants spelled out to the IRS agent making the audit that the tax law specifically indicated this particular medical reimbursement plan was allowable.

IRS answered that it would, indeed, be all right if the plan covered the other fifty employees of the company, as well as the two stockholder-officers. Tax deficiencies were proposed against both the corporation and Brown and Andros, but the accountants refused to interpret the law the IRS way.

In Tax Court, the judge declared that there was nothing in the law requiring all employees to be covered. He concluded that if Congress had not written such a requirement into the law, even though IRS had at the time urged it to do so, the Tax Court was not going to write it in now.

"In fact," said the court, "it would be unfortunate if the payments made by the corporation failed to qualify simply because the employees who received them also happened to be stockholders."

The corporation was allowed to deduct the medical expenses, and the two beneficiaries had no taxable income from the medical payments made in their behalf.

If a taxpayer undergoes an operation for hernia or for removal of his tonsils there is no doubt that the item is a medical expense. IRS will always grant that fact without argument. But if a taxpayer comes up with something unusual, he will have to explain. IRS gets upset when a taxpayer or his problem is "different."

Here, in quick succession, are four cases—out of perhaps thousands of "different" cases—that IRS questioned. In each instance, the taxpayer wanted a deduction for medical expense and IRS said it was not allowable. Two of the cases went to court for decision and IRS won one of them. Two other cases were decided in favor of the taxpayer by the IRS itself after the taxpayer gave battle.

One case involved a San Francisco dancer who specialized in the exotic on stage. She paid a plastic surgeon $2,500 to straighten her nose and enlarge her breasts with a series of silicone injections. She deducted payment for the surgery as a medical expense on her federal income tax return.

A woman revenue agent audited the dancer's tax return. She sympathized with the taxpayer's desire to improve her appearance, but told her, "A medical expense is money paid to prevent or alleviate a physical or mental defect or illness. How can I allow such a deduction for you?"

"My bustline and my nose were physical defects in my kind of work," the dancer argued.

The revenue agent argued back, "By the same reasoning you ought to be able to deduct the cost of the food you eat, since it is consumed for the purpose of giving you the strength to work. The tax law doesn't stretch that far."

The dancer insisted she was entitled to the deduction, that she had spent $2,500 to help her income, which income was then subject to tax. Therefore, she was entitled to some tax relief for the expenditures, just as she was permitted to deduct her union dues and the cost of her exotic and expensive costumes.

The flaw in her argument was that the $2,500 spent in one year would help to produce income over many years.

"I've got ten years to go," reasoned the dancer. "Then I'll be through with this kind of work."

The woman revenue agent relented to the tune of $250 a year for ten years as a tax deduction, on the theory that the bust building and nose straightening were for business purposes and that the cost should be allowed as an offset to the business income earned and reported on the tax return.

Then there was the librarian who had spent thousands of dollars on psychiatrists in trying to overcome an excessive shyness. She had journeyed to a clinic in Paris that treated emotional problems through an offbeat process that changed the patient's handwriting. The trip had cost $2,000 for transportation and fees.

When she returned home, the librarian informed her friends that she felt she had acquired in Paris a more outgoing personality, that the trip and the five weeks of treatment at the clinic had done her a lot of good. Privately, her friends credited her changed outlook to the fact of her having been in Paris.

She claimed the expenditure of $2,000 as a medical expense on her tax return for the year. In previous years she had been allowed deductions for fees paid to psychiatrists who, she now reasoned, had not helped her a fraction as much as the Paris clinicians.

The IRS asked to look at the bills, cancelled checks, and airline tickets that would substantiate her claim. After examining the proofs, the agent said to her, "I don't see how it can be accepted as deductible. If you had gone to Paris for a surgical operation that you couldn't get anywhere else, then your travel expenses might be allowed. But this Paris venture is quack medicine."

The librarian was no longer shy. "Quackery or not," she retorted, "I'm entitled to the deduction. There are cases and rulings allowing deductions for payments for almost anything, so long as the purpose is to prevent or treat disease. Why, I heard of a tax ruling that allowed a deduction for the fee paid an Indian medicine man when he performed a dance to drive evil spirits from a person who was sick."

Faced with such determination, the IRS agent read up on the medicine man case. There was such a ruling. He allowed the librarian the claimed deduction in full for the trip and treatment in Paris.

A U.S. Post Office clerk in Washington, D.C., didn't do well at all when he tried to deduct expenses for what had been a good time. He was suffering from varicose veins when he read that dancing would help to relieve or even cure the condition. At a dance studio, the manager told him that dancing lessons and dancing would, of course, be very helpful to anyone with varicose veins.

"In fact," the manager emphasized, "dancing will be so helpful that you can probably take a deduction on your income tax return for the cost of the lessons as a medical expense."

The clerk signed up for a $2,200 course and the dancing really did make him feel better. He deducted that $2,200 on his income tax return.

When IRS said, "You cannot deduct the cost of your dancing lessons as a medical expense," the post office clerk appealed the decision to the

Tax Court. The dance studio's lawyer represented him before the judge.

The Tax Court was particularly interested in the postal clerk's work. The judge wanted to know why he hadn't sought transfer to a mail carrier route if he believed exercise would relieve or cure the condition of varicose veins. Why had he been content to work at what was essentially a sedentary job? The clerk had no answer.

The job factor, plus the fact that no doctor had prescribed dancing as treatment for the circulatory condition, convinced the judge that whatever value the dance lessons might have had either socially or physically, they had no medical value.

Then there is the cost of a diet as a possible medical expense. It is surprising how many people want the government to exempt such cost. Very few taxpayers win an argument in that direction. An occasional stalwart defender does succeed, however.

If a diet is an addition to the regular diet, and is exclusively for treatment of an illness, the taxpayer has a medical expense. But when the diet is a substitute for the regular diet in order to provide ordinary nourishment, he does not have a deductible medical expense, even though the diet has been prescribed by a doctor. If he had gone on the drinking man's diet when that fad was sweeping the country, IRS wouldn't have let him deduct the cost as a medical expense, and no one is known to have offered to fight for it. A salt-free diet, however, is another matter.

One taxpayer, a Southern Pacific Railroad locomotive engineer, had to eat many meals away from home. Sometimes he had to pay an additional charge in order to get salt-free dishes. He insisted to IRS that the extra amount he paid, over and above what the food regularly cost, was a deductible medical expense. IRS disagreed, but the Tax Court allowed a deduction.

However, when the railroad man claimed in a later year that the extra cost of renting a kitchenette while on vacation was incurred in order to allow his wife to prepare his salt-free meals and, therefore, the difference between the cost of the kitchenette and accommodations without should be deductible, the IRS disallowed the deduction and the courts backed up the decision.

IRS is not a bureau made up of fools, and a taxpayer had better not try to make its people look like fools. For example, a Californian who had installed a fallout shelter on his property was not allowed to deduct the cost of building it as a medical expense. IRS said that the danger of radiation sickness was too remote for the shelter to be categorized as preventive medicine.

A newspaper reader wrote to an editor: "The law says that amounts paid to prevent disease are deductible as medical expense. Some people live to eat, but others eat to live and that describes me. I eat nothing but health foods and so I intend to deduct all my food bills as medical expense."

The idea sounds good, but the courts say, "Not a chance!"

CHAPTER TWELVE

Using the Tax Power to Punish

That the power to tax involves the power to destroy (is) not to be denied.
— Justice John Marshall, 1819

Under our constitutional system, a person is presumed to be innocent of a crime until he is found guilty under due process of law. In a civil tax case, the situation is not always so simple or clear-cut. A taxpayer, for example, can find himself in serious trouble, faced with the burden of proving he did not commit a crime, even though he has not been charged with a crime.

The United States Supreme Court has, on numerous occasions, told the Internal Revenue Service to stop worrying about the morals of taxpayers and confine its attention to the business of collecting taxes. But the IRS can't seem to follow the court's advice. It continues to build tax cases against people who have become embroiled in other sections of the law and it gathers evidence against these people from studies of their participation in crimes and misdemeanors that in themselves have nothing to do with taxes.

There is on record the case of a stockbroker who took his case all the way to the Supreme Court and was directly responsible for making the IRS fall flat on its tax-collecting face.

The stockbroker, found guilty of fraud and sentenced to serve nearly five years in prison, was also fined $18,000. In his prison cell, he found some consolation in the thought that he could deduct $23,000 on his income tax for the legal expense he had incurred while trying to keep out of prison. IRS examined his return and threw up its defenses. The stockbroker was told he couldn't take such a deduction.

IRS contended that legal expenses absorbed during an unsuccessful criminal case were not a necessary part of a stockbroker's business and that to allow a deduction for such an item would mean that all U.S. taxpayers were, in fact, paying for his attempt to avoid penalty for an act of fraud.

When the case came before the Tax Court, the judge agreed with IRS. The stockbroker, though, was as tough as he was sharp. He appealed and his case reached the United States Supreme Court. The fact that the fraud charges had arisen directly from the stockbroker's business of selling stock meant, to the Supreme Court, that the expenses were a "necessary" part of the broker's business. "Necessary," for tax purposes, means "appropriate or helpful" to the taxpayer's business, the court said.

If IRS were permitted to allow such expenses, would it thus really help to frustrate some clear national policy? That was the basic issue, as the Supreme Court saw it, and the court said it also felt that Congress had *already* put into the securities laws its idea of what was fit punishment for the crime the stockbroker had committed.

Since the taxpayer had a right to employ lawyers to help him in his defense when charged with a crime, and since Congress had never clearly stated that expenses of even an illegal business were nondeductible, the Supreme Court reversed the IRS and the Tax Court. The high court's opinion was that if the stockbroker could *not* deduct the $23,000 of legal expenses, he was being punished twice for the crime—once when he went to prison, and again when the IRS refused to permit the deduction. The court ruled that he was entitled to a tax deduction of $23,000 for his legal expenses.

There is something reassuring in the Supreme Court's written opinion in which it declined to distort the income tax laws:

> We start with the proposition that the federal income tax is a tax on net income, not a sanction against wrongdoing. . . . Congress has authorized the imposition of severe punishment upon those found guilty of the serious criminal offenses with which the respondent was charged and of which he was convicted. But we can find no warrant for attaching to that punishment an additional financial burden that Congress has neither expressly nor implicitly directed.

To deny a deduction for expenses incurred in the unsuccessful defense of a criminal prosecution would impose such a burden in a measure dependent not on the seriousness of the offense or the actual sentence imposed by the Court, but on the cost of the defense and the defendant's particular tax bracket. We decline to distort the income tax laws to serve a purpose for which they were neither intended nor designed by Congress.

While no good citizen can approve of wrongdoing, it makes thoughtful people uneasy to see the tax laws used to punish people indirectly for things that the government cannot punish directly, or to punish a person a second time for something for which he has already been punished.

Actually, a person who has been convicted of a crime and sent to prison may be better off in one way than you, who have never committed a crime, if the IRS starts an investigation.

In prison, a man loses many of his rights as a citizen, including the right to vote. Yet in prison a taxpayer enjoys rights that may not be enjoyed by a free, law-abiding citizen. The reason is that a taxpayer who is sitting in his home or office, with no police in the vicinity, usually does not have the toughness of moral fiber and technical knowledge of his rights to help him refuse to answer questions put by investigators sent to interrogate him during a so-called fishing expedition. (Oftentimes, a taxpayer has no idea why the investigators are questioning him, and they aren't usually very cooperative in explaining what the fishing is all about.)

IRS has sometimes operated on the basis that when a taxpayer is not in the custody of a law enforcement agent, he need *not* be advised by the IRS of his absolute right to have an attorney present during an interview by IRS special agents, which is to say investigators. But a taxpayer who is a convict has already learned what his rights are, and he will fare much better when facing IRS—precisely because he is in prison.

A certain taxpayer with the alias of Swensson battled IRS on that very point. He appealed a conviction on a tax fraud charge and his argument was that, under the Miranda decision of the United States Supreme Court, the information obtained from him during an interview by the revenue agent had been obtained improperly and so could not be used against him. The IRS argued that the Miranda requirement, which provided that the accused be informed he could have an attorney present and that an attorney would be provided if he couldn't afford one, did not apply because, at the time of the interview, there was no certainty that a criminal tax case would ever develop and, anyhow, the taxpayer was not in the custody of federal officials, but was in a state prison for a completely unrelated charge.

The Supreme Court said no to both of those arguments, commenting on tax investigations in these words: "Such investigations frequently lead to criminal prosecutions, just as the one here did. . . . We reject the contention that tax investigations are immune from the Miranda requirements for warnings to be given a person in custody."

To show how a taxpayer can get into tax trouble when he has done no wrong, but has been investigated by U.S. Treasury agents on suspicion of doing wrong in another direction, there is the case of Bob Lenhart, a Kansas railroad employee, and his wife, who used their savings of $18,000 to buy a tavern. Each payday the establishment cashed checks for railroad workers. That simple service got the couple into tax trouble.

Treasury agents raided the tavern on a tip that punchboards were operating and they seized all the tavern's bookkeeping records. The Lenharts were charged with gambling, tried before a jury, and found *not* guilty. IRS, meanwhile, had taken a look at the tavern's books and began an investigation of the railroad man and his wife. It was looking for evidence of tax fraud. This is what the IRS found:

In their last income tax return the couple had reported a profit of $10,000 on the tavern operation. The government's accountants totaled up the tavern's bank deposits and concluded, from the large amounts of cash deposited, that the profit on the business was actually $50,000 for that year, not $10,000.

At the trial the man and wife testified they had reported their sales from the tavern's cash register tapes and had kept a record of the sales in a notebook. The IRS agent testified he had not seen the notebook. He said the seized records hadn't even been turned over to him until long after the raid.

The Tax Court judge indicated he thought the tavernkeeper was being given a raw deal. He said:

"At most, this record reveals ample proof of inadequate record keeping by the taxpayer, and perhaps a penchant for unbusinesslike methods in his operation of the tavern. It should be emphasized that the understatement of taxpayer's income, covering the single taxable year, was computed by IRS under a method which is based upon the principle that unexplained bank deposits are evidence of taxable income.

"However, it is undisputed that the taxpayer engaged in a large check-cashing operation and that a large part of the deposits in both bank accounts was from the check-cashing operation, and there is no evidence that the taxpayer made a profit on that operation. In fact, under these circumstances it would seem that the bank deposits method of computing income would be inept and unreliable."

The couple didn't have to pay a deficiency, but their experience should provide a lesson: the IRS may presume a taxpayer to be guilty of something even when it doesn't know what it may be.

Another thing the IRS people try to do with a lawbreaker, or a suspected lawbreaker, is to disallow any tax deduction such a taxpayer may try to take on his income tax return for a payment he may have made in violation of a *state* law. A rather sharp insurance broker managed, however, to make some illegal payments and to get a tax benefit from the payments.

The state law required the broker—Ormsby—to collect the full amount of premiums for all insurance he sold, and it prohibited commission payments to a person not licensed as an insurance salesman. In order to get big customers, the broker violated the state law. In some cases, he allowed the customer to pay him an amount less than was charged in the regular billing. He then would receipt the bill "paid in full." In other cases, the customer paid the full amount billed, but Ormsby later made out a check to the customer for a rebate. Since the insurance man paid only the net amount of the premium to the insurance underwriters after deducting his commission, the rebates and discounts came out of his commission income.

"You have to pay tax on the full amount of the commission income," the IRS ruled. Its agents contended that the broker was *not* entitled to deduct the rebates and discounts, since his payment of them was a clear violation of state law.

Ormsby argued, "But I'm not claiming these amounts as deductions. These people bought the insurance from me at a reduced price, and I never earned the full commission from them in the first place."

The IRS dismissed the argument as a play on words.

The Tax Court judge, however, detected a difference. The income tax is a tax on income, and an amount that was never income to the taxpayer cannot be taxed. From the moment of the sale of insurance, the broker was not entitled to the full amount that he billed his customer, but only to a reduced amount. That being the case, the insurance broker never had the income in question. Accordingly, the standards applying to the allowability of deductions didn't apply to his situation.

As you can see, the IRS likes everything to conform, to be cut and dried and as legal as can be. That's why a midwestern labor leader—not James Hoffa, in this case—came to fight the tax collectors about $125,000 in legal fees and expenses paid out by his local over a four-year period to help him win a long court fight against an indictment on extortion charges. He thought his reasoning was sound enough to beat IRS. It was not. The union local itself was not charged with a criminal offense, nor were the charges of extortion linked to the labor leader's union position. The local's other officers felt, however, that if the leader were convicted, the publicity would damage both the local and the labor movement generally. That's why the local had paid out the $125,000.

The union chief didn't report it as income on his tax return. The IRS said he should have. He argued that the $125,000 was a gift. The IRS countered with the opinion that labor unions weren't in business to make gifts, and that the leader had thus received income that he had failed to support.

When the case reached the Tax Court, the labor big shot also argued that even if the $125,000 were income, the legal fees and related expenses should constitute a deductible business expense. The deduction of $125,000 would thus offset the income of $125,000.

The only trouble with that argument was that the court could not see what trade or business the labor leader had in which the $125,000 would be a legitimate expense. He had salary from his local, salary from the local's health and welfare fund, and salary from a business corporation as his only sources of earned income. The charge of extortion had not arisen from any of those sources. The Tax Court held that the government was entitled to collect income taxes on the $125,000.

Not everyone did it, of course, but the practice of making kickbacks was widespread in the southern city in which an optician named Thomas manufactured eyeglasses. He paid so-called referral fees to ophthalmologists who prescribed the glasses and suggested to the patients that they have Thomas fill the prescriptions. Thomas did what he had to do to get business—meaning that he kicked back to the doctors.

An IRS agent would not allow deduction of the amounts of the referral fees on the basis that they were against public policy. Thomas charged that the federal tax law was being used to punish him for doing something that wasn't a crime.

"If we allow you to take a tax deduction for those payments," said IRS, "we are subsidizing an unethical way of obtaining business."

Thomas maintained that the income tax applied to the earnings of both priest and prostitute, that the tax was a tax on the net income after deducting the necessary expenses of producing that income. He conceded that if a payment was actually illegal under state or federal law, then there might be a basis for not allowing a tax deduction. But no such law forbade the payments.

When the IRS refused to alter its position, Thomas went to court. After a trial court and an appeals court had turned him down, the United States Supreme Court allowed him to take deductions on his income tax returns for payments classified as kickbacks.

IRS does win some kickback cases, although why it should lose some and win others may be difficult to define as reasonable.

A drapery manufacturer built its business by making kickbacks and lavish gifts to customers. IRS refused to let the company take any tax deductions for either the kickbacks or the gifts (see chapter 21).

The firm had begun business operations as a small supplier of custom-made draperies to house trailer builders. It was a tough business, but kickbacks made things easier. While IRS was quite willing to tax the drapery manufacturer's income earned from the kickback method of doing business, it sanctimoniously refused to allow the company any tax deductions for the expense of getting such business.

Company officials told IRS that it ought to permit deduction of any expenses whatsoever that were necessary to produce the income IRS was taxing. The government's answer was that kickbacks violated public policy and therefore were not deductible items.

"What public policy? There is no federal law against kickbacks," cried the company's owner. "There are only state laws on kickbacks. Why should you use the federal tax law to punish me for violating a state law that I haven't even been charged in the state courts with violating?"

The Tax Court judge seemed to sympathize to some extent with the drapery people. He realized that disallowing the payments because IRS didn't think they were "nice" was carrying the tax law too far. However, he upheld the IRS ruling. The drapery firm had not proved that the kickbacks were "ordinary" in the industry. While the owner testified that "everyone was doing it," he actually introduced no evidence proving that anyone else was following such procedures. Would his competitors come forward and publicly testify that they made kickbacks? They didn't.

A business expense, to be allowed as a tax deduction, must be both "ordinary" and "necessary," but the manufacturer had proved only the "necessary" half of its case. It couldn't prove the "ordinary" half. It lost the case and paid the tax.

CHAPTER THIRTEEN

Tax Cheats and Fraud

The neglect of truthfulness leads to hypocrisy, but the exaggeration of truthfulness leads to destructive fanaticism.

—Hans Küng
in *Truthfulness: The Future of the Church.*

Since the beginning of history human beings in every land have committed crimes, and not the least of the criminals has been the citizen who cheated the tax collector. Not until recent decades, however, has the tax cheater lost caste. Once he was considered to be rather clever. He may have aroused the lethal anger of the king, but the king's other heavily taxed subjects secretly admired him all the way to the gallows. In the United States, the tax criminal isn't at all popular. Nobody who has voluntarily paid taxes until it hurt is going to make a Robin Hood-like hero out of a citizen who has avoided paying his legitimate taxes.

Individual tax fraud cases are interesting, as is almost all creative crime. Sometimes, the nature of the tax frauds amuses us; at other times we are astonished and outraged.

The most effective weapon IRS uses to detect tax cheats is the revenue agent who can sift through masses of boring detail, yet remain alert to small things on paper that don't ring true. A big operator who was caught by such an agent was a contractor named Sorenson involved in the construction of a $2.5 million hotel and convention center in an eastern state. Simultaneously, he was building himself a $100,000 home in the country and charging all the costs to the hotel construction job. If such a procedure went undetected, the government would, in effect, be paying much of the cost of the home through the taxes evaded by Sorenson when he understated the profit on the hotel project.

The big operator's tax return eventually came up for audit. At the start, the revenue agent assigned to give the return a routine examination had not a glimmer of suspicion anything might be out of order. He couldn't examine every bill paid by the contractor. So he selected a sampling of bills and checked them one by one.

The smallest was an invoice for $83 for a personalized and illuminated mailbox. After having checked scores of bills for larger sums and found everything okay, the agent might well have passed over the $83 item, but he paused in his paper work to wonder why a hotel needed a mailbox.

Before he finished, he learned that the mailbox, and almost $100,000 of other expenses, was for the house in the country, not the hotel. The house was ultimately sold to meet the unpaid taxes and penalties. The contractor went to prison for tax evasion.

Brocamonte, owner of a phony gourmet restaurant, tried to get by without paying wages to his waitresses. He hired girls who were attending college or studying music, ballet, or art, and all they received for their work were two not-so-fancy meals a day and tips. On the restaurant tax return, Brocamonte claimed a deduction of $10,000 for salaries to waitresses.

Then there was the ice cream. To help make the down payment on his restaurant building, Brocamonte had borrowed $2,500 from his ice cream supplier, who then added $1.35 to the price of each drum of ice cream until the loan of $2,500 was repaid. The restaurateur had bills for the ice cream, so how could the IRS ever figure out that part of the price per container was not for ice cream but for repayment on a nondeductible loan?

And there was the jukebox. Brocamonte got 40 percent of the take on the jukebox. This money went directly into his pocket and not onto his tax return.

Then one of the waitresses sent a letter to the IRS. A revenue agent visited the restaurant. He found out about the girls and the no-wage setup. Further investigation brought to light the undercover deal concerning the ice cream. He heard the jukebox blaring and found out about that, too.

As for Brocamonte, he learned all about the tax law, tax deficiencies, and fraud penalties.

When a taxpayer with a guilty conscience has an honest difference of opinion with IRS on how much tax is due on reported income, he may hasten to pay the additional tax IRS demands in order to get the revenue people off his back. Can IRS come back at the taxpayer later and charge that it has decided the return was fraudulent and that the payment of additional tax is proof he understated his tax on the return in question?

A purchasing agent for a fabric-processing firm in Los Angeles was accused by IRS of receiving from salesmen gifts that were unreported taxable income. The purchasing agent—Palmer—denied getting the gifts. IRS wasn't at that time charging the taxpayer with fraud, but it was trying to collect additional tax that its agent insisted was due. To avoid legal expense and annoyance, Palmer paid $4,000 the government said he owed.

A year later a federal grand jury indicted him on a criminal charge of fraud for not having included the gifts in his tax return. IRS argued that it didn't have to prove that the purchasing agent had underpaid his original tax, because he had already admitted it by paying the $4,000 additional tax. All the tax bureau had to do was to prove that his underpayment was willful and that, therefore, he had intended to defraud the government.

"No," said Palmer. "I paid you the money only because it would have cost me too much to argue with IRS. Now I should have a chance to show that I never really owed any additional tax."

The judge recognized that facts found by some government agencies are not subject to challenge in court unless clearly wrong. No such rule applies to investigative agencies, such as the FBI. To make their findings presumptively correct in a criminal matter would be to allow them to act as both prosecutor and jury. Since every tax audit is a potential criminal matter, the judge felt that the same rule should apply to the IRS as applied to the FBI. He held that IRS would have to prove both (1) the tax underpayment and (2) the fraudulent intent.

Bryant, another purchasing agent, didn't tell the accountant who prepared his tax return that he had been pocketing cash kickbacks from a lumber supplier in his southern city. If he had, he would have lost his job with a furniture manufacturer. The accountant worked down the hall from the purchasing office at the same manufacturing company and would have been obligated to tell on him.

Soon after, IRS made a routine audit of the lumber supplier's returns. The supplier, it was revealed, had been faced with a hard decision about the kickback payments it had made. If it claimed them as tax deductions, it might be asked to name the person to whom the payments were made and the reason they were made. If it did not claim them as tax deductions, the IRS might be suspicious that the money had been taken by some of the stockholder-officers of the supplier corporation. IRS might then try to charge the officers with taxable income or tax fraud. The supplier finally had elected to show the payments as business expenses paid to Bryant, the purchasing agent.

The IRS agent who audited the lumber supplier's return put through a request to have Bryant's tax return pulled for examination. At first, Bryant denied having received the kickback payments. Then, faced with the evidence, he changed his stand and admitted all. He said that his failure to report the income was not because he wanted to defraud the government, but because he wanted to protect his job.

The Tax Court judge said: "Even though a non-tax motive is present, that does not establish an absence of fraudulent intent. The fear of disclosing a fraudulent transaction is not a valid excuse for failure to report income." The court found that the failure to report the kickbacks was due to fraud.

Some tax cheats blame their troubles on mistakes made by their accountants. A dance studio operator turned over information regarding his business to the public accountant who kept his books and prepared his income tax returns. However, some of the business income was not reported on tax returns. The IRS went after the dance man for tax fraud.

"It's the accountant's fault," the studio operator pleaded. "He got all of the information from me. Any data not reported is the result of his errors."

The judge's decision was stated as follows: "The court is satisfied that the taxpayer underpaid his income tax in each of the years in question. Our problem is not the measure of those tax deficiencies, but whether there was fraud.

"We are not unaware that recurrent omission of substantial amounts of income is, in and of itself, strong evidence of fraud. But under the circumstances of this case, where there is evidence of reliance on an accountant properly to perform his duties, the claimed omissions do not seem to us to require the application of this doctrine.

"We do have our strong suspicions that fraud may have been present, but the IRS had not flushed out the necessary evidence to cause us to so find." The dance man won.

While it is up to the taxpayer to disprove any IRS contentions as to what is the correct amount of his tax, the shoe is on the other foot when it comes to establishing the existence of fraud. IRS has to prove that the taxpayer committed tax fraud.

Taxpayers are presumed to be innocent until found guilty. They have certain rights. We should be concerned that the IRS not forget it, and particularly not forget it when dealing with the 99.999 percent of taxpayers who are honest.

The IRS can dig out tax fraud without violating a taxpayer's rights. It does so every day, as in the case of a revenue agent who was auditing the tax return of a New York State physician named Herrick. The doctor didn't keep copies of his bank deposit slips. The bank did. The daily deposit slips had separate spaces to show the amount of currency and the amount of checks deposited.

The tax man examined the bank's copies of the deposit slips for two years and found not one slip on which anything but checks was listed. He then asked Dr. Herrick's office girl whether any cash payments from patients ever came in. She said yes, some came in every day and were turned over to the doctor rather than being entered in the books. The doctor went to federal prison.

A man wrote to William L. Raby, one of the authors of this book, in care of the *Salt Lake Tribune,* where his tax column is regularly published:

Dear Mr. Raby:

You mentioned once that a wife can't be taken as a dependent on the tax return if she has any income of her own. You also said that if a joint return is filed, income of both husband and wife have to be reported. However, I just want you to know that you're wrong on the first point, even though you may be right on the second.

Our income isn't very much, and my wife has income only from baby-sitting and none of those people filed any tax returns on her. I make out the income tax return as my separate return and show her as a dependent. I don't have to report her income. IRS has been accepting this for years.   O.N.

The published reply to the letter said:

The fact that you've been doing something that isn't proper and have gotten away with it for years simply means you've gotten away with it for years. It doesn't prove it's proper.

By not reporting the baby-sitting income you are evading taxes. Furthermore, if you keep on doing it, you are committing a criminal act because you now know that it is wrong.

It's one thing to take advantage of loopholes, or to press for interpreting ambiguity in the way most favorable to yourself, but what you are doing is just plain wrong. Any idiot can cheat. Wise up and pay up, or figure out some legal way to cut your tax bill.

Even if you're not guilty of tax cheating, be careful what you tell an IRS agent. Long after both you and the agent have forgotten what you said, your words—or his version of them—may come back to haunt you. Diligent agents make notations of what you tell them, and the notes go into the IRS files, as a Florida racetrack bettor being tried for tax fraud learned to his sorrow. In court he argued that the government had shown no possible sources of unreported income to explain why his increase in net worth should be viewed as resulting from income on which he had evaded tax.

Up came the government with a memorandum from the revenue agent who had first questioned the bettor. The memorandum said the taxpayer had told the agent his income for the previous year had included $4,000 of racetrack winnings that had been reported under the heading of miscellaneous income. The inference was clear that if there were reported racetrack winnings in one year, there could be unreported winnings in other years.

The presiding judge allowed the memorandum to be received into evidence. The taxpayer was convicted.

In another case involving too much talk, two former tax officials were charged with conspiring to help a Connecticut man, found guilty of tax fraud, to escape prosecution. The government introduced transcripts of telephone conversations the two men had had with a third federal tax official. It had been routine practice for this official, and his predecessors, to have secretaries with earphones listen in and transcribe all official telephone conversations. The judge allowed the transcripts to be received in evidence and the two tax officials were convicted.

If your income tax return is audited, remember that it is easy for revenue agents to misunderstand what you say. You have no opportunity to audit what you say. Only if things go against you will your words with the agent be resurrected. Statements you made that might help you remain untouched in the file.

Another thing to remember is that the IRS is curious. An agent reading his morning newspaper came across a news story that detailed how a gypsy palmist in Chicago had persuaded a retired subway motorman that his stomach trouble was due to cancer caused by an obsession for money that offended certain spirits. She said the remedy was to have the money cleansed of the curses. He would then soon be well. The palmist volunteered to perform the cleansing operation.

The aging man turned $5,000 over to her. After some months it occurred to him that the palmist was never going to return the $5,000. As a result, he took her to court, where the judge awarded him $5,000 actual damages, plus $5,000 punitive damages.

The IRS then went after the palmist to collect tax on the $5,000 she was supposed to have cleansed.

The gypsy had a clever answer to the charge that she had received $5,000 as a result of the swindle. The $5,000, she said, was really given to her daughter, then seventeen years old, as a love gift. The daughter testified that she and the man of advanced years had been involved in an affair for more than two years and that she had been in love with him.

The Tax Court judge said he had noted that the daughter was an "exotically attractive young woman," but he couldn't believe she was in love with a sixty-eight-year-old man suffering from stomach trouble. Nor could he believe that she and the man had had any sort of romantic relationship. He commented that the gypsy palmist's "witnesses were uniformly unimpressive in candor, credibility, and demeanor." The judge went on to express doubt that the man had ever been alone with the girl and concluded that the palmist owed $1,156.52 of income tax on the $5,000 she had obtained from the ex-motorman.

Until 1965, any racetrack winnings a taxpayer may have had probably went unnoticed and tax-free unless he reported them voluntarily. To-day, honesty is somewhat enforced by a law requiring tracks to report the name, address, and social security number of any winner of more than $600.

A Long Island racetrack bettor saw the new law as his big op-portunity to make some money, instead of losing by it.

The big track winnings come on the daily double. A bettor who selects the winners of the sixth and seventh races is eligible to bet on the winners of the eight and ninth races. If he has all four winners, he may get several thousand dollars for the tickets.

The Long Islander followed this pattern of activity: At the track he would try to locate an obviously amateur bettor who had a winning ticket. Then he would approach the man (or woman) and explain the consequences in tax penalties if the amateur were to cash the ticket himself: the winnings would have to be reported as taxable income. The schemer would buy the rich ticket from the amateur for between 80 and 95 percent of what it would pay at a cashier's cage and then, for $10, would have the ticket cashed by a hanger-on type who would give the track cashier his own name and address as the winner. In one racing season, a typical hanger-on collected on thirty-one winning tickets totaling $78,000.

The scheme had seemed foolproof, but another fringe operator who had cashed many such tickets at $10 a set was worried about what IRS might do about his own income tax return. He didn't have the money to pay on $40,000 of $50,000 of "winnings." He went to the IRS and blew the whistle on the operation. The Long Islander was tried and convicted for conspiring to deprive the government of essential tax information, one of the many casualties of new ideas to beat the tax collectors.

One would think, from the countless number of published cases of those who have been unable to cheat the government, that potential crooks would give up any such ideas aborning.

Ed Smith, an eastern chain laundry owner with a rough reputation, was convicted of federal tax evasion and owed the government more than $5 million in personal taxes. The corporations he controlled owed more than $3.5 million. He went to prison and the corporations were taken over by the government.

After two and a half years, he was freed on parole. Meanwhile, government-appointed receivers had been operating the corporations and attempting to find investors willing to buy them. The newly freed ex-convict set out to get financing so that he could become the buyer.

In the past, Smith had used devious and unpleasant procedures to acquire laundry routes. When prospective buyers learned that he was out of prison and interested in getting back his former businesses, they were fearful that if they went ahead and bought them from the receiver, Smith would open competitive laundries and conduct raids on routes in a move to expand his new operation.

The receivers, trying to get the most money for the tax collectors from the sale of the assets, asked a United States judge to enter an order barring Smith from entering into the laundry business in any area where he would be competing with his former corporations.

The judge said: "To permit him to depreciate the value of the assets by warning off otherwise willing and competent bidders, and permitting him to reacquire the very assets he used to defraud the government and reduce the amount the government might realize in taxes, would result in a situation completely shocking to this Court and a situation which this Court in good conscience cannot possibly permit."

The court ordered the former laundry operator and current parolee to keep his hands off the customers, the goodwill, and all the other assets connected with the corporations he formerly had controlled.

A Florida jeweler who had been embezzling money from his partnership died before he could prepare an income tax return. The executor of the estate, who knew nothing of the thievery, prepared, signed, and filed an income tax return for the jeweler's final year of life.

The theft from the partnership was ultimately uncovered, and the partnership claimed a theft loss on its federal income tax return. The IRS allowed the loss deduction to the partnership, but it charged the jeweler's estate with a fraud penalty.

The executor asked, "How can you charge the man with fraud when he died before his tax return was prepared? For all you know, he may have intended to report the stolen money as income."

To this an IRS agent had a plain answer: the money hadn't been reported.

"I didn't report it because I didn't know about it," the executor explained. "You certainly aren't charging me with fraud, are you?"

The agent said IRS was not charging the executor with fraud, but that it intended to collect a fraud penalty from the estate because of the omission of the stolen funds from the dead jeweler's final income tax return. The executor took his grievance to the Tax Court.

"Fraud requires a state of mind, a fraudulent intent," the executor argued before the court. "How can you impute a fraudulent intent to a man who is dead before the fraudulent action takes place?"

The Tax Court decided that no one could. IRS lost.

It is always surprising to learn that some people, alive and well, don't file income tax returns. The self-employed owner of a Kansas auto repair shop was one who did not. He filed no return for 1944, nor for any year after 1944. When IRS caught up with him and he was charged with tax fraud, he agreed that he was guilty for the year 1944, but claimed that he was not guilty of such fraud for the years after 1944.

No tax returns were filed after 1944, he said, not to avoid the payment of the income taxes he owed, but only to prevent IRS from discovering that he had failed to file a tax return for 1944. He further reasoned: If he had filed a tax return in 1945, IRS would want to know why there was none for 1944. Then, when it came time to file for 1946, IRS would want to know why he hadn't filed a 1945 tax return. This peculiarly inspired evasion, he explained, had gone on year after year for two decades.

The Kansas garageman stressed that the important factor was his motive, which was not to avoid payment of taxes but to avoid criminal action for not filing returns. He argued that since the tax law says, "If any part of any underpayment . . . of tax required to be shown on a return is due to fraud . . . then penalties shall be imposed," he was really not guilty of tax fraud because the underpayment was due to something else—the desire to avoid detection.

The judge who decided the case said he was indeed intrigued with the ingenuity of the argument, but he had to conclude that a man whose only excuse for not filing a tax return was that he didn't want to be prosecuted for tax evasion had in reality only one purpose for not filing the tax returns, and that was tax evasion itself. Any other meaning to the law would mean that there could be no such crime as tax fraud, since every tax evader could argue that he wasn't really trying to evade tax but only trying to avoid detection for having evaded the tax.

Honest men get into trouble with IRS in cases of fraud and they sometimes can obtain justice only by taking IRS to court. In one case, a man unfortunate enough to be robbed was outraged when the IRS tried to tax him.

A Rhode Island investor named Rowan and his long-time friend, Schmidt, were equal owners of a contracting corporation. When Schmidt died, Rowan took over operation of the business. He soon discovered that his friend had been stealing. Some items of income had never been reported on the corporate books and, of course, had never been reported on Schmidt's personal tax return.

Being an honest man, the Rhode Islander told IRS about the embezzlement. The tax collectors decided the corporation should pay additional taxes for each year involved, based on the amounts embezzled by Schmidt, because the amounts were really income to the corporation. In addition, IRS said the corporation must pay 50 percent of the amounts as a fraud penalty, plus 6 percent interest per year.

Rowan demanded to know why, in all good logic and fairness, the corporation should have to pay a fraud penalty when it was the victim of the embezzlement rather than the perpetrator of it. IRS was unmoved by his protest.

In desperation Rowan sought help in the Tax Court. There the judge agreed that it seemed unfair to tax the victim, although the tax returns had been signed by Schmidt as a duly authorized corporate officer and with full knowledge of the fact that they were false. As the judge viewed the law, this constituted fraud on behalf of the corporation. The corporation would have to pay.

The Rhode Islander appealed the decision. In the appeals court, the judges said the investor was right, that for fraud to be charged to the corporation the corporate officer must have been acting in the corporation's behalf and not, as in this case, robbing the corporation in his own behalf.

An important fact to keep in mind is that being found "not guilty" in a tax matter is not the same as being found "innocent."

A big-city ward politician was charged with criminal tax fraud for failing to report on his income tax return some substantial campaign contributions that he had used for personal purposes. A jury found him "not guilty." The verdict meant that the politician was free of criminal tax charges. He no longer had to worry about going to prison. He was a long way, however, from being through with the tax people.

IRS charged that the politician owed $6,000 in taxes on the campaign contributions they insisted he had used for personal purposes. Interest at 6 percent per year, plus a 50 percent fraud penalty, brought the total tax deficiency to $10,800. IRS demanded payment.

"You can't do this," the politician protested. "The jury found I didn't use any of that money for personal purposes. Isn't there something called double jeopardy?"

IRS explained that, yes, the jury had decided that it hadn't been shown beyond a reasonable doubt that the politician had "willfully evaded" his tax. That, however, had been a criminal proceeding. Now there was the matter of the tax claim, which was not criminal. IRS did not have to prove fraud "beyond a reasonable doubt." All it had to do was show some evidence of fraud and then it could collect all it was seeking.

The politician paid. In the next campaign, he cleverly emphasized his acquittal on the criminal tax charges, but kept quiet about what had happened when he learned that "not guilty" did not mean "innocent."

Have you ever wondered what you would do if you found on a vacant bus seat an unmarked, unidentifiable briefcase stuffed with bundles of $10 and $20 bills to the amount of $25,000?

A certain New Orleans bookkeeper had such an experience. When he brought the treasure home, he examined the bills and found them unmarked. His wife persuaded him not to tell the police or the tax people. The couple jointly rented a bank safe-deposit box and stashed the money there. Then they began, each in his own way, to tackle the problem of how to benefit from possession of the money while the husband continued to earn $165 a week.

The wife bought lots of clothes and luxuries, and wasn't embarrassed by bills that remained unpaid after some months. She had the secret knowledge that she could take some of the tens and twenties out of the safe-deposit box any time she wanted to pay up. She planned to take an extended trip to Europe just as soon as it was safe to spend the money.

The bookkeeper spent all his spare time trying to figure out, without finding a reassuring answer, a foolproof system of spending the hidden money without attracting the attention of the IRS.

When tax time arrived, the couple didn't report the $25,000 on their return, although the law required such disclosure. Then the bookkeeper died.

The new widow mourned him briefly and then stopped by the bank to snatch the tens and twenties on her way to a travel agency. Her plans were foiled, however. The deposit box had been rented in both their names and, as a consequence of the bookeeper's death, it had been sealed prior to inventory by the tax people.

A bank was named administrator of the dead man's estate and a lawyer was hired to handle the work. Between the two, they got $3,000 of the money found on the bus seat. IRS wanted to know where the cached $25,000 had come from, but the widow wouldn't tell. So IRS assumed it was ill-gotten gain from a tax fraud scheme and grabbed $10,000 in tax, an additional $5,000 for fraud penalties, and $1,800 in interest. The widow's charge account creditors sued her and took $5,000. She was left with $200 in cash.

Another form of found treasure, or windfall, is the money IRS pays to individuals who inform on tax evaders. Informing is a sorry business that often turns up unpleasant people, like the greedy and less than grateful Seattle woman who had suspected that her family doctor was not reporting cash fees for house calls.

By talking to some of his other patients, checking with the office nurse, and doing some smart guesswork, she was able to list specific calls at homes where, she suspected, the doctor had pocketed cash fees.

The excitement triggered by her sleuthing opened her mouth a little too much. She told her sister. Then she sat down and wrote to the IRS, detailing the information about the doctor and asking for the usual informer's fee. While she was writing the letter, her more enterprising sister was *telephoning* the same information to IRS.

Once the government had its grips on the doctor, both the Seattle sisters applied to IRS for the informer's fee. IRS paid the fee to the sister who had telephoned the information, because its records listed her as the first informant in the case. The sisters now don't speak to each other. The sister who telephoned collected a reward of $500.

In another case, the informer was an embittered St. Louis bookkeeper who "betrayed" his employer of twenty-five years. The employer was convicted of tax fraud, and the bookkeeper was paid a whopping $10,000 as an informer's fee.

After the employer emerged from federal incarceration, he set out to learn who had turned him in.

IRS keeps such information secret, but the bitter bookkeeper could not. He boasted a little about his maneuver to some people and the news eventually trickled back to his former employer. The smug tone of the boasting, as reported to him by old friends, caused the businessman to suspect that his former employee hadn't paid tax on the informer's fee. The ex-employer himself turned informer, and in due course the bookkeeper was convicted of tax fraud. Presumably, the new IRS data-processing system will keep future informers from getting by without paying tax on their gains.

A taxpayer named Ray and his employee, Hulda, had a cozy arrangement. Ray, who owned the business, ran everything outside the office. Hulda ran the office.

Once Hulda had hoped she could also get to run Ray, but Mrs. Ray was firmly in the driver's seat and not apt to be dislodged. Since matrimony was out of the question and Ray had never provided a retirement program for his employees, Hulda decided to set aside something for her old age—financed by Ray and without his knowledge.

For six years, Hulda covered her thefts of cash from the business by juggling her entries in the books. She managed to steal $50,000 by the time Ray announced he was going to sell the business. The prospective buyer's auditors were due the next week to check the books. Hulda took off that night for Mexico City. Ray didn't prefer criminal charges against her but, of course, reported the theft as a loss on his income tax return.

After two years, homesick and down to $25,000, Hulda ventured back to the United States and deposited the money in a big-city bank near the border. She telephoned Ray and offered to return the remaining $25,000 if he wouldn't prosecute her. She wanted to live in peace. He said he would think about it. Actually, he should have taken the next plane to Hulda and grabbed the money from her.

The revenue people had a line on Hulda, both through their watching station in Mexico and from an advice received from her bank on the unusual size of the cash deposit in the account she had opened. While Ray was thinking about her offer, the IRS swooped down on Hulda's bank account and grabbed the $25,000 for tax deficiencies. She had failed to pay income tax on the money she had embezzled over the years.

This was difficult for Ray to accept. Hulda had embezzled him out of $50,000, and then the government had thwarted his chance of getting back $25,000 of it. He, the victim, had to pay her income taxes.

CHAPTER FOURTEEN

Divorce and Taxes

An income tax form is like a laundry list—either way you lose your shirt.
——Fred Allen

A man who may have thought everything was nicely settled when a divorce decree was signed by the judge often is snapped out of his state of euphoria when the Internal Revenue Service calls on him. Changes in marital status often are accompanied by unusual property settlements, so you can understand why IRS looks slit-eyed at any tax return from a newly divorced husband or wife that comes up for audit, and why the odds are high that year-of-divorce returns will get an audit.

A middle-age lothario named Caraska who owned a hardware store in Oregon had been caught in embarrassing circumstances in the company of a lady taxi driver. His wife sued for divorce and, in the settlement, she received a certain installment note on property Caraska had sold. The note had a balance of $40,000 due, which gave her a very comfortable source of income when added to all the other money and possessions the hardware man had to provide. IRS learned of the note in a tax audit.

While he had been receiving the collections on the installment note during the years of his marriage, Caraska had properly reported 60 percent of the principal payments as income. That 60 percent was profit on the sale of the property, on which he had elected to pay tax as the collections came in rather than at the time of the sale. He also had reported the interest payments received.

After he gave the note to his ex-wife, the man reported no income on it. On her income tax return, the ex-wife had reported as income only the interest she had received, not the 60 percent of principal.

The IRS auditor argued with Caraska that he had really sold the note for $40,000 when he turned it over to his ex-wife, that he had paid his debt to her with the note, and that therefore he should have reported $24,000 of income (60 percent profit percentage times $40,000 note balance). The hardware man squirmed, and he protested, but he lost the argument and paid.

Then the IRS audited the ex-wife's return. With her, the revenue agent attacked with a different argument. He said she stood in the tax shoes of her ex-husband, the hardware man, and just as he had to pick up part of the principal payment as income based on the note, so she had to pick up as income 60 percent of the principal payments she had received. That's what IRS told her.

She protested and took the IRS into Tax Court. The judge agreed that if Caraska's transfer of the note to her was to be treated on his tax return as if he had sold the note for its $40,000 face amount, then the tax cost of the note to the ex-wife should be that same $40,000. That being the tax cost, no part of the principal payments would be treated as profit. The IRS, implied the judge, should be content with collecting income tax once on the $24,000 profit.

Just what kind of tax mess can a man with two wives get into? The owner of an auto muffler repair and replacement establishment, who advertised his business as "The Muffler King," found out.

When he and his wife decided to part, they divided their property. She would not give him a divorce, although for tax purposes they were legally separated. She and their daughter went to live in another city.

If the muffler king were to file a separate return as a single person that year, his income tax would be $3,500 more than if he filed as a married man. He was "remarried" and living with another "wife" and reasoned that she could be the wife to file a joint return with him. But on that return the two taxpayers took a deduction of $600 for his daughter by his "other wife," the real mother of the dependent. That deduction brought IRS in to look at the return, since it showed a dependent child not living with the taxpayers—an obvious tip-off for a tax audit. The agent wanted to see a certified copy of the divorce decree that he presumed had canceled out the first marriage. Of course, there was no decree.

The startled revenue agent said, "You can't file a joint return with the woman you describe as your second wife. If you haven't divorced wife number one, you cannot be legally married to a wife number two."

The muffler king was concerned about the $3,500 added tax. "I ought to be able to file a joint return with some wife. How about getting my first wife to sign it?"

His answer was in the state law that said parties to a bigamous marriage may not deny the validity of that marriage. The idea of the law was to protect the legitimacy of any children—present or future—of an illegal marriage.

The taxpayer was stuck for that year. He couldn't file a joint return with the second "wife" because they weren't legally married, nor with the first wife because a joint return with her would be an attempt to deny the validity of the so-called second marriage. He paid the additional $3,500 demanded by IRS.

The case had a happier tax ending the next year, after the muffler king and his bigamous wife went to Mexico, where he got a Mexican divorce and they obtained a Mexican marriage certificate. On the subsequent April 15, they filed a joint tax return, and presumably IRS let it stand as filed.

However, a divorce obtained in good faith below the border can get a man in tax trouble that may haunt him and other taxpayers for years to come.

One interesting case involved an oil man named Moore who had obtained a divorce in Mexico but came back to be married to a second wife in the United States.

Moore's first wife had refused to give him a divorce. When she learned that he had divorced her in Mexico and married someone else, she went to court.

Over the man's protest, the court decided the first wife's complaint was in order, that the Mexican divorce was not valid in New York and that the subsequent marriage in Nevada was bigamous.

In came the IRS, which had noted that the oil man had been filing joint income tax returns with his second wife. The revenue agent wanted more tax money because, he said, a taxpayer couldn't file a joint income tax return with a woman to whom he was not legally married. Moore took the argument to the Tax Court, but the Tax Court said that IRS was exactly right. Soon after, the oil man died and his estate appealed the Tax Court decision to the U.S. Circuit Court of Appeals.

The appeals court didn't go along with the legalistic-moralistic approach of the IRS. It was concerned about preserving certainty and uniformity in the federal tax system. The way it saw the problem, if a divorce in one place (Mexico) would not be recognized in some other place (New York) but would be recognized as valid in still another place (Nevada), then the divorce and a subsequent remarriage both ought to be recognized as valid for federal tax purposes.

Otherwise, a man whose divorce and remarriage were held valid in Nevada could file a joint return if he lived there, but would have to file as a single man if he lived in New York and New York held the divorce invalid—and if he went to Arizona, his status might never be resolved. The court didn't like the effect of a rule like that, and it concluded that the taxpayer had indeed been married to his second wife for tax purposes and his joint returns could stand as filed.

The issue in the case is still alive. IRS lost the court fight, but it has announced that it will not follow the court decision.

If you think it is the man who pays and pays, you could find proof in the case of a man named Vaughan, who was certain he was getting a bargain when he traded $70,000 worth of stock for a divorce. His wife took the stock and went her way.

The IRS agent who audited his income tax return noted that Vaughan indeed had profited by the deal, because the stock had originally cost him only $15,000. The agent said the taxpaying ex-husband owed income tax on the difference between the $70,000 value of the stock when his wife got it and the original purchase price of $15,000. The tax on the profit of $55,000 came to about $14,000.

"If anyone has to pay tax," argued Vaughan, "it should be my ex-wife. She got the stock. As a matter of fact, I ought to get a deduction."

The agent didn't agree at all. In his opinion, the situation could be compared to one in which Vaughan might have owed $70,000 on a bank loan and used the stock to pay it off, and that would be the same as having sold the stock for $70,000. Vaughan said it wasn't fair. He decided he would rather fight in all the courts of the land than pay.

A minority of the U.S. Supreme Court justices who ultimately decided the case reasoned that IRS could hardly liken the obligation of an ex-husband to support his ex-wife to a note owed to a bank.

The majority held that the amount of support Vaughan owed his ex-wife could not, of course, be calculated as easily as the amount owed on a note, but it seemed to them that by agreeing to pay her $70,000 to get out of his life, the deal established that what he owed her in the way of support was worth $70,000. Therefore, for $70,000 he had sold stock that originally had cost him $15,000. While the $70,000 discharged his obligation to support his former wife, he now had to fork up another $14,000 as part of his tax obligation to support his government.

The IRS interest in divorce in connection with tax matters also extends to child support. A Toledo mother received $3,000 for child support during the tax year from her former husband, and her father chipped in with $8,500 to help her out. She had a job, and her own earnings came to $2,600. She claimed in her tax return that she was furnishing more than half the cost of supporting her five children.

How can $2,600 be more than half of $14,100? Mathematically it cannot, but in tax matters peculiar things are possible.

If the $3,000 from her ex-husband had been received as alimony, the money could have been considered as her contribution to the support of the children. Her husband then would have obtained a deduction for the alimony and she would have had to report it as income. But the $3,000 was not alimony. Clearly, it was child support. Without the grandfather's contribution of $8,500, the mother would thus have been furnishing only $2,600 out of $5,600 for child support, and that would have meant that the father could deduct $600 for each child as a dependent on his tax return.

The IRS got involved because both the mother and the father were claiming the children as dependents.

"Neither of you is entitled to the dependency deduction" was the IRS decision. According to IRS, the grandfather, who hadn't tried to claim a tax benefit from his $8,500 contribution to the family, was entitled to take the five dependency exemptions, since he had furnished more than half the cost of supporting the children.

"It was a gift," said the mother. "My father gave me the money with no strings attached. I put it in my bank account and used it as I thought best. So when I spent it on the children, I was spending *my own money.*"

The Tax Court found that the grandfather had indeed made a gift, and it ruled that at the moment of the gift the money became the mother's. When she spent it, it was just the same as spending money she had earned.

The IRS often insists on proof of the cost of child support. Sometimes that can be very difficult. Look at this case, for example:

A court order forced Al Lucchese to provide $100 a month to support his fourteen-year-old daughter, Lucinda. The amount itself was not deductible on his income tax return, but as a father he figured he was entitled to take the usual $600 deduction for a dependent. He was wrong.

A revenue agent who was auditing Lucchese's return asked him to prove he had the right to take the deduction. The father laid out on the agent's desk a dozen $100 checks that had gone through his bank account, all endorsed and cashed by Lucinda's mother. The agent demanded, "Show me that $1,200 is more than half of the total amount spent on the child's support."

Lucinda's mother wouldn't tell her ex-husband how much was being spent on the daughter. Perhaps she and her new husband were also taking her daughter as a dependent. Lucchese didn't know, because his ex-wife wouldn't say. He argued with the IRS agent that, if his ex-wife wasn't listing Lucinda as a dependent on her tax return, that should be conclusive proof that he was furnishing more than half the support.

The agent didn't offer to find out. He muttered something about each return standing alone and said that he couldn't disclose information on one taxpayer's return to another taxpayer.

Some lawyers used to insert a clause in divorce decrees that required the wife to furnish the ex-husband with an affidavit once a year listing the total cost of supporting the children in her custody. Lucchese's lawyer hadn't arranged for such an accounting, so he had to pay $200 additional in taxes and never found out whether he was being treated unfairly.

The tax law that made it rough for Lucchese has been changed. If the couple involved in a divorce agree in writing on who is to get the dependency deduction for a child, that person will get the dependency exemption of $600 so long as he or she contributes at least $600 a year for the child's support. In the absence of such an agreement, if the parent who is claiming the exemption for one or more children has contributed at least $1,200 to their support (no matter how many children), he is presumed to have furnished over half their support unless the other parent produces proof to the contrary.

While these rules and specified amounts may seem arbitrary, the arrangement should cut down on the number of tax cases involving husbands who lose dependency deductions because their former wives have refused to say how much it cost to support the children.

When you see how hard IRS will fight to collect a relatively small amount of taxes that in all common sense and justice simply could not be owed, it makes you feel warm and good when the Tax Court sets the tax collectors down, as it did in the following case, which involved a question of whether a marriage had ended in divorce or annulment.

The decision sought was important, because in some states an annulment revokes the marriage from the very beginning so that legally the man and woman are considered never to have been married.

A middle-aged woman—Aileen—who had obtained an annulment reasoned that if she had never been married to the man—Henry—the monthly payments he was making to her could not be alimony. If the money were not alimony, then she should not have to pay income tax on it. Henry didn't reason that way. On his income tax return he deducted the payments he had made to Aileen as alimony.

IRS didn't want Henry to take the tax deduction, and it wanted Aileen to pay tax on the payments, which it said were income. She reported no income at all.

"It's not income to me," Aileen said. "He fraudulently induced me to marry him by concealing his impotency from me. What he is paying me is damages for the injury his fraud did to me. It is not alimony."

The IRS understood her frame of mind, but did not agree with her conclusions. An agent said, "Even though what you're receiving is damages, it is still taxable income." Whereupon IRS said both Henry and Aileen owed additional taxes —the woman on the "damage" payments she was receiving but hadn't reported as income, and the man because IRS said he was not entitled to deduct the "damage" payments he was making.

In Tax Court the judge learned Aileen had been a widow at the time of the questionable marriage to the man, who was a widower. Her widow's pension had been cut off. After six months together, she and Henry agreed to call it quits. Only after her lawyer suggested that an annulment rather than a divorce might allow her to get back her widow's pension was Henry's alleged impotency mentioned.

The judge concluded that, for all practical purposes, they had been married. He decided that the payments she received were, indeed, alimony—taxable to her and deductible by Henry. Aileen had to pay added tax, but Henry did not.

Another woman taxpayer didn't marry the man who wooed her, but she caused him to go to court for relief when IRS sanctioned—in fact, if not in principle—her financial shenanigans. Her name was Joan, and she was engaged to marry a trusting soul named Frank.

Sometime before the scheduled wedding she sat down with Frank and explained that because marriage was a contract, she thought he ought to put up some substantial earnest money—like $10,000—in advance of the ceremony. That idea seemed reasonable to Frank. He took $10,000 out of his bank account and opened a joint account with Joan.

Then she decided she could do better for herself. She withdrew the $10,000 from their account and informed Frank she was going to marry another man, whose name was Rodolfo.

Frank confronted Rodolfo. "You stole my sweetheart and my money," he said. "I miss my money."

After much argument, Rodolfo and Joan returned $4,000 to Frank.

In due course, Frank made out his income tax return and claimed a deduction for the unrecovered $6,000 that Joan, and presumably Rodolfo, was enjoying. He figured that Joan had stolen the money from him, and when IRS questioned his return he argued that he was entitled to a loss because of the theft.

IRS didn't agree. In fact, the auditing agent told him, "All Joan did was withdraw money from her own bank account. That is hardly theft."

Frank persisted until he got the case into court. "No theft loss here," ruled the tax judge, "but it does seem that Joan really owed you that $10,000, since she never delivered on the contract for which you put up the cash. When you were able to get back only $4,000, you suffered a bad debt loss of $6,000."

Since a nonbusiness bad debt is a capital loss, Frank could deduct $6,000 from his income at the rate of $1,000 a year for six years.

Sometimes IRS appears to have drawn a proper bead on a doubtful tax avoidance scheme, but misfires because it has no proof against the taxpayer.

The Tax Court in Ohio was confronted with the unusual question of whether a husband had an inalienable right to live in a house owned by his wife or could be kicked out of it by her any time she wanted to. The answer meant $5,000 to a widow—Mrs. MacDonald.

IRS had said that her late husband, after putting the home in her name, had continued to live in it for eleven years, or until he died.

Now, a federal tax is charged against the property of a person who dies leaving an estate of more than $60,000. If the house belonged to the husband, then its total value was taxable and the government could collect an additional $5,000 from the widow. To discourage tax dodging, the law gives IRS the right to treat property as still owned by a person when he dies, even though he has given away the property, if he has retained the right to use the property or receive the income from it.

Mrs. MacDonald objected to paying the $5,000 tax and she contended that the house had really been given to her, without any strings attached, by her late husband. The IRS agent handling the case said she had to pay.

Later, in Tax Court, the judge accepted the idea that the husband's continued use of the house was suspicious evidence of a plan to beat the tax. However, the wife had testified that there never had been any agreement giving the husband a *right* to continue living there. The judge felt that IRS needed more than suspicion to collect $5,000. In fact, the judge said, the husband had put himself at his wife's mercy. Had the husband and wife separated, the wife could have kept the house and the husband would have had to move out if she told him to. The widow didn't have to pay the claimed tax of $5,000.

Wives often aren't that smart about business and taxes. When they sign without reading the business papers their husbands put before them, they expose themselves to possible tax penalties that the courts may find difficult to set aside. The law is cold. A wife's lack of knowledge of what is spelled out in the papers will not save her from trouble if a misdeed has been committed by her husband.

A Hawaiian woman who had inherited a family business let her husband John manage it. Every year he prepared their federal income tax returns. She dutifully signed her name each year on the tax form where he told her to sign. Later, it turned out that John was a thief. He had embezzled more than $250,000 from his wife's business and had run away.

She got a divorce and tried to salvage the almost bankrupt business. Then, long after John had left, an IRS agent came to call on her, making inquiries about the joint income tax returns that were filed during the years the embezzlement had been taking place. Specifically, he asked if John had reported the quarter of a million dollars he had embezzled as income on those tax returns? He had not. The agent informed the ex-wife that she would have to pay considerable added tax.

"Are you out of your mind?" she exclaimed. "He embezzled money from me. Now you want me to pay his income tax on the money he embezzled?"

"You filed a joint return," the agent reminded her. "On a joint return, both you and your husband are liable for any tax due on any income of either of you. The money embezzled from the business was income to your husband. You are liable for the tax he didn't pay on it because of the joint return that you filed with him. You wouldn't want us to show more kindness to embezzlers than to honest taxpayers, would you?"

The wife could not convince IRS that it should temper the tax law with a little common sense, so she went to Tax Court.

The Tax Court judge found himself constrained to go along with IRS, though he did say, "It seems extremely harsh that petitioner should be liable for tax based on money embezzled from her." He went on to add that wives should be more careful about filing joint tax returns with their husbands.

The judges of the U.S. Circuit Court of Appeals to whom the Tax Court's decision was appealed were appalled at the result, commenting that "an affirmance of the Tax Court would visit upon the innocent wife payment of $237,496 for taxes and fraud penalties, computed substantially upon money alleged to have been embezzled or taken without authority from her."

They were unwilling to approve such a harsh result and searched through the facts in the record for some other approach. They found that the husband had given the business a note for the money he had taken, and had even made payments on the note. They learned that the husband had never been prosecuted for embezzlement or any other crime. They concluded that the amounts taken by the husband could be thought of as "unauthorized loans" rather than amounts embezzled. Accordingly, they held that the wife did not have to pay tax on them.

In spite of the unusual problems that can and do arise, a joint return—reporting all income and deductions of both husband and wife—is almost always better than separate returns, although an Arizona architect and his former wife might not agree. They discovered that filing a joint return lost them the right to take a tax deduction.

Although they were divorced, the decree was not yet final, so the couple could still legitimately file a joint federal income tax return. He was paying her alimony, which would provide him with a tax deduction if he filed a separate return. On the joint return, her $3,000 of alimony income offset and eliminated his $3,000 alimony expense deduction. It was just as if there were no alimony—except for one minor point.

The former wife had paid $800 to her attorney for his work in getting her the alimony award. Since the alimony would be taxable income to her on a separate return, the $800 legal fee would be deductible on the same return as an expense of producing that income. Because a joint return reports all income and deductions of both husband and wife, the

Arizonans took a tax deduction for the $800 fee on their joint return. An IRS agent threw out the $800 deduction for legal expenses.

"There's no alimony income reported on this return," he said. "Therefore, you can't get a deduction for the legal expenses of producing the alimony."

The architect argued—first with IRS and then before a Tax Court judge—that Congress had never intended to punish taxpayers for filing joint returns, that the idea of a joint return was that any deduction could be taken on it that could be taken by either husband or wife filing separately.

The judge saw it IRS's way. For tax purposes, the wife could not be said to have alimony income when she had filed a joint return with the husband who was paying the alimony. If there was no income, then there could be no deduction for expenses of producing the income.

CHAPTER FIFTEEN

Travel and Entertainment

People who squawk about their income taxes may be divided into two classes. They are: Men and women.

—Anonymous

It is doubtful if anybody has ever compiled a won-and-lost tally of all the cases decided by the courts on arguments with the Internal Revenue Service over income tax deductions for travel and entertainment expense. It does seem, however, that IRS has won a majority of the arguments—not 90 percent, but probably 60 or 70 percent.

The tax collectors' excellent batting average is not to be credited to their greater intelligence or tougher fighting ability, but to the difficulty taxpayers have in proving such expenses. Expenses of producing income are deductible, if you can prove them. Personal living expenses are not deductible.

A taxpayer's attitude about expenses is different from a tax agent's, perhaps simply because their day-to-day experience, taste, and habits are different.

A successful New York businessman may take a customer to "21" for lunch or dinner, where the tab for two can be as high as $40 or $50, with a tip of 5 or 10 percent to the captain and 20 percent to the waiters. When four editors lunch or dine at Locke-Ober's in Boston, the check is comparably high. The same goes for lunch or dinner at Jack's in San Francisco and at Chasen's or Scandia in Los Angeles.

So what happens when a revenue agent calls in a businessman for a tax audit that includes questions about expensive restaurant entertainment? The low-ranking agent, who probably has never been seated at a "21," a Jack's, or the Wrigley Building Restaurant in Chicago, often finds it difficult to accept the premise that such expense is *necessary* entertainment. His every inclination is to disallow the expense. Why, he doesn't drink Bloody Mary's for lunch and he has never had stuffed shrimp or a Boston steak at Locke-Ober's. Some people live like millionaires and expect the government to pay for it, he says to himself.

The rich luncheons do, however, develop business that produces income that is taxed for money to operate the government. So the agent concentrates on making the taxpayer *prove* the expense, and prove its connection with his business, not on doing what he'd like to do—tell the taxpayer he ought to take his customers to restaurants that feature $2 specials.

Many travel and entertainment expenditures are partly business and partly personal, and even the taxpayer himself cannot always make a clear-cut distinction between the two elements. He must, however, for the burden of proper substantiation of these expenses rests upon him. He must prove that the *primary* reason for the expense is business. Sometimes that is difficult, as a salesman for a paper products company discovered when he was called in by IRS to substantiate a deduction for $1,150 spent during the year on drinks and luncheons for customers and prospects. The amount included tips calculated at 15 percent.

The salesman, Jim Cipperly, had saved the canceled checks drawn for most of the $1,000 spent on food and liquor. He had nothing to show for $150 in tips.

"You've shown that you spent some money at restaurants and cocktail lounges," the IRS auditor said, "but you haven't proved that the money was spent for business."

Cipperly's office calendar showed the names of the customers with whom he had had appointments. He spent careful hours analyzing the checks and charges totaling $1,000 and, with the help of the calendar, he made up a list that showed the name of the person with whom he had lunched each day and the amount spent.

"That's no good," said the IRS. "A diary of expenses is proof only if prepared at the time the expenses occur."

About this time the salesman decided that he was not going to get anywhere trying to win his point against the revenue agent. Accordingly, he petitioned the Tax Court to take a look at the expense list.

The judge listened to Cipperly's explanation of how he did his entertaining and kept track of the costs. The judge was persuaded. He said, "We think the canceled checks, plus the summary prepared by the taxpayer, establish the amount spent at each luncheon meeting, the date and the restaurant where each luncheon was held, the business purpose, and the name of each customer entertained. This has weight in corroborating the taxpayer's testimony with regard to the meals and the canceled checks. This evidence establishes at least a minimal compliance with the IRS substantiation requirements. The taxpayer is entitled to his deduction, including the cash tips of 15 percent."

A local salesman in El Paso had a different problem. He normally left home early in the morning, ate breakfast and lunch while covering his route, and was home for dinner. He deducted the cost of his morning and noon meals as business travel expenses. IRS disallowed the deductions. The daily trips didn't require the salesman to sleep or rest, the IRS said, and if he didn't have to pause for sleep or rest while on a trip, he was not far enough away from his tax home to be entitled to deduct his meals.

The El Paso man paid the added tax IRS wanted, then sued to get his money back. A U.S. District Court judge decreed that he was entitled to his money. The IRS appealed the decision. The U.S. Circuit Court of Appeals found that the district court was right and that the salesman was entitled to get his money back. Again, the IRS appealed—this time to the U.S. Supreme Court.

To convince the Supreme Court that he was entitled to deduct the cost of his meals, the El Paso salesman had to show his meal expenses differed from, say, the nondeductible meal costs of an office worker who ate his breakfast on his way to work and his lunch in the restaurant around the corner. Was the salesman entitled to deduct his meals simply because he traveled more miles between eating them?

Said the Supreme Court: "Any rule in this area must make some rather arbitrary distinction. . . ." The court decided that the IRS was correct and the salesman was not entitled to deduct the cost of his meals.

Thus, if you travel on one-day trips, your transportation expenses may be deductible, but your meals may not be. Companies that reimburse their employees for meals on trips that do not qualify as "travel away from home" because of no necessity for sleep or rest may have to treat the meal allowance as additional compensation and take out withholding tax and social security from payments made to the employee.

A housewife in Canton, Ohio, wondered about her husband's explanation of his overnight stays on short trips to Akron. She wrote to a tax practitioner for enlightenment:

> My husband used to come home each night from his business trips to Akron. Now he stays overnight every time. He tells me that he has to stay overnight if the expenses of his trip are to be deductible. Frankly, I think he's got some woman there. Is there any tax rule that says he can't come home at night?

The tax man made this reply:

> It all depends on the type of job he has. Normally, his business transportation expenses (plane fare, auto) would be deductible regardless of whether he stays overnight. However, his meals would not normally be deductible unless he were away overnight.
>
> For most people, the cost of staying overnight, if they didn't have to, would be more than any tax benefit they would get from deducting their meals. So you may be right about his having a girl friend in Akron. Quoting the tax law to him won't solve that problem. Maybe you should improve the service at home so he won't find it quite so taxing to get home at night, or go with him next time.

If a wife goes with her husband on a business trip, to a romantic foreign land, for example, he had better not attempt to deduct her expenses when he estimates his income tax, unless she really helped him to earn his salary on the trip. Here's how a Chicagoan did it:

Sparrold owned a meat-packing company with a half interest in a Mexican cattle business that he routinely inspected two or three times a year. His Spanish was so meager that he couldn't converse easily with range bosses, cowboys, and government officials. He couldn't read the company's business records because they were written in Spanish. His wife could read and speak Spanish fluently. She had been a teacher of Spanish in the Chicago school system.

The couple made two trips to Mexico—one in March and another in December, when the weather wasn't too good in Chicago. Later, the Chicago company deducted all of the expenses on its tax return, including a substantial amount for entertainment related to the cattle business. Each trip covered three weeks.

The IRS agent who audited the company's income tax return treated the business trip expense accounts of both Sparrold and his wife as so much malarkey. In his opinion, any business they did in Mexico could have been done in one week instead of three, and so he disallowed two-thirds of the businessman's own expenses. He also rejected the usefulness of the wife as an interpreter. All the expenses claimed for her were thrown out.

The meat-packer succeeded in getting the IRS to reverse its agent's ruling on *his* expenses, but the IRS review officials would not accept the idea that Mrs. Sparrold was a necessary business partner on a cold-weather trip to sunny Mexico. So he went to court.

The court noted that when a businessman hires an accountant to interpret the financial aspects of his business, or a lawyer to interpret the wage and hour law, such expenses are a deductible business expense. It noted, too, that a businessman in a foreign land needs an interpreter who will be responsive to his thoughts and whom he can trust implicitly. The judge held that the wife's expenses were a deductible business expense because of her services as interpreter for her husband.

It is obvious that IRS will not, as a bureaucratic policy, believe that a wife's presence on a business trip is primarily for business purposes. A well-known motion picture impresario discovered that when he tangled with IRS over the deductibility of the expenses involved in taking his wife with him on several foreign trips, including a trip around the world.

While the tax collector would not allow the deduction, a district court judge in California decided the case on the basis of the evidence, rather than on the basis of whether it might be fun to take a trip around the world.

The evidence showed that the producer's company was engaged in providing family-type entertainment around the world. For many years the company had paid the expenses of wives accompanying their husbands on business trips. In fact, the company had insisted that the wives accompany the executives, if at all possible.

A man traveling with his wife projects a wholesome image. He can entertain and be entertained without embarrassment. A man traveling alone is difficult for many hosts to handle. In turn, he often encounters difficulties in social situations. In addition, when a man is traveling with his wife, and especially a man of the producer's prominence, there may be newspaper interviews and photographs in which the wife will appear with her husband. With the wife along, there may be additional publicity from feature articles done from the woman's viewpoint, with the resulting projection of the company's image as a disseminator of family entertainment. The producer was allowed the claimed deduction.

But the fact that IRS has lost a case like this in court will not cut down its attacks in the future on deductibility of similar expenses. Although taxpayers may be entitled to deduct the expenses of taking their wives with them on business trips when they can show that their reasons are primarily business, they should expect that if IRS learns about it they may either have to pay extra taxes or have a court fight on their hands before they are finished.

Another traveling man, named Gleason, whose wife sometimes accompanied him, came up against some IRS frowns because the IRS reasoned that the couple did not have a proper home.

His job was to travel the country selling a fund-raising organization's services to churches, hospitals, youth agencies, schools, and other non-profit organizations. He was paid a salary, and he was reimbursed for travel expenses whenever he was away from Atlanta. If his wife went with him on a sales trip, the company also absorbed her expenses. He had lived in Atlanta all his life, and he was now in his mid-sixties.

Gleason's tax problem arose because he and his wife had disposed of their home after their three children had grown up. When the salesman and his wife were in Atlanta, they stayed with his widowed sister-in-law. Her address was their mailing address, and they stored some of their possessions in the basement of her house. Both he and his wife voted in Atlanta. They had their bank accounts there, registered their automobiles there, and belonged to Atlanta church, fraternal, and social groups.

On his tax returns, Gleason did not report the expense reimbursements paid to him. The accountant who prepared his returns reasoned that inclusion of the reimbursement in gross income would be a washout—that Gleason was entitled to deduct the expense items anyway—so why bother?

The IRS was bothered, however.

"None of these are deductible," the IRS agent said, "because they are not travel expenses while away from home. We don't question the amounts. But you cannot be away from home if you have no home!"

"Atlanta is my home," Gleason replied and took his problem to the Tax Court.

"Surely 'home' is not where the heart lies," declared the Tax Court judge. "If this were true, it would open the floodgates for the deduction of all kinds of personal living expenses, for many of us have moved from our birthplaces, return often to visit our relatives and friends, and intend some day to go back 'home' to stay."

Then the judge explained why he thought most of the expense in this case was not deductible. "A salesman gets to deduct meals, lodging, and so forth while away from home because he has a double burden of expenses—one set of expenses at his permanent home and other expenses, which partially duplicate those home expenses, while on the road. Where there is no duplication of expenses at all, there is no basis for a tax deduction."

The court ruled, however, that the Atlanta salesman could deduct the monies expended for transportation.

The question of where a taxpayer's home is situated comes up again and again in struggles with the tax bureau, especially if the "home" in question is a part-time or temporary place of abode.

For tax purposes, "temporary" means for less than a year. If a temporary job assignment is expected to last longer than a year, then the assignment is classified "indefinite." At stake in the case of John Munce, an electronics technician in Dallas, was whether the $12-per-day allowance he got from his employer was taxable income. If the job assignment was "indefinite," as the IRS contended, then the $12 per day was taxable and $990 more tax was due.

Munce's employer had described the assignment as "indefinite." But Munce insisted to IRS that it really was "temporary," because the company's employee manual defined "indefinite" as "expected to last at least 60 but not more than 365 days."

"But why did you buy a house and move your family and all of your belongings to a 'temporary' job site?" the IRS agent asked the technician.

"I bought a house because I couldn't find a decent one to rent. I took the family with me because I thought it important that my growing children have a father, and I didn't know how long the assignment would last."

The agent stubbornly replied that if Munce did not know how long he would be there, the assignment was indefinite. Therefore, $990 in additional tax was due.

Munce asked the Tax Court to settle the conflict. Unhappily for Munce, he was directed to pay the additional tax for the reason that he had actually spent two years on the temporary assignment and could not, when the assignment began, have reasonably anticipated that the job would be done in less than a year.

A seventy-nine-year-old man who lived in Florida had been employed for some twenty years as an auditor at racetracks in Florida. Then, because of his age, he had trouble getting work in Florida. He traveled north, to racetracks in Rhode Island and New York, and found employment. Most of his working time was spent near Pawtucket, Rhode Island.

On his income tax return, the man deducted $1,404 as automobile expenses in traveling from Florida to the northern tracks, and he charged $2,343 in expenses for meals and lodging while "away from home on business." The relatively large expense deductions caught the IRS eye, and the tax return was audited. The IRS determined that his "home" for tax purposes was Pawtucket, not Florida, and it refused to allow him any deduction for auto or living expenses.

The IRS said that where the auditor lived was not his "tax home." Rather, his "tax home" was where he carried on most of his activity, spent most of his time, and earned most of his income—regardless of where he maintained his family residence.

The old man believed the ruling might be reasonable if his jobs in Rhode Island and New York were permanent, but he thought his case was different because of his age. Each job was only for the duration of a particular race meet, and he could not count on getting another job at that track for the next meet. At seventy-nine, people don't, as a rule, obtain long-term employment.

While the Tax Court is not a court that applies principles of equity, the judges do apply common sense. The judge who heard the IRS argument and the race auditor's story concluded that "because of petitioner's age and the temporary character of employment, it was highly unreasonable to expect him to move his permanent residence from Coral Gables to Pawtucket."

The judge, accordingly, allowed the old man to deduct all the expenses that IRS had disallowed.

A prominent major league baseball player struck out in a contest he waged with IRS over where his home was.

Although the man played for a team in the Los Angeles area, he maintained a home for his wife and children in Spokane, Washington. He spent less than ninety days of each year in Los Angeles and about the same amount of time in the other cities where his team regularly played. The remaining six months of the year were spent in Spokane.

The tax law allows a deduction for business expenses while traveling away from home. Was Spokane or Los Angeles the home of the baseball player?

He took the position that Spokane was his tax home and deducted his Los Angeles living expenses on his federal income tax return. The IRS declared that Los Angeles was his home, and that he could deduct only those expenses that were incurred on road trips away from Los Angeles.

The IRS reasoning was that business expenses could arise only when it was the nature of the business that forced the player to travel, and not his personal preference, that he could have lived in Los Angeles but chose instead to live in Spokane, and that it was strictly a personal preference, not something that should give rise to a tax deduction.

The player's attorney argued that his situation was similar to the tax situation of two skaters who had obtained deductions for travel expenses while away from their northern homes as members of the annual Ice Follies extravaganza.

There was, however, one important difference between the tax problems of the skaters and those of the ballplayer. The Ice Follies had a business office in Los Angeles, and the show had its annual premiere in Los Angeles each September. Then the Ice Follies went on tour and that year's show never returned to Los Angeles. Therefore, Los Angeles was not a logical place for the skaters' home. In the player's case, his team played half its games in Los Angeles, and Los Angeles was the base to which it returned after each road tour.

The ballplayer lost. He did not get a tax deduction for living expenses while he was in Los Angeles, away from his real home, and the court ruling has, of course, affected almost every sports figure in the country, from the youngest rookie pitcher to the most famous football lineman or basketball star.

Fame in tax matters often comes unsought and unwanted. So it came to a wire lather and sometime wire lather foreman. He drove his car from home to his construction work—his bag of tools beside him—every day. Since he had to drive in order to work, he was convinced that he ought to get a tax deduction for using his car as transportation.

The Tax Court first said no, he was commuting to and from work. Commuting expenses are not deductible. The lather appealed the Tax Court decision to the Circuit Court of Appeals. The appeals judges said the Tax Court was wrong and that he was entitled to deduct some part of his car expense, that if it were possible to store his tools at the various construction sites, the cost of storage should be the maximum amount he could deduct. They said further that if there were no way of storing the tools but he would have driven to work anyway (regardless of the fact that he had to lug his tools with him), the Tax Court then was instructed to divide his car expenses between the part that represented the cost of transporting the tools and the part that represented the cost of transporting Sullivan.

The Tax Court duly reconsidered and concluded that at least $410 had been spent on getting to and from work and that the latter should be allowed to deduct $137 of it as the cost of transporting the tools.

He saved only $27 in taxes by twice arguing his case before the Tax Court and once before the Circuit Court of Appeals, yet the tax proposition that he established is an important one and could save money for many taxpayers who use their cars to transport both themselves and the tools of their trade to and from work.

Tax arguments on auto expenses are frequent, and many of them are settled in court. A Dr. Wells thought he had a solid reason for deducting 100 percent of his automobile expenses. He drove an expensive sports car on his medical rounds and his wife had an expensive sedan for her personal use. On his income tax return the doctor claimed that all the expenses for operating the sports car were business expenses.

"Don't you ever use the car for personal things—like going to parties?" asked the revenue agent who audited his return.

Dr. Wells explained he was always on call and that he and his wife went to parties in their separate cars, so that if an emergency called him away she wouldn't be without transportation.

"Don't you use the car for commuting from your home to your office?" asked the revenue agent.

The doctor said he went from home either on a house call or to the hospital, and only got to his office later in the day.

"You can't take a deduction for the personal part of your use of the car," insisted the revenue agent.

The agent didn't quite know how to go about calculating the personal portion, but he told the doctor that some part of the use of the car for social purposes was personal, and that all of the use of the car for getting to his first business call of the day, and back home from his last call of the day, was also personal. Similarly, the use of the car to go to and from lunch was personal, although Dr. Wells insisted that he normally had lunch at any convenient place in the course of his rounds—quite frequently at the hospital. The agent was willing to allow the doctor to deduct 50 percent of his auto expenses.

The doctor struck back at what he considered a capriciously unfair ruling. He took his case to the Tax Court, where the judge ruled that a deduction of 70 percent of the expense for operating his auto would be fair.

When a Boston nurse attempted to deduct her auto expenses, she learned that IRS did not consider she was traveling on professional business when she made house calls. She had several patients whom she tended regularly in their homes. One day, she would be at the home of Mrs. Jones, the next day at Mr. Smith's, the third at Mrs. Black's, and so on. There were five such patients. She usually spent one day a week with each.

The nurse told IRS that she was in business, just like a lawyer or a doctor, and that the expense of driving from her home to the homes of her patients should be allowed as a deduction on her income tax return. IRS replied that the auto expenses were more like the expenses of getting to one's place of work, which are not deductible.

In Tax Court, the judge decided IRS was correct and that the nurse was an employee who had five employers. Having more than one employer did not in itself make her travel expenses deductible.

The authors, incidentally, have *never* found anyone, among the many with whom they have discussed this case, who thought the ruling was at all fair.

One tax practitioner wryly remarked, "If the nurse had been a call girl with a greater customer turnover, she might have fared better." (Call girls, by the way, might, under the law, be permitted as independent contractors to deduct their transportation expense to and from the places where they meet their clients.)

If you have a situation anything like the case of the traveling nurse, watch out if and when the IRS audits your return. IRS examiners are using the nurse's case as a precedent to disallow many travel expense deductions.

It is interesting to note the speed with which IRS acts when it wins a tax case, in order to take maximum, or even undue, advantage of the victory, as contrasted to its usual very laggard pace in changing policy when it loses a tax case.

John Black, an Idaho insurance agent, estimated that he drove his car 26,250 miles on business during the year. He computed his auto expense deduction on his tax return on the basis of ten cents per mile for the first 15,000 miles, and seven cents per mile for the miles over 15,000, for a total deduction of $2,287.50. When his tax return was audited, the IRS allowed him only 40 percent of the amount.

"You didn't prove how many miles you traveled on business," the revenue agent said.

After much argument, and unable to convince the agent of his veracity, Black appealed to the Tax Court.

There he testified that he had a record of the addresses of the various clients he called on, and the dates of the calls. He also testified that he had recorded his business mileage for one month of the year in question, and during that month had driven 2,600 miles on business out of a total mileage of 3,000. In the following year he had kept an extremely careful record of his business driving, and it had ranged from 500 to 600 miles per week. He said that in the year under controversy he certainly had driven no less for business purposes than he had in the later year.

The IRS argued before the court that Black had not proved his right to the deduction he claimed. He should have kept a weekly mileage record during the year.

The judge didn't agree with the IRS. He allowed Black the automobile expenses he had claimed and pointed out, "When a taxpayer has shown error in the IRS determination, that determination ceases to be presumptively correct, and it is necessary for this court to make a proper determination based upon all the evidence of record. The evidence in this record, as a whole, supports the total of 26,250 miles driven by the taxpayer for business purposes, as claimed by the taxpayer on his federal income tax return."

Another traveling salesman, Nelson by name, contended with IRS that there were categories other than mileage, food, and lodging that should be allowable as deductions on an income tax return—trying to keep his customers' goodwill, for instance, when he had little or nothing to sell.

Nelson had been a successful wholesale salesman of costume jewelry when he had a serious disagreement with his bosses and quit his job. While looking for a new line to sell, he continued to cover his old territory, making goodwill calls on his former customers. He deducted the travel and entertainment expenses on his income tax return, although he had little income to report for that year.

IRS understandably was suspicious of a return that showed more expenses than income. The revenue agent who audited the return told Nelson that, because he was not trying to sell anything on his calls, his expenses were not expenses of producing income and could not be taken off on his tax return.

In Tax Court, the salesman argued that he shouldn't have to pay the added tax IRS wanted from him. After all, he said, during World War II, when many companies had no merchandise to sell, they had continued to advertise. Would the judge disallow such advertising expenses because, due to a temporary emergency, the advertiser had no merchandise?

The IRS lawyer, on the other hand, reminded the judge that a few years earlier the court had decided a case in which a lawyer from North Dakota went to Washington to take a job but kept his law office open for thirteen years against the day he would leave the government job and go back to practicing law. The judge had decided that the lawyer couldn't deduct his law office expenses since he was not actually practicing law.

Nelson, the jewelry salesman, countered that there was no similarity in the two situations. He had been trying to find a new line of jewelry to sell and had no other work, whereas the lawyer was working for salary. He likened his case to that of a laid-off worker who continued to pay his union dues while looking for another job. The union dues would be deductible.

The judge conceded that there was no doubt Nelson was actively trying to line up a suitable connection in the costume jewelry field, and that if he didn't cultivate his customers in the meantime, both his ability to get a new line and his income after he got it would be damaged. The judge, therefore, ruled that the salesman's expenses for keeping the goodwill of his old customers were incurred for the production of future income, and he was entitled to deduct them.

Owners of yachts, especially big ones, don't do so well in Tax Court—like the consulting engineer from Bridgeport, Connecticut, who listed his thirteen-and-a-half-ton, forty-five-foot diesel yacht on his tax return as one of his "personal effects." He told an IRS agent it was only logical that if an automobile could be a personal effect, then a yacht could be.

The tax law allows a deduction for the cost of moving "household goods" and "personal effects" to a new place of employment. The engineer would be entitled to deduct the costs of moving his yacht from Bridgeport to Florida if the yacht qualified as a personal effect. Otherwise, no deduction would be permissible. The deduction for moving expenses was put into the tax law in 1964 to make it easier for employers to transfer employees and to hire employees in one region of the country for work in another. Then, in 1965, the IRS ruled that the expense of moving a personal automobile was deductible as a moving expense, although a car might seem a little large to be called a "personal effect." Somewhat later, IRS ruled that "household goods" and "personal effects" included household pets.

You can understand why, when the engineer tried to deduct the cost of moving his yacht, the IRS people choked. And the Tax Court judge who was asked to review the IRS decision disallowing the yacht as a personal effect said, in his ruling: "Congress did not choose to include personal property generally or all chattel property in Section 217, but limited the covered property to items having intimate association with the home or the person at the former residence. Accordingly, we must conclude and hold that the taxpayer may not deduct any portion of the expenses he incurred in having his yacht sailed to Florida as moving expenses for household goods and personal effects."

A West Coast tax expert also tried to stretch things a bit on his tax return by likening his yacht to a roadside billboard.

A business that rents a billboard to advertise its services can deduct the expense on its income tax return. Although licensed tax experts are prohibited by their code of ethics from using billboards, this sharp tax consultant came up with a gimmick for a floating billboard that he thought would bring him business and also get him a tax deduction.

He bought a small yacht. He christened the craft *1120*, the number of the tax form filed by corporations. The tax specialist hoped that other yachtsmen, intrigued by the unusual name, would ask him what it meant. He then would let it be known that he was an expert in corporate tax matters. Since yachtsmen usually are men of means, he could expect some of them to consult him professionally. Some did.

The tax expert deducted all his yacht expenses on his income tax return. The amount was lumped into a category of "travel and entertainment," and since the total was not notably high, his tax return was not questioned by IRS.

Then one year a question was added to the business income schedule of the individual income tax return form that asked whether the taxpayer had deducted expenses for a list of things that included "a pleasure boat or yacht." If he checked "Yes," the tax specialist knew he was in for an audit. He couldn't check "No." That would be falsifying a return. Could he ignore the question and not answer it? The yachtsman-tax specialist consulted another specialist, who said, "Not answering for the reason that you're afraid of an audit isn't a good enough reason. By not answering the question, you're implying that your answer isn't 'yes.' "

The yachtsman reluctantly checked "Yes," and of course his return was audited. The yacht expense was thrown out by IRS and he was told he would have to pay more tax. He appealed to the Tax Court. He explained why he had named the yacht *1120* and compared the yacht to a billboard that a bank or an insurance firm might use to sell services.

The judge admitted the idea was unique, but indicated that of itself the name hardly proved the yacht was principally used for business rather than pleasure. The billboard comparison fell flat, too. The judge said it was difficult to visualize someone *enjoying* an advertising billboard, whereas the tax specialist obviously enjoyed his yachting. He sank the tax specialist's tax gimmick and found none of the yacht expenses deductible.

CHAPTER SIXTEEN

Charitable Contributions

The income tax division of our government should be mighty glad the taxpayers have what it takes.

—Author Unidentified

The Bible admonishes us to do our good works in private, on the theory that charity done for one's own benefit is not charity at all. The Internal Revenue Service uses a similar philosophy in testing whether your charitable contributions are deductible on your income tax return.

In addition to being a genuine gift, a deductible charitable contribution must be made to a so-called qualified American organization. Therefore, a gift made to a needy individual, regardless of how charitable the motive, is *not* deductible. Even a gift to a university that is earmarked for use in research by a specified professor will *not* get you a deduction for a charitable contribution. And if you know someone who wants to remember the church he attended as a boy in the old country, tell him that the IRS rules don't permit an income tax deduction for a gift made to a church in a foreign land.

The IRS has properly suffered a lot of days in court in its endeavors to disallow deductions for charitable contributions that are not run-of-the-mill. Surprisingly, it has lost many innings, usually to taxpayers who stood up and fought for what they did about charity.

When a woman made a "gift" to the building fund of a church-operated home for the aged, the IRS said it was not deductible as a contribution because she later became a resident of the home and the gift obviously was made in the expectation she would receive extra special treatment. A Circuit Court of Appeals, however, overruled IRS and allowed the deduction.

On the other hand, payments made by doctors to a hospital were disallowed as charitable contributions by both IRS and the Tax Court on the basis that the payments were really made in order to provide the doctors with a place to send their patients.

A corporation that gave stock and money to a college to "soften it up," with the expectation that the college might later sell the corporation some land, was allowed to take a deduction for the gift because the court believed that the intent to donate was the dominant motive, even though some benefit, in the form of favorable consideration, was anticipated by the corporation.

When a bank donated land to build a state highway, the IRS disallowed the deduction on the basis that the real purpose of the bank's gifts was to increase the value of its remaining property. A court, however, decreed that the primary purpose of the gift was to benefit the public, even though the bank achieved some incidental advantages. The contribution was, therefore, allowed as a deduction.

Money is not the only gift for which you can take a deduction. If you render services to a tax-exempt charitable organization and don't have your expenses reimbursed, you can deduct the costs of your meals and lodging while traveling for the organization, plus your transportation (five cents per mile if you use your car).

The cost of attending your church's national conference is deductible if you were there in some official capacity.

If you are a nurse's aide or Red Cross worker and must wear a uniform, the cost of that uniform is deductible, as long as it cannot be used for general wear.

You can also deduct gifts of property. Many taxpayers give clothing, toys, and similar items to charitable organizations at some time during the year. The amount you're entitled to deduct in such cases is not what the property would have brought from a junk dealer—which is what the IRS so uncharitably contends—but rather the amount somebody who wanted to buy such property might reasonably have paid. That's difficult to prove, however, and taxpayers often get into arguments with revenue agents over how to establish even what was given, let alone what it was worth. Nevertheless, if you keep records and are fair and reasonable about the deduction you claim, you should be able to make it stand up.

Things that sometimes aren't considered to be normal property can also produce a legitimate charitable contribution deduction. For example, the owners of a two-story building in Oklahoma donated to a charitable organization the right to build additional stories atop the existing building. The IRS allowed a deduction for the fair market value, as determined by appraisers, of the air rights thus contributed.

When the IRS turns out to be so reasonable about rights in the sky, you'd think it would be more reasonable on matters of religion. It took a drubbing in the following situation, and almost anyone would have expected it.

A California produce man belonged to a church with no distinctive, identifying name. It lacked a written character, constitution, and bylaws, and it had no permanent headquarters, comprehensive records, or bank account. Its only operational guide was the Holy Bible.

The members held regular meetings for Bible study, worship, and evangelism. They sponsored radio broadcasts and printed and distributed Bible literature, and their ministers regularly performed marriage ceremonies that were accepted by the state of California as valid. Yet IRS disallowed the Californian's contribution of $2,100 to the church because, it said, the church was not an organization, only a collection of individuals. The church did not have a bank account nor did it own a building. The produce merchant paid $500 deficiency in his tax, then sued to get his money back.

At the trial, the IRS contended that the contribution was not deductible because the produce man claimed the church had been organized in Jerusalem, in ancient Palestine, in the year 33 A.D., and deductions are allowed only for charitable contributions made to American organizations. The judge remarked that the church was obviously located in the United States. Other arguments were quickly disposed of, and he stated that the $2,100 contribution was fully deductible. He ruled that IRS should return to the Californian the $500 of tax which it had improperly extracted from him.

When a religious-minded person cannot prove he has made a contribution entered on his tax return, he has little chance of setting IRS down. A devout and hardworking couple—Mr. and Mrs. Dolford—with a total income of $6,000 a year, donated $1,200 a year to charitable organizations. They claimed this amount as a deduction on their tax return, but failed to show the names of the beneficiaries as required by the law.

When asked for some proof that the $1,200 was contributed, the Dolfords told an IRS agent that because of their religious beliefs they could not reveal the amounts, dates, or recipients of their charitable gifts. "Our gifts must remain private knowledge between God and ourselves," they told him. The agent thereupon disallowed their deduction.

"This is an unconstitutional infringement on our freedom of religion," the couple complained when they went to the Tax Court.

The Tax Court judge said he didn't doubt the taxpayers' honesty or the sincerity of the Dolfords' religious beliefs, but that they must abide by the law. If they would not list the beneficiaries, the Tax Court couldn't help them. The IRS was held to be correct, and the couple was ordered to pay additional income tax of $170.

An organization that felt differently about publicity was a railroad that was willing to have the whole world know what a nice thing it had done for an old friend. Nevertheless, it got into a tax fight.

A famous railroad had served an equally well-known town in one of the Rocky Mountain states for many years, and a particular old steam locomotive in its "graveyard" of outdated equipment was closely related to the history of the city. The city council asked the railroad to donate the iron steed to its Pioneer Association so it could be placed on public display on a new siding to be laid in a city park. The rail executives, mindful of the new generations that had never seen a steam engine puff its way into town, agreed to make the donation.

On its federal income tax return, the railroad claimed a deduction of the $6,000 value of the locomotive as a contribution for the use of the city. The IRS wouldn't accept the claim for such deduction on the grounds that the Pioneer Association wasn't a charitable organization. IRS also contended that the locomotive had been given to the Pioneer Association, not to the city.

In Tax Court the railroad argued that the tax law only required that the contribution be "for the use of" the city, and that the locomotive had been given to the Pioneer Association at the city's request for permanent exhibition on city property. The judge decided the railroad was entitled to the tax deduction.

IRS didn't have a very good understanding of how a railroad is linked to the history of many western towns. It didn't understand, either, very much about another western institution—a cattle rancher who will fight.

G. T. Macomb, operator of a Texas ranch, donated some cattle to a nearby YMCA. The organization then sold the cattle for $4,000. The rancher's tax return made no reduction in his expenses for the cost of raising the cattle he had donated to the Y. And he listed the $4,000 received by the YMCA as a charitable contribution.

The IRS disagreed. It contended Macomb was trying to get a double deduction. He had already deducted as ranch expenses the cost of feed, veterinary medicines, and everything else involved in raising the cattle. To give him an additional $4,000 charitable contribution deduction would mean that he had deducted both what the cattle cost him and what they had brought at the time of sale.

Macomb paid the extra tax IRS demanded, then brought suit in the local U.S. District Court for a refund. The judge held that the rancher had done right and was entitled to the full $4,000 deduction on the cattle donated to the Y.

Contributions of tangible things like railroad locomotives and cattle are clearly defined. They have, or once had, an ascertainable market value. What about intangibles like a man's time and talent?

An artist who creates a painting can get a deduction for its fair market value if he contributes it to a nonprofit organization. This is so even though the cost of the painting is mainly estimated in terms of the artist's time. A civic leader who has donated countless hours to nonprofit organizations cannot, however, get a tax deduction for the time he has put in.

The distinction is that the artist has donated a piece of property with fair market value, while the civic leader has donated only his services. Services are not property.

What about the scientist or educator who has written scholarly articles and donated them to nonprofit organizations for publication in professional journals?

A noted chemist-educator in Boston wrote ten articles for publication in learned journals distributed by such organizations as the American Institute of Physics. When he made out his income tax return, he totaled up all the time he had put in producing the articles, covering several prior years as well as the current one, and claimed a charitable contribution deduction of $35,000.

The IRS agent who visited the professor asked one question, "Would any publication pay money for one of your articles?"

The professor had to say no, that his work was a contribution to scientific knowledge and could not have a dollars-and-cents price put on it.

The revenue agent quickly pointed out that the tax law allows a deduction only for property that does have a dollars-and-cents value. The professor then took his problem to a tax practitioner.

"Do these journals that published your material ever pay for articles?" asked the tax adviser. The professor explained that the only payment was in scientific prestige, academic promotions, and broader job opportunities. The tax man advised him to settle with IRS for whatever deduction it would allow for the charitable contributions—cost of paper, postage, secretarial help, expenses for conducting experiments, and cost of travel. The IRS agent conceded a $200 deduction, a far cry from the original claim of $35,000.

Something more tangible was involved when a home-building operator named Franklin decided he no longer had use for a closet full of artist's paintings of the expensive custom-built houses he had erected. Although he had already deducted the $5,500 cost of the paintings as part of the cost of building the homes, he decided to turn them into tax deductions again. In so doing, he created an unusual tax case from which both he and IRS came out winners.

Franklin made a big ceremony out of his formal presentation of fifteen of the paintings to his state university's school of architecture. He then deducted $15,000 on his income tax return as a contribution to the university.

The IRS was willing to agree that he was entitled to a deduction for the fair market value of the paintings. But the bureau wasn't exactly stupid about art. It had art experts on call who looked at the paintings and judged that a general tax allowance for them would be more like $25 per painting, rather than $1,000 each. And it was less than gentle in reminding the builder that the university had stuffed his valuable gifts out of sight in a storeroom.

Franklin then brought his own art expert, who said the paintings were, in his opinion, worth substantially more and that he could get between $10,000 and $15,000 for the lot if a buyer could be found. The expert was forced in good conscience to admit there wasn't much hope of easily finding a buyer.

In the end, IRS agreed to allow the builder $5,000 of the $15,000 deduction he had claimed. The IRS books will show that auditing this tax return recovered for the government $6,000 in tax.

Everyone won—especially the builder. Giving away the paintings saved him $3,000 in tax, although he had tried to save $9,000. Deducting the $5,000 original cost of the paintings had saved him $3,300 in tax. Thus, $5,500 spent on artwork actually returned him $6,500 in tax savings.

Here is an important note about paintings: If you can buy for $25 a painting that a year later is worth $1,000 when, for example, you give it to a school, you are making a good profit from your tax savings. The $1,000, *if you can substantiate it,* will be deductible. In a tax bracket where $1 of deduction will save you 20 cents in taxes, the painting for which you paid $25 has saved you $200 in tax—a neat profit of $175. And, in a 70 percent tax bracket, the profit is $675! *If* you can substantiate it.

There is, of course, the cooperative art dealer who will be glad to testify for you. How effective will his testimony be? This is what the Tax Court said about one such dealer: "Although it was clear that he was knowledgeable in the field or art generally, we had no confidence in his valuations, which appeared to be highly inflated. He impressed us as a cynical person, with flexible scruples."

How does the Tax Court treat taxpayers who claim such inflated tax deductions? In one recent case, a Des Moines taxpayer had donated paintings that he claimed were worth $19,200. The IRS asserted they were worth no more than their original cost of $1,700. The Tax Court allowed a deduction of $4,200.

The Iowan paid only the amount of tax he would have had to pay in the first place, and possibly less than if he had originally claimed only $4,200; plus interest at 6 percent, which was deductible; plus the expenses of fighting the tax case—also deductible. And there were no penalties.

Perhaps many struggling artists have been able to continue their work because American taxpayers, who have found that art can cut their tax bills, are buying pictures. The practice may be a present-day equivalent of the WPA artists' projects of the 1930s.

IRS may be on shaky legs when it gets involved in art, but it stands fairly solid on school matters. If a taxpayer gives something to a tax-exempt school, he has a tax deduction. If he pays something to the same school as tuition, he does not. Sometimes you can't tell the difference. In one case IRS thought it could.

An Illinois couple, Mr. & Mrs. Green, sent two children to a non-profit, tax-exempt grammar school that emphasized progressive teaching and Christian ethics. The school charged no tuition. It was supported by contributions from parents, churches, and others interested in its work. The Greens deducted from their federal income tax return $1,075 they had paid to the school, claiming that it was a charitable contribution.

The IRS auditing agent got interested in the donation when he discovered that the taxpayers' children attended the school that was the object of their charity. He disallowed the entire $1,075 and said an additional tax of $320 was owing.

The Greens appealed to the Appellate Division of the IRS, which said it recognized that the problem was not clear-cut. The Appellate Division suggested the parents find out what it had cost the school to educate their children during that year. This they did. The school estimated the cost at about $200 per pupil. The Appellate Division thereupon suggested, "Suppose we disallow $400 as being, in effect, tuition for the two children, but allow you to deduct $675 as a charitable contribution. How would that strike you?"

It struck the Greens as being quite fair.

An ailing St. Paul widow was convinced that IRS was anything but fair. Before being admitted to a home for the infirm and aged, she had donated $7,500 to its reserve funds. Later, when she became a resident, she paid $95 per month for board and room, plus an infirmary charge, the same as the other residents who could afford to pay.

On her income tax return, the widow had claimed the $7,500 donation as a charitable contribution. This was a substantial deduction for a woman of modest income, so the IRS audited her return. IRS didn't believe that the $7,500 was a legitimate contribution, but rather was a payment made to persuade the home to admit the invalid, even though she was under sixty-five. Therefore, the IRS ruled, the $7,500 was a payment for services and not a charitable contribution. Then the woman died.

The executor of her estate argued with IRS that the $7,500 was a charitable contribution in fact, and that, although the home may have been influenced by it in considering her application for residence, the home was under no legal obligation to do so. The contribution had been made with no strings attached.

The Tax Court ruled in favor of IRS, but an appeal to the U.S. Court of Appeals brought a reprimand both to the IRS and to the Tax Court. The appeals court held that what somebody might expect to happen didn't destroy what actually *did* happen, even in a tax case. There was no evidence that the contribution had opened the doors of the home to the widow, and there was no doubt that the $7,500 had been given to the home with no legal strings attached. The court of appeals ruled that it had been proper for her to take the deduction. Therefore, the IRS could not collect a deficiency in tax from her estate.

CHAPTER SEVENTEEN

The IRS Does Not Respect Age

In levying taxes and in shearing sheep, it is well to stop when you get down to the skin.

—Austin O'Malley

The evidence is clear that the Internal Revenue Service does not respect age. A revenue agent digging for more taxes in the return of an elderly couple with very limited resources is likely to be just as hardhearted with them as with a millionaire whose accountants have helped him avoid taxes. One of the standard procedures of an IRS agent is to get technical. Usually, he will stick to the letter of the law, and woe to the oldster who is easily intimidated.

A bereaved widow or widower may expect a detailed examination of the final tax return of the dead spouse. While a ghoulish expertise in poring over returns of the deceased may help to obtain more tax collections for the government, the consequence to older taxpayers is all too often an unpleasant, sometimes searingly painful ordeal.

A widow in Georgia did not think she had taxable income when her husband's employer paid her $25,000 as a death benefit. The husband had worked for the state, and the money she received came from a retirement program set up by state law for the state's employees.

The income tax law says, "Gross income does not include amounts received under a life insurance contract if such amounts are paid by reason of the death of the insured." The IRS came up with the contention that the death benefits received by the widow were taxable, that they did not fit into the life insurance category because there was no insurance contract in the normal meaning of the word, that is, no contract with a life insurance company.

Her lawyer countered with the argument that the key elements of a life insurance contract are "a binding arrangement of risk shifting and risk distribution." The dead husband, along with twenty thousand other state employees, had paid into the state fund. By virtue of his payments, he and his survivors were entitled to certain benefits—including the $25,000 death benefit. The Tax Court judge who tried the case agreed that the Georgia husband certainly had "shifted the economic risk that could arise from his death from his survivors to the fund."

As to the IRS argument that a contract with a life insurance company was needed to permit the $25,000 death benefit to escape income tax, the judge said, "Tax law deals in economic realities, not legal abstractions. The right to look to the substance of a transaction is not a right reserved for the exclusive benefit of the IRS to use or not to use—depending on the amount of tax to be realized. The taxpayer has the same right." And the substance of the matter, as concluded, was that the $25,000 payment was life insurance and not subject to federal income tax.

The IRS can get technical in another direction and come out of the fray looking like the mustachioed villain in the nineteenth century melodrama. If you have ever seen an old-time melodrama restaged in a summer theater presentation, you will recollect how the widow, about to lose her modest home to the cruel mortgage holder, is saved at the last minute from being thrown out into the snow when her long lost son comes galloping up with the money in his valise.

The widow in this case had already sold her house, but she was the target of a claim by IRS for a whopping tax deficiency that would take a deep cut out of her substance. After some weeks of meeting with a revenue agent and submitting to his questions about her dead husband's income tax returns, she moved from their old residence in Bellaire, Texas, to Timmons Lane in Houston.

On February 12, 1968, the IRS sent her a formal notice stating she owed more taxes on her husband's return. Under the law, if a taxpayer does not ask the Tax Court to review such a notice within ninety days of the date of the notice, the taxpayer must pay the additional tax.

The notice of the deficiency was mailed by IRS to the old Bellaire address but, for some reason never determined, it was not delivered and was returned to IRS marked "unclaimed," with the Bellaire address crossed out and the Houston address penciled in. The IRS made no attempt to remail the notice to the Houston address, which in all common sense it should have done.

In June of 1968, the Texas widow's attorney wrote the IRS to inquire where the tax matter stood. On July 1—in reply—the IRS remailed the February 12 notice of deficiency it had been holding, this time to the attorney. On August 1, the widow formally petitioned the Tax Court.

"Don't listen to her, judge," the IRS said to the Tax Court. "She had precisely ninety days from February 12 in which to file her petition with the court, that is, until May 11, but she didn't file until August 1. She has no choice except to pay the tax."

"That's ridiculous," the woman's lawyer retorted. "She wasn't aware that IRS had sent her a notice until after the ninety-day period was past."

The judge had to agree that IRS was at least partially right. "It is well settled," said he, "that the ninety-day period runs from the date the notice of deficiency was mailed. And it is immaterial that the notice was returned undelivered, for actual receipt of the notice by the taxpayer is not required."

But even when the villain seems to have the technicalities on his side, the widow usually manages to enjoy a happy ending. If actual receipt of the notice does not matter in law, how could the Bellaire-Houston widow achieve a happy ending? The judge found a way.

The address on the IRS notice to the widow had been changed by someone, presumably the post office, since she had left instructions to have her mail forwarded from Bellaire to Houston.

"We do not think this mailing can be said to have been completed within the meaning of the statute," the judge stated, "because the post office diverted it. A taxpayer cannot be held responsible for this. IRS should have known, at the time the notice was returned to them, that something was wrong and it was in a position to do something about it. It is our opinion that July 1 should be considered the mailing date (not February 12), which makes the petition filed within ninety days thereof timely."

The judge ruled that the IRS was wrong, that the Tax Court should hear the Houston woman's complaint, and that she would not have to pay any additional tax, in any event, until after the Tax Court decision was handed down. She would first have an opportunity to receive a fair hearing on the IRS action.

While the tax people insist that all they want is to collect the fair amount each taxpayer owes, they often seem to go out of their way to trip taxpayers on technicalities. It is easy to understand the Internal Revenue Service's wish to send a Bobby Baker to prison. But why should our government's mighty taxing arm deny tax and interest deductions to residents of a nonprofit apartment development for the elderly? Yet that is just what IRS did.

Some senior citizens in a midwestern city each paid $3,000 to buy a voting membership in a nonprofit apartment building. Each member paid from $85 to $90 a month as his share of the operating expenses, including interest and taxes.

The tax law allows tenant-stockholders of cooperative apartments to deduct on their personal income tax returns their share of the interest and taxes paid by the cooperative. The manager of the building in this case told the elderly tenants how much they were entitled to deduct. The way he figured it, they certainly were tenants, and they certainly were the only stockholders the building corporation had.

IRS audited the tax returns of the senior citizens. In any normal meaning of the word, the nonprofit apartment corporation was a "cooperative apartment development." IRS agreed to that meaning, but it seized upon the technical language of the law that said the deductions for interest and taxes (worth possibly $175 or less in tax benefits to each of the pension-pinched senior citizens) could be allowed only to "tenant stockholders."

"Yours is a nonprofit corporation and has no stockholders," said IRS. "Therefore, the members are entitled to no deductions."

The manager of the development battled IRS in behalf of the senior citizens. When he finally realized that he was making no progress, he retained a lawyer to take the case to court. The old people lost on the technicality that without stock there could be no stockholders. Although they owned and operated the cooperative, the elderly taxpayers were held by the court to be tenants only and not stockholders. Their claims for interest and tax deductions were denied.

From the day her husband died, Mrs. Hampton, a watercolorist, ceased to live in the house she and her husband had jointly owned, a house valued in his estate at $30,000. She listed it for sale at that price. After a year of many nibbles but no bites, Mrs. Hampton reduced the asking price to $28,000. Neglect and vandalism took their toll. Three years after her husband died, the elderly artist sold the house for $24,000. Could she deduct the $6,000 loss ($30,000 estate value less $24,000 selling price) on her federal income tax return?

The accountant who regularly prepared her tax returns advised Mrs. Hampton that she could not deduct the loss, because it was a loss on the sale of a personal residence. She felt, however, that it was only fair she should get some tax benefit and her attorney agreed with her. She consulted another tax expert, who advised her that she was entitled to a capital loss of $6,000. On her tax return, she took the loss as an offset to other income she had had for that year.

The revenue agent who audited her return disallowed the deduction. He said that although she might have had a loss if she had inherited the property without previously owning it, the fact was that she had owned the house jointly with her husband until his death. It had been her personal residence, and this, not the fact that she had acquired part of her interest in the property because of her husband's death, was the important thing.

The lawyer accused the IRS agent of splitting hairs. He contended there was no real difference whether the husband had owned the property in his own name and left it to his widow, or had taken title to it in both their names so that she would get it when he died. She would figure her gain or loss on the sale of the property based upon the value of the property on the date her husband died, and not based upon what he had originally invested in it. Thus, the argument went, for tax purposes she had acquired the property on the date of his death.

Since Mrs. Hampton had never lived in the property after that date, it was not her personal residence. After that date, it was an investment asset on which she was trying to realize the most she could.

Faced with such logic, IRS backed down and admitted it had perhaps been unfair. The loss deduction taken by Mrs. Hampton, the watercolorist, was allowed.

A woman named Dorothy, put on retirement before her time, didn't do as well in arguing with an IRS agent and she had to go to court to get relief. She suffered from asthma and, at fifty, had reached the point where she could no longer work, so the telephone company's pension committee voted to give her the same retirement benefits she could otherwise have started to draw at age fifty-five.

IRS did not at first require that she report the $90-a-week retirement pay as taxable income. For five carefree years, Dorothy paid no tax on income that actually was sick pay. However, because she could have retired when she reached fifty-five regardless of the condition of her health, a young revenue agent auditing her return challenged her failure to report the retirement pay as income after she passed fifty-five. The agent said to her, "Since you could have retired at fifty-five anyway, what you are receiving now is retirement pay rather than disability pay."

Dorothy couldn't see it that way. The revenue agent had assumed that, because she could have retired at fifty-five, she would have. The agent didn't understand about the girls at the telephone company. They liked their work.

When the case was tried in Tax Court, Dorothy produced statistics to show that only 15 percent of the telephone company's female employees actually retired at age fifty-five. Most of them knew their jobs so well, and so much enjoyed their on-the-job friendships, the court was told, that they worked on through age sixty-five.

Dorothy explained that the only reason she was drawing $90 a week was because of her asthma. If it weren't for that, she would still be working. Therefore, she argued, the $90 a week was excludable sick pay and not taxable retirement pay.

The young revenue agent had not understood, perhaps, how anybody who could retire might not want to, but the sixty-seven-year-old judge who ruled that Dorothy owed no tax had a different outlook. He understood that lots of people would rather work, not because of a money problem but because they *liked* to work and didn't want the problems that accompany idleness.

Good tax planning can often help elderly people solve some of their tax problems before they crop up. Here is a rather complicated example.

The wills of a Nebraska couple in their sixties bequeathed their $40,000 home to their church. But that provision for a post-death bequest wasn't worth a nickel to them in figuring their current income tax bill. Their taxes, on a total income of $20,000 per year, were running well over $3,000 a year.

The pastor of their church also had a problem. He wanted to show a good financial statement to his trustees, but he couldn't include in it the probability of the church someday inheriting a house. So he figured out a way to help the couple save income tax and help himself in the matter of a stronger financial statement.

The Nebraska couple deeded the house over to the church. The church got immediate title, but with the provision that the couple had the right to live in the house, or receive the rent from it, as long as either of them lived.

By transferring title to the church, even though they held the right to use the house for the rest of their lives, the couple could get an immediate income tax benefit. The effect was the same as leaving the house to the church after their deaths, except that transferring the title meant they couldn't change their minds later. They took a contribution deduction of $16,000 on their income tax return in the year they signed the deed.

Of course, the elderly taxpayers weren't able to use the whole $16,000 deduction in that year, because charitable contributions can only be deducted in an amount up to 30 percent of total income. The unused portion, however, could be carried over and subtracted in later years, until all of it had been accounted for. Giving the house to the church saved those two good church members approximately $1,300 a year on their tax return for three years. Yet they kept right on living in the house.

The minister could then show that his church owned a $40,000 house, subject to the right of the couple to live in it until they died.

Anybody who pays income taxes can probably cut his tax bill with a little advance planning. The case of a retired Ohio carpenter and his wife, who have $180 a month in social security benefits coming in, plus $5,000 a year in interest and dividends paid to the husband on their life savings, helps to prove the premise. Their income tax would be $260 if it weren't for something called the retirement income credit. That credit equalizes the tax situation of people who provide, in part, for their own retirement, and of people who rely entirely on tax-free social security benefits without any planning.

The carpenter's wife has no retirement income of her own, and the maximum retirement income for which she and her husband can get special tax consideration is $2,286, less the amount of their social security benefits. Those benefits amount to $2,160 per year ($180 times twelve). The couple thus can reduce their tax by 15 percent of $126 ($2,286 minus $2,160), a reduction of only $18.90. A help, to be sure, but not much.

If the wife herself were receiving some of the interest or dividends, the couple could do much better. Suppose the husband puts savings accounts producing $1,608 per year of interest into the joint ownership of his wife and himself. Her half of the interest would be $804 per year. Since she earned at least $600 a year in each of ten previous years, she would now be eligible for a retirement income credit in her own right. Her credit would be 15 percent of the $804 of interest, which is $120.60.

Nor is that all. The husband is still entitled to a retirement income credit. He must subtract his two-thirds of the social security benefits from $1,524. The social security is $2,160, and his two-thirds is $1,440. Therefore, his retirement income eligible for the credit is $84 ($1,524 minus $1,440). The 15 percent on $84 is $12.60. The total credit is thus increased from $18.90 to $133.20 ($120.60 plus $12.60)—and the tax they have to pay is cut from $260 to $126.80.

A simple change in their tax setup has decreased by $114.30 a year the amount of cash they have to lay out for income tax.

CHAPTER EIGHTEEN

Real Estate

Taxes are what we pay for civilized society.

—Justice Oliver Wendell Holmes

It is fortunate that Americans can go to the Tax Court of the United States for escape from some of the arbitrary and seemingly capricious rulings of the Internal Revenue Service, especially in real estate matters. Take, for example, what could have happened to the tax bill of a partnership that owned an office building in New Jersey.

The construction company that erected the building had said in its application for a loan that the owner of the building was to be a corporation or partnership to be formed for the project. The stockholders of the corporation then became 50–50 partners in the project with an outsider as financier. All the partners, as individuals, provided from the loan the necessary money to finance construction of the building, which was thus owned and operated by the partnership.

Eighteen months after the building was completed, the outsider—the lone 50 percent partner—bought out the interest of the other 50 percent partners, the corporation's stockholders. The stockholders made a $100,000 profit on the transaction.

The IRS wouldn't accept the transaction as reported. IRS contended that the $100,000 profit should not only be taxed to the individuals, who had reported their $100,000 gain, but should also be taxed to the corporation. As the tax people saw the transaction, the corporation had put together a package deal, consisting of an option to purchase land, an agreement to lease the building, and a commitment for a loan on the property. The corporation had sold that package for $100,000.

The New Jersey corporation vigorously objected to the order to pay an additional $40,000 of income tax on money it had never seen, and took its objection to the Tax Court.

The Tax Court judge ruled: "We are very doubtful that the corporation's real estate package, which the IRS claims it sold for $100,000, would hold together under close scrutiny. . . . It can be argued that at one time during the course of the undertaking, the corporation might have sold the real estate package to the unrelated individual, but we are not concerned with what it might have done; the incidence of taxation follows what was actually done. The stockholders were entitled to either have the corporation enter into the project and reap some of the profit or keep the corporation out of it and make it their own project."

The judge concluded that the corporation had not become a part of the project and that the profit had been received by the stockholders. He also declared that the profit had been properly taxed to the stockholders and could not be taxed a second time to the corporation.

You would think IRS would be more reasonable in its approach to taxing profits of risk takers. It sometimes appears that IRS would prefer to preserve slums and encourage the decay of the central city, and that, of course, doesn't make sense.

A landlord leased a gasoline station in Tucson for ninety-nine years. Under the lease, the tenant-marketer had the right to tear down the buildings on the property and replace them with something else.

Each year in his tax return the landlord deducted part of the $80,000 original cost of the gas station as depreciation, offsetting his rental income from the tenant. After three years, the tenant tore down the gas station and put up a parking garage. The landlord took a deduction on his tax return for the $48,000 remainder of the original cost of the gas station building.

You have probably guessed it! The IRS disallowed the deduction of $48,000 and told the landlord that, instead of deducting $48,000 in one year, he could deduct $500 a year for the remaining ninety-six years of the lease. That didn't seem very reasonable to the landlord, who was already past sixty.

He went to court and the U.S. Circuit Court of Appeals finally told the IRS that its own regulations required it to allow the landlord his $48,000 claim for deduction.

But that wasn't the end of it. Three and a half years passed. All over the country business tenants under long-term leases were asking landlords for permission to tear down old buildings and replace them with new ones. The landlords, undoubtedly relying on the appeals court decision to give them tax deductions for demolition losses, granted such permission much more readily than they otherwise might have done.

That was good for progress. Some of the demolished buildings had been slum dwellings, and others involved urban renewal and beautification projects. Replacement of old, inefficient, and ugly buildings with new ones is favored by all civic-minded and progressive people and business communities everywhere.

Now, nobody believes IRS really disapproves of progress as a policy, but such an official attitude would seem to be behind a revenue ruling issued by IRS late in 1967. In that ruling the tax bureau announced that it would not follow the appeals court decision in the case just cited, that it would ignore the court's interpretation of the IRS regulations and would, therefore, not allow landlords to take loss deductions when their tenants demolished old buildings in order to put up new ones. The law is the law only when the men in IRS find the law to their taste.

Other federal bureaus are responsible for their own brand of peculiar and idiotic reasoning, as evidenced by the following case.

The government decided to take over a housing project at an army base in the West. While the owner of the housing area—a man named Zimmerman—couldn't stop the government from taking it, he did have the right to request a court to determine how much he should be paid for it. He intended to exercise that right.

In order to take over the project through condemnation, which it did in the month of December, the government had to deposit $137,000 with the local U.S. District Court. However, the owner didn't yet have the right to take and use the money.

When Zimmerman filed his tax return for the year in which the $137,000 deposit was made, he included a memorandum to the effect that the government had taken over the property, but that he was not yet reporting the gain on the sale because the amount of the sale price had yet to be determined by the court.

The IRS decided that the sale had, in fact, taken place in December, when the deposit was made, and it told Zimmerman he must pay an additional $70,000 of income tax. This Zimmerman reluctantly did, and then brought suit for refund of the $70,000 in the very same U.S. District Court that had handled the condemnation case.

The judge had not liked the way the government had proceeded in the condemnation case, and he didn't find its position in the tax case to be any more acceptable. Rejecting the IRS argument that title to the property had passed to the government when the deposit was made with the court in December, the judge said, "The only trouble with the government's present claim is that its own act, its own uncertainty, its own parsimonious position, left the property owner in a position where he did not possess the present unfettered right to use these funds as his own for any purpose."

The judge concluded that one branch of the government should not "be permitted to take one position in a condemnation case when it seems appropriate for it to do so, and then another branch of the same government jump to an opposite position in a later tax proceeding when such position supports the government's claim." He ordered IRS to refund to Zimmerman the $70,000 tax he had paid under protest.

Note that in the Zimmerman case the U.S. Treasury was in a hurry to declare a deal made. In another, unrelated case, IRS decided it would be to its advantage to declare that land had not yet been purchased by a Mississippi contractor when, indeed, it had.

In that case, a junior college had condemned some real estate owned by the contractor. To avoid having to pay federal income tax on his gain on the involuntary sale of the property to the school, the contractor would have to spend the money to buy other real estate by the end of the following year.

It would seem a simple matter to determine whether somebody has or has not purchased real estate. In this case, the southerner thought he had purchased real estate, but it turned out that the IRS thought he had not.

Ten days before the twelve-month deadline, the contractor paid for a piece of real estate that would be suitable for subdividing only if he could obtain an access road and water service. The purchase contract provided that if the access road and water service were not made available within the following six months, then the contractor could transfer the property back to the seller and his money would be refunded.

The contractor treated the deal as a purchase of real estate that allowed him to avoid having to pay tax on the previous sale of land to the junior college. The IRS insisted that the purchase was incomplete until both the road and the water supply were put in.

The taxpayer's most telling argument in reply was that the contract didn't compel him to turn the property back even if the access road and the water did not become available—although he had a *right* to turn it back. Based on that circumstance, and the fact is that he had become liable for the real estate taxes on the proposed subdivision land, had the right to take possession of the property, and had gone ahead and tried to get a water district formed, he ultimately was allowed to treat the purchase of the property as sufficient to avoid having to pay tax on the involuntary sale to the junior college.

He had, indeed, bought the property.

In an Ohio condemnation case, H. L. Ronman held out for a bigger price when the state highway commission offered him $10,000 for a twenty-foot strip of land in front of his house. The land was needed for a highway, and so the state took it in condemnation proceedings.

The elderly landowner went to court and asked for $50,000. The court gave him $20,000, plus interest at 6 percent a year for the two years that had elapsed since the land was taken over for the highway. The total amount came to $22,400.

On his tax return Ronman reported the $20,000 principal payment but not the $2,400 in interest. He had been advised by his lawyer that interest paid by a state is not subject to federal income tax.

Three years later, an IRS agent checked Ronman's income tax return while examining returns of all who had received payments for land along the new highway. The agent asked why the interest income hadn't been declared.

"The interest isn't taxable," Ronman explained.

"You're wrong. You owe $700 more tax on that $2,400 of interest," the revenue agent told him.

"It'll be a cold day when I pay it," replied the old man, and went to see his lawyer.

The lawyer did some research and returned with the interpretation that although the tax law says that no income tax is due on interest paid on the "obligations" of a state, the courts have decreed that Congress meant only interest that was paid when the state borrowed money. The court had given the old man $2,400 of interest because of the two-year delay in his getting the fair value of his land, but the state had not borrowed money from him.

"I'd like to fight it anyway," said the taxpayer. "How much will it cost to go to court?"

The lawyer estimated a fee of $1,000. The old man grumbled and paid the $700 tax bill. Principle bowed to cash considerations.

In another fascinating case, a promoter arranged for a partnership to purchase some undeveloped Oklahoma farmland. The investors put up $10,000 as a down payment on the purchase of $100,000, and out of that the promoter received $5,000 for putting the package together. He also got an interest in the partnership.

The promoter then went out and formed a land development coporation, bringing in some new investors. The idea was that the corporation would purchase the land from the partnership, subdivide it, and sell off the lots to builders and individual investors. Seven months after the partnership purchased the land, it sold the holdings to the land development corporation for a profit to the partnership of almost $30,000. The promoter received another $6,000 in commission, plus four acres of the land as a bonus.

The capital gains provision of the tax law provides that partnership profit is ordinarily taxed much more lightly to the partners if it is capital gain than if it is ordinary income. Only half of a capital gain is included in income for most taxpayers. Thus, if a partner would normally pay tax on a dollar of income at 30 percent, a dollar of capital gain would cost him only 15 percent tax.

The IRS ruled that the partnership's gain on the sale of the Oklahoma land was ordinary income because the sole business of the partnership was to hold the land for sale. Gain on the sale of property that is sold in the ordinary course of a trade or business is ordinary income, rather than capital gain.

However, the promoter argued—and the Tax Court agreed—that the gain was not the result of any activity on the part of the partnership itself. While the partnership did acquire the land and did hold it for sale, the $30,000 gain was an increase in value and was not caused by the partnership. The partnership, said the Tax Court, was not really engaged in the business of developing land. It was simply a way for a number of individuals to invest in land they hoped would go up in value. Under those circumstances, the Tax Court said the partners were entitled to treat their profit as capital gain even though they had held the land for only seven months.

A taxpayer named Girard, born on a relatively small Kansas farm, went to a state university. After graduation, he returned to the farm to work it. By the time his parents died and he inherited the farm, it was obvious to him that he could not raise wheat with an operation as small as his. He decided to get out of the business of farming.

As farmland, the property was worth somewhere between $250 and $500 an acre. The farm, however, was not far from a growing city, and Girard determined that the land might be worth as much as $1,500 to $2,000 an acre for residential purposes. He decided to subdivide it and sell off individual parcels. He put in water and sewer service and gravel streets, and started selling lots. He reported his profit on the sale of the land as long-term capital gain.

"You ceased to be in the business of farming and went into the real estate subdivision business," the IRS said in disallowing the claim. "Your profit is the result of the sale of property which you are holding for sale to your customers in the ordinary course of that trade or business."

The result was that Girard owed twice as much tax on ordinary income. He brought IRS to court.

The Tax Court noted that he had always been a farmer, that he had honestly thought he couldn't realize the true value of the family farm other than through subdividing it, that the improvements he had made were the minimal improvements required by local subdivision law, and that he had not bought additional land to replace the parcels that were sold. Nor had he constructed any buildings on the land. Girard had done no advertising in connection with the subdivision, a real estate agent who had handled the subdivision had done very little advertising.

The court concluded that the ex-farmer was not in the real estate business, even though he was engaged in subdividing real property, and that his gain from the sale of the subdivided land could be taxed as capital gain.

Property near the Nevada-California state line at South Lake Tahoe, California, acquires much of its value from the presence of gambling casinos just across the Nevada state line. Casinos mean tourists, and tourists mean business. Adjacent property owners are in a position to prosper.

A physician leased property along U.S. Route 50, not far inside the Nevada state line. He paid $350 a month for a small complex that included a dwelling in good condition, a real estate shack, and another dwelling that was substandard. The complex was a few hundred feet from his medical office. He hoped that eventually he could buy the property on which his office was located, combine it with the complex, and so have a parcel of land large enough for a motel. The lease for the complex provided that he could purchase it at any time within five years and, if he did so, 25 percent of the rent paid would apply against the purchase price.

Meanwhile, the doctor deducted the $350 per month rent on his income tax return—$4,200 for the year.

The IRS took the stand that the deduction was out of order. It insisted that the 25 percent that could apply against the purchase price was not a tax-deductible item. In the IRS view that $1,050 per year was part of the cost of purchasing the property. "That is the law," the doctor was told.

The Tax Court was annoyed. "The law is what we, not you, say it is," the judge informed IRS. "An amount paid as rental of a property under a contract giving the lessee an option to purchase will not be considered not to be a rental merely because the amount of the rental payments or a portion thereof will be credited on the purchase price of the property if the option to purchase is exercised. The substance of the transaction will be considered."

The Tax Court then looked at what had happened. "There was no agreement requiring the doctor to purchase the property. If the doctor did choose to exercise the option to purchase the property, a substantial down payment over and above the credit from the rental payments would be required." The Tax Court allowed the doctor to deduct the entire $4,200.

CHAPTER NINETEEN

The Capital Gains Struggle

The gathering storm of rebellion against the awful burden of taxes should at last convince the local and federal governments that they have plucked too many feathers from us geese.

—*"Isn't It The Truth!"*

in the *Arizona Daily Star*

A bargain is something you value that you buy for less than its real worth. Any time you can get something at 50 percent off the regular price, you have an exceptional bargain. That is what capital gains means to you in figuring your taxable income. A dollar of capital gains income will be marked down fifty cents. It may be slashed even more if you are in a tax bracket of over 50 percent on your ordinary income. This is so because the top tax on your long-term capital gains can be limited to 25 percent by an alternative computation. Thus, a taxpayer who would pay seventy cents tax on an added dollar of salary income will pay only twenty-five cents on an added dollar of capital gains income.

The Internal Revenue Service and taxpayers are struggling against each other all the time over the question of whether a particular gain to a taxpayer should receive capital gains treatment or be considered as ordinary income. When IRS leans too hard on taxpayers, however, Congress sometimes steps in and makes special rules that soften the harshness of high tax rates by generously classifying many categories of income as producing capital gains.

Taxpayers stretch way out in order to have gains treated as capital. IRS fights the stretching as a policy and it fights congressional generosity, too, by treating such income as producing ordinary gain.

Many decisions made both by the IRS and the Tax Court illustrate how the taxpayers continually try to stretch the law and how the tax collectors continually try to tighten it.

A New York television writer had a deal under which he received a salary plus a 5 percent interest in the shows he wrote. Most of the shows weren't big time, so the 5 percent didn't amount to much until, one day, one of them hit the jackpot and was sold to a network for a million dollars.

The writer received the expected 5 percent bonanza of $50,000. After his first elation had cooled down, he suddenly was hit with the revelation that if he piled that fat check on top of his regular income, the government tax collectors would take $27,500 of it. It didn't seem fair when compared to a normal business deal. If he had owned 5 percent of the stock of a corporation, for example, or 5 percent interest in real estate, his gains on the sale of such holdings would be capital gain, his tax would be no more than 25 percent of the gain, and on a $50,000 bonanza he would have to pay only $12,500 in tax. He would be able to keep $37,500.

His New York lawyer thought that a 5 percent interest in a television show wasn't any different from any other investment asset. So the writer reported it on his income tax return as a capital gain and paid only $12,500 of tax on it. The IRS came after him for $15,000 additional tax, a total of $27,500.

The Tax Court judge who had to decide whether the $50,000 windfall was ordinary income (tax of $27,500) or capital gain (tax of $12,500) held that if the television show had not been sold, the writer would have continued to receive 5 percent of the net profits of the show and it would have been taxable to him as regular income. He would have been receiving the money as compensation for writing the show. When the show was sold, however, he received the money that much faster, but it still was payment for his writing services. The writer had to pay $15,000 more in taxes.

The court may have interpreted the law correctly, but few, if any, writers think it is a fair law. A business operator can hold a business for a year, enjoy its income during the period, then sell it and take a capital gain on the profit. A writer can work for many years on a book or a television story and then, when he sells it, be forced to pay tax on the proceeds as ordinary income.

The Tax Court was established to promote uniformity in the interpretation of the tax law throughout the country, but, as shown in this book and in IRS' own records, it often doesn't work out that way. Here is an example of a single tax problem that had two opposing answers, each of them right, depending on geography.

Two brothers named Jones purchased, as partners, a master franchise to market a trademarked soft ice cream product in two states. The partners sold subfranchises, which granted exclusive rights to the use of the soft ice cream trademark and freezer-mixer machine in parts of the two-state area. They received a lump sum on each sale, plus royalties for each gallon of formula mix used by purchasers of the subfranchises.

On their tax returns, the brother-partners included as capital gain the amounts received from the sales of the subfranchises. That meant that only half of each dollar of payment they received was included as income. IRS decided that the amounts in question were part of the operating receipts of the business and insisted that the income be taxed like any other income—all of it and not just half of it.

The Jones brothers went to the Tax Court, which decided that IRS was right, that the proceeds from the sale of the contracts should be taxed as ordinary income, not capital gain. This is the point at which the different answers came in.

One brother, a resident of Texas, appealed the Tax Court decision to the Circuit Court of Appeals in New Orleans. The other brother lived in Seattle, so he appealed to the Court of Appeals in San Francisco. The New Orleans court ruled that the sales of the subfranchises were sales of the exclusive and perpetual right to use the trademark in specified territories and the income should be capital gain. The San Francisco court ruled that the restrictions on the purchasers of the subfranchises did not, in fact, give them a complete and exclusive right to use the trademark in their territories. Therefore, the proceeds of the sales of the subfranchises were ordinary income.

Whereas technicalities most often work against the taxpayer, there are cases in which IRS has lost on a technical point. Jim Littleton, the branch sales manager of a large eastern company, had a chance to buy stock in the company at bargain terms. He could buy 150 shares at $25 a share. The market price was $85. He couldn't lose.

On June 2 of the tax year in question, Littleton wrote to the company treasurer and asked for the stock. On June 6, the treasurer sent him written instructions and enclosed a purchase form for him to sign. On June 14, the sales manager put the signed form into the intracompany mail with his check for $3,750 in payment for the stock. On June 20, the company recorded in its books that it had issued him 150 shares of stock. On December 15—note the lapse of time—the sales manager sold the stock for $12,750.

If Littleton had held the stock for more than six months, his profit would be a long-term capital gain and he would be required by law to pay tax on only $4,500 of the $9,000 gain. If he had held the stock for six months or less, the gain would be a short-term capital gain and the full $9,000 would be subject to tax.

When did he buy the stock? Was it June 14, when he put the signed form and the check into the intracompany mail? Or was it June 20, when the company issued the stock certificate to him? December 15, when he sold the stock, was more than six months after June 14, but less than six months from June 20.

On his income tax return, Littleton showed June 14 as the date of purchase and figured his tax on the gain as a long-term capital gain, reporting only $4,500 of the $9,000 as income. IRS said that June 20 was the day he purchased the stock, and therefore the gain was short-term capital gain. He would have to pay tax on $9,000 rather than on $4,500. The sales manager asked a U.S. Court of Appeals to decide.

The court observed that it was very significant that an intracompany mail system was used in sending the purchase form to be signed. The stock was acquired, said the appeals court, at the moment the signed form and check were deposited in the intracompany mail on June 14. Therefore, since the stock was sold on December 15, six months and one day later, Littleton was entitled to a long-term capital gain.

It may seem that capital gain cases are won and lost with almost seesaw regularity, and there is good reason for this opinion. Kaberstad, the operator of a small chain of Texas liquor stores, sold the stores for

$75,000 when he was able to get brand-name merchandise at prices that would allow him to compete with cut-rate liquor stores. Then he brought an antitrust suit against the producers, wholesalers, distributors, and retailers of the name-brand liquors. The suit was settled out of court. The former liquor merchant received $53,000 in settlement.

The sale of the liquor business had produced a slight gain, which was taxed as a capital gain. Since only half of a capital gain has to be reported as income, Kaberstad decided that the $53,000 he received in the antitrust settlement could also be reported as capital gain on his tax return. IRS disagreed. Revenue agents viewed the $53,000 settlement as reimbursement to the former store proprietor for lost profits, and therefore they wanted to tax the full amount of $53,000 rather than half of it.

Kaberstad argued that his inability to get name-brand liquors at competitive prices had dissipated the goodwill his business had had with its customers. Accordingly, the selling price of his business had been much less than it should have been. If he had obtained $53,000 additional when he sold the business, the $53,000 would have been capital gain. This was the same thing, as he saw it.

He took his case to a Tax Court judge, who decided that any goodwill involved in the liquor business, at least based on the facts that had been brought out in this case, was attached to the name brands of liquor that he, as a liquor store proprietor, had not been able to obtain at competitive prices. Since he hadn't owned the name brands, he could hardly sell them. It was his inability to get the use of the goodwill of the brand names that had led to the antitrust suit.

If Kaberstad was arguing that what he had received was payment for the goodwill of his business, it would have to be a goodwill that he owned and not goodwill that he had not been able to use.

The judge concluded that the $53,000 was ordinary income and not capital gain.

Inventors get a special capital gains tax break. If you, as an inventor, should license a manufacturer to use a patent, the royalties you receive can be only half income if the royalty contract is written to comply with the tax law. Many other arrangements can be set up to produce capital gain when they might otherwise produce ordinary income, a fact that has the taxpayer trying to find new capital gain gimmicks and the tax collector trying to nullify them.

For instance, owners of small corporations often would like to get money out of reserves and pay tax on only half of it. The IRS would like the distribution to be treated as a dividend, all of it subject to tax. At one time, taxpayers used a three-layered cake called the "preferred stock bailout." In such a case, the corporation gave its own preferred stock shares to the stockholders. These were and are tax-free. The stockholders would then sell the preferred stock to an insurance company, and the corporation would buy the preferred stock back from the insurance company. Sale of the preferred stock by the stockholders to the insurance companies produced capital gain.

IRS had the law changed so that such a transaction would produce ordinary income to the selling stockholders. On the other hand, when new corporations are formed there is no reason why preferred stock and common stock can't both be issued right at the start. This same type of three-layered cake can then be used later to get some of the earnings out at capital gain rates.

The problems of capital gains get quite complex, but the savings open to you from having substantial amounts achieve capital gain instead of ordinary income treatment may make it worthwhile to take the trouble of learning as much as possible. Here is a letter of inquiry from a Miami taxpayer who should have done some homework on taxes before he sold his business:

> Dear Sir: Last August I heard from a Michigan office of the IRS (my former home was in Michigan) that they wanted to see my books, records, personal bank accounts, and copies of my 1964, 1965, and 1966 1040 returns! Later, a local IRS man went over the contract whereby I sold my business in 1965. The contract said that I was being paid $25,000 for an agreement not to compete with the purchaser. This was nonsense. My age, my ulcers and bad hearing, the fact that I was selling so I could move to Florida, all meant that I was not going to go back into business in competition with the buyer.
>
> Now the IRS says that I owe them $4,000 on this 1965 return,

since the $25,000 I had treated as capital gain is really ordinary income. I had a so-called IRS District Conference, and all it was composed of was one man from IRS and I might just as well have done my talking to the clock on the wall.

While I am resigned to paying this tax, I can still voice my opinions regarding what I think is a vicious situation and I sincerely believe that some drastic changes should be made in the laws. I would like to know if there are any groups or organizations dedicated to controlling or correcting the activities of the IRS and if so, I would add my voice to the throng.

The reply to this man's letter stated that the lawyers and the accountants who are engaged in tax practice are the only people who can protect taxpayers in their dealings with the IRS. From what the Michigan man said, it would appear that the real culprit in his case was not the IRS, but the attorney who drafted the agreement under which the business was sold and/or the certified public accountant who reviewed it for tax consequences.

However, the seller has not yet come to the end of the road when he has had a District Conference at the IRS office. If, in fact, it was physically impossible for him to compete with the buyer of his business, and both he and the buyer knew it, this might carry some weight in reaching a compromise settlement of the case with the Appellate Division of the IRS.

The rule is clear if an amount is allocated in an agreement to permit no competition between the buyer and the seller of a business, this controls the tax consequences to both of them. If, however, the agreement is pointless and fraudulent, the Michigan-Florida man, for example, might be able to get the Tax Court to treat the proceeds to him as capital gain and not ordinary income.

As you must have noted, the IRS is seldom caught napping in capital gain matters. In one case, it even donned the costume of motion picture critic. When the movie *A Streetcar Named Desire,* starring Vivian Leigh and Marlon Brando, was originally released, it was widely hailed as "a work of art." The IRS didn't think so. It thought of *Streetcar* as "a depreciable asset."

Unlike most aesthetic judgments, the validity of the IRS opinion had an immediate cash impact. It meant $67,500 in income tax.

The film version of *Streetcar* originally belonged to a California corporation. Then it was sold to its controlling stockholder. On the corporate tax return, the sale of *Streetcar* was reported as producing a capital gain. It was exactly here that IRS entered the picture, contending that *Streetcar* was a depreciable asset. Consequently, the gain on its sale to a stockholder who controlled the selling corporation would be ordinary income rather than capital gain.

The stockholder had realized no income from the picture because of the terms of a distributing agreement between the film producer and his corporation. The corporation argued that since *Streetcar* had produced no income to the stockholder, the picture was not a depreciable asset to him.

But the Tax Court concluded that, although the stockholder did not actually realize any income during the two years involved, his *Streetcar* had a lot of mileage left in it—and so it could have been depreciated.

The gain was ordinary income, and the $67,500 tax deficiency had to be paid.

CHAPTER TWENTY

The Special Agent

The power to tax carries with it the power to embarrass and destroy.
—Justice Willis Van Devanter, 1920

There is one sure way to tell if you are being investigated as a tax evader. Should an Internal Revenue agent call on you at your home or office without having first telephoned for an appointment, it is sensible to be immediately suspicious. Even if he does have an appointment, you had better demand that he thoroughly identify himself before you let him in. If his identification card has these words printed on it—*Special Agent*—watch out! You have been tagged.

It has been charged by innumerable taxpayers that when a special agent first called on them they thought he was just another tax collector type. They didn't realize he was a *special* agent, nor did the words special agent enlighten them.

A special agent is, in fact, a detective. He is required to identify himself properly, just as a policeman must advise you that he is a policeman. IRS now instructs its special agents to explain their mission and to warn the taxpayer under investigation that what he says may be used against him and that he has a right to consult a lawyer before talking.

That wasn't always the policy, and it still may not be a policy that is always followed conscientiously by an IRS detective. Not so long ago a Minnesota auto parts distributor received a visit from two revenue agents. One identified himself simply as a revenue agent. The other said he was a *special* agent. They asked to review his financial records. The word special didn't ring a bell in the taxpayer's consciousness. He gave them permission to look at his books.

At the end of the day, after the two IRS men had left, the distributor's bookkeeper reported that one of the agents had snapped photographs of some of the records. He said that the tone of some of the questions asked by the *special* agent could only be described as menacing.

When the two agents reappeared next day, the distributor picked up his private phone and called his lawyer, who immediately warned him that the presence of the *special* agent marked the investigation as a possible fraud case. The lawyer arrived on the scene in a hurry. He ordered both agents off the premises and demanded they give up the photographs they had made of the records. The agents agreed to leave, but refused to relinquish the records. They carried them off the premises.

The lawyer then brought suit in behalf of the Minnesota distributor against the IRS agents to force them to return the photos and records. The suit contended that the revenue agents should have notified the distributor the audit was not routine, but instead was an investigation for possible tax fraud prosecution. A further charge was made to the effect that the distributor's constitutional rights against self-incrimination had been violated.

This is how the judge ruled: In a criminal matter, such as a gas station stickup, the "what" of the crime is known. The police are seeking the "who" of the criminal, trying to link a man with the crime. In a tax matter, the "who" is known. It is the "what" of whether a crime has been committed that is not known. The taxpayer is not taken into custody during the investigation, and hence needs no warning from IRS to preserve his right against self-incrimination. The judge concluded that IRS could keep the evidence it had gathered.

If the IRS should charge you with tax fraud, it has the burden of proving that you have committed the fraud. Different judges interpret that rule in different ways, however, and a taxpayer often is found by one judge to have committed a fraud when another judge might rule that he has not.

In one recent case decided by six judges, five agreed that "when all the circumstances . . . are considered, it appears that the existence of a fraudulent intent . . . has been established by clear and convincing evidence."

The sixth judge didn't agree, and his dissent explained what the IRS had done to a taxpayer the judge considered to be innocent of any wrongdoing:

> The government seeks to impose a 50 percent fraud penalty in this case, in addition to the other penalties already assessed, with such zeal and enthusiasm that it is puzzling on the one hand and somewhat frightening on the other.
>
> The case that the government has put together is made by piling inference on top of inference and suspicion on top of suspicion without any substantial, much less clear and convincing, evidence to support it. Statements attributed to the taxpayer that are clearly favorable to him have been skillfully and artfully interpreted by the government by inference and innuendo in such a way as to give them a meaning never intended by him, and as so interpreted and changed have actually been used against him.
>
> His acts and conduct, even when he was cooperating with the investigative agents of the Internal Revenue Service, have been interpreted by the government from the beginning as suspicious and fraudulent, even though the taxpayer had no such intent. From the outset, his every act and deed have been considered suspect by the government, and it has handled the case on that basis.
>
> As was said in another fraud penalty case, "The case on the issues where the burden was on the IRS was presented and tried too much on the theory 'Give a dog an ill name and hang him.' "

Fortunately for all of us, the courts are more zealous than is IRS in endeavoring to protect the rights of taxpayers. When two special agents from the IRS dropped in on an Oklahoma radio station owner one day and asked for his records, he said he didn't have them, that they were at his accountant's office. Then the taxpayer, suspecting that IRS might be trying to build a tax fraud case against him, rushed across town to the accountant's office, grabbed all his books and records, and ran.

When the agents reached the accountant's office a few minutes later, they were too late. The broadcaster had beat them to it.

IRS then went to court, demanding that the judge order the broadcaster to turn the documents in question over to its agents. IRS argued that the records were the property of the accountant and, therefore, the taxpayer could not claim he had a right to refuse to produce them under the Fifth Amendment provision of the Constitution that says an individual cannot be forced to incriminate himself.

The appeals court upheld a decision of the district court to reject that argument.

The IRS lawyers contended that the accountant could force the broadcaster to turn the records back to him, since they were the accountant's property. If he did that, then the government would be able to subpoena the records from the broadcaster. The appeals court disposed of that argument, saying, "That the government might obtain these documents without compelling the taxpayer to incriminate himself is hardly a justification for compelling him to incriminate himself. We cannot ignore the dictates of the Fifth Amendment on the ground that it would be more convenient or efficient to do so."

Both courts held that the broadcaster could refuse to turn over his papers to the IRS, and that IRS could do nothing about it.

A taxpayer under investigation should be aware of the difference in types of tax fraud. Criminal tax fraud can result in a fine and imprisonment, while civil tax fraud results in a penalty of 50 percent of the tax deficiency partially or wholly tainted with the fraud.

To cover its bases, the IRS almost always proceeds against the taxpayer on the criminal fraud charge first. If the taxpayer is convicted on the criminal charge, the IRS then can proceed to collect the tax deficiency plus the fraud penalty and interest. But that would be over and above the criminal penalty.

If the taxpayer were fined $10,000 on the criminal charge, he might find himself faced with any amount of tax deficiency that the government felt it could reasonably charge—plus a 50 percent fraud penalty and 6 percent per year interest charge.

Once the government has established that any part of the deficiency for a given year is due to fraud, the taxpayer then has the burden of proving what his correct tax liability was, of disproving the contentions of IRS. And, as pointed out elsewhere in this book, if any part of the deficiency for a year is due to fraud, there is no limit to how long after that the government can institute a tax proceeding. In the next chapter of this book, we will discuss a case where more than a quarter of a century passed before the IRS charged there was a tax deficiency due to fraud.

If a taxpayer is acquitted on a criminal fraud charge, he may still be charged with civil tax fraud. Obviously, the fact of his acquittal will help his case in the civil court, but there are taxpayers who have been found not guilty on the criminal charge and yet found to have committed fraud for purposes of the imposition of the 50 percent fraud penalty.

Therefore, it is important never to get involved in a situation where fraud could be logically suspected. This means being able to explain all your bank deposits and all your sources of income, and being able to justify all tax deductions taken. If you are in a business or profession where you handle a great deal of cash, your office procedures should be such that every penny is accounted for and deposited intact in your bank account.

If you do something on the advice of an attorney or accountant, make sure that he is considered by his fellow professionals to be competent and that his advice to you is in writing. And if you obtain advice from IRS about your tax case, make sure you keep records of the name of the person to whom you talk, the date, and the exact advice given and received.

When matters get sticky, people who have advised taxpayers sometimes turn out to have completely forgotten what they said. In addition, taxpayers frequently misunderstand the oral advice given to them. In most cases, written memos can prevent confusion and help a taxpayer to avoid a fraud charge.

In one important case, the Ninth Circuit Court of Appeals faced the problem of a lawyer who apparently had been prosecuted and convicted for tax evasion primarily because he was a supporter of unpopular causes. The comments of the judges may be the best way of presenting the nature of the *persecution* of the lawyer. The judges said:

> In the special agent's two and one-half years of investigation, he interviewed some five hundred, perhaps as many as fifteen hundred,

persons. If any of those persons made statements which would have been helpful to ———, the government's attitude was that ——— had no right to know that, unless he found it out by his own effort at his own expense. . . . The government uses its resources, here for two and one-half years, to build up its case and its charts. Then it gets its indictment. The taxpayer still has no notice of wherein he is charged with criminal conduct. At the trial, or shortly before, he begins to learn the enormous amount of detail in the government's case. If he is financially able, and is lucky, he may acquire a tax expert who, in helping him to cross-examine the government's special agent and giving direct testimony for the defense, will largely demolish the government's case. But, as in the instant case, it may leave a remnant, a vestigium somewhat above the level of *de minimis,* so he may still, as in this case, be headed for the penitentiary.

What has happened to him is that the government has not assumed the burden of proving, beyond a reasonable doubt, that he is guilty. It has assumed only the burden, with its unlimited resources and time, of preparing a mass of documentary evidence and charts incomprehensible to a layman, all prepared by the government itself, and saying to the taxpayer, "Your task is to prove that *all* of what is contained in the charts is false, not merely that it is 96 percent false, but that it is all false. You do not have the time, nor the resources, that the government had, but that is your misfortune."

. . . The judgments which the special agent formed and embodied in his recommendation that ——— be criminally prosecuted can only be described as grotesque. His two and one-half years of investigation had convinced him that ——— had evaded taxes in the amount of $11,465.74 for the year 1955. The trial resulted in a finding that [his] taxes for 1955 would have been $414.78. The special agent determined [his] taxes to be 27 times as much as the Court found them to be. On an examination testing his accuracy, the special agent would have scored less than 4 out of a possible 100 . . . for 1956, the special agent's report said ——— should have paid a tax of $5,225.77. The Court found that ——— had no taxable income for 1956, but had a losss of $9,231.59. The special agent's examination score for 1956 would be, then, some almost incalculable number below zero.

The special agent was, so far as the record shows, technically competent and experienced. Such gross miscalculations as we have recited make it evident that some element, foreign to the functions and duties of a government tax officer, was corroding his judgment. Whether that corrosive element was that he had views differing from [his] about the Lawyer's Guild, or about "Cuba, Laos, China, etc." or about other political and social problems, or was something else that we cannot even imagine, the consequence is that we have no confidence whatever in the special agent's conclusions in this case. Yet he was not only the government's investigator but the government's principal witness in the trial. . . .

It is interesting that the special agent, in his report to his superior recommending that ——— be criminally prosecuted, said:

> "It is concluded that the taxpayer should be prosecuted for attempted income tax evasion for the years 1955 through 1958 and that the evidence is sufficient to secure a conviction. Inasmuch as the taxpayer is a well-known attorney in the ——— area, it is believed that this case would have a definite beneficial effect in this community."

Thus the special agent sought to upgrade the moral standards of taxpayers. . . .

This Court will not place its stamp of approval upon a witchhunt, a crusade to rid society of unorthodox thinkers and actors by using federal income tax laws and federal courts to put such people in the penitentiary.

Perhaps the upsetting thing about this case is that few less-than-rich Americans could withstand two and a half years of dedicated endeavor by an IRS agent investigating their personal affairs, without having it discovered that sometime they had made a mistake, zigged when they should have zagged, or violated some minor law. Furthermore, saddling a practicing attorney with a two-and-one-half-year investigation, in which his office routine is constantly interrupted, hundreds of his clients and business associates are interrogated, and he is placed under the constant strain of not knowing why he is being investigated, constitutes a cruel and unusual punishment in itself, regardless of any subsequent trial and conviction or acquittal.

When the average taxpayer is interrogated by agents of the IRS, is he really in a position to supply completely free answers? And can we assume that his statements are being made of his own free will?

A gas station operator—Wojiewkowski—whose return had previously been audited by a regular IRS agent was informed at the time a special agent was brought into the case that he did not have to answer any questions, that he did not have to show any of his records, and that anything he did say or produce might be used against him. Nevertheless, he gave the IRS agents free access to his records and, of his own free will, went to the IRS office to answer questions.

Later he hired an attorney, and the attorney petitioned a court to suppress the statement that had been obtained from Wojiewkowski by the IRS. The judge was faced with the question of whether the taxpayer had given the statement of his own free will. This is what the judge said:

> Defendant was as much an accused as any other suspected of violating a federal criminal law and was entitled to the same constitutional warnings. True, he had been told at the filling station that he need not answer questions, but now he was suddenly confronted with the solemnity and seclusion of a hearing room occupied by two governmental interrogators and a reporter. The door was closed and defendant was asked to stand and be sworn. It was then that the questioning began.
>
> Query: Under these circumstances, mindful of the surroundings, the capabilities of this defendant, the extent the investigation had reached, had he been effectively deprived of his freedom of action in any significant way so that he would feel compelled to answer the questions put to him? I believe so. Deprivation of freedom of action cannot be treated separately and in isolation, but must be evaluated in the light of what influence the atmosphere and surroundings of

governmental-oriented facilities had on the free choice of the person being interrogated.

Coercion can be mental as well as physical. Whether the test of coercion be a subjective one or determined by its effect on a man possessed of average resistance is not important here because coercion was present under either test. In such a setting, the need for counsel to protect the Fifth Amendment privilege comprehends not merely a right to consult with counsel prior to questioning, but also to have counsel present during any questioning, if the defendant so desires.

Mindful of the civil audit powers bestowed on Internal Revenue agents by federal law and the inherent aura of authority associated therewith, fundamental fairness required the revenue agents at the question-and-answer session to inform the defendant, in understandable and explicit terms, that a criminal prosecution might be contemplated and that the defendant had the right to remain silent.

I'm influenced by my impression of this defendant and what must have been his personal sensation on that day. That the defendant did not realize his predicament is evident from the fact that after the hearing he asked the revenue agent "to figure up what I owed him, you know, so I could get them straightened out. . . ."

The statement that the IRS had obtained from Wojiewkowski was ordered suppressed and the government was not allowed to use it in attempting to build a criminal case against him.

Many conscientious IRS agents are impatient with procedural safeguards that appear to limit their activities in dealing with the public. That type of bureaucrat is much more interested in performing his job efficiently than he is in observing the spirit and strict letter of procedural law. He argues that the innocent have nothing to fear from him and that he can more readily apprehend the guilty if given more power. He further claims, paradoxically, that the procedural safeguards actually injure the innocent by allowing well-advised and shrewd culprits to continue in their criminal activities with legal impunity. Finally, he points out, quite correctly, that corrupt or lazy agents of the IRS are encouraged to use the excuse of powerlessness as a cover for their own negligence or inactivity.

Efficient IRS agents who are intent only on doing a good job are constantly seeking increased powers. The more honest and capable they are, the more they resent the implication that in their zealousness to employ expanded powers they might ride roughshod over the rights of the taxpayer.

We shall return to this problem in the next chapter, dealing with our recommendations for procedural improvement. But the lessons of this chapter should be remembered any time you deal with IRS. Although a minute portion of tax audits blossom into criminal investigations, every tax audit has such a potential. When a criminal investigation starts, you need expert professional advice from a lawyer. Probably a majority of persons convicted of tax fraud have themselves provided the evidence on which they were convicted.

CHAPTER TWENTY-ONE

Recommendations

His horse went dead, and his mule went lame,
And he lost six cows in a poker game;
Then a hurricane came on a Summer day,
And blew the house where he lived away;
An earthquake came when that was gone,
And swallowed the land the house stood on.
And then the tax collector came around,
And charged him up with the hole in the ground.

—Author Unidentified,
from H. L. Mencken's
A New Dictionary of Quotations

People get very much the type of government they deserve. In the long run, that's the government they have demanded. There are a number of indications that have made many of us—taxpayers and government officials alike—strongly aware of the fact that our federal tax administration may not be what the American people demand or deserve. The anecdotal examples used to illustrate the various tax agruments presented in this book make the same point.

The many charges made against the Internal Revenue Service by both taxpayers and the tax courts reinforce our feeling that there is a problem. We are concerned that the prevailing idea that a federal taxpayer has privileges but few rights is obsolete in today's society.

We advance the argument that the taking of deductions in arriving at taxable income should be a right; that being able to effectively contest a proposed deficiency in tax should also be a right; and that the taxpayer should be given the right to call to account government officials who act illegally or who subject a taxpayer to persecution.

The tax bureau's administrative procedures were laid out originally when tax rates were low and only the well-to-do paid income taxes. Still adequate for the taxpayer who has it made in the world of money, these administrative procedures do not provide adequate remedies to the present-day average taxpayer.

The IRS must operate within the fences of the system erected for it by Congress, and with all the disabilities inherent in a large-scale operation where ambitious men may be most interested in furthering their own careers and frightened men may be most concerned with protecting their jobs. On the whole, the IRS does an outstanding job—within the fencing. We recommend, however, that some of the fencing should be changed. With modification, the climate in which administration is carried on also will change.

This chapter will cover seven specific recommendations, spelling out the basic idea that a serious reexamination of the relationships between the government and the taxpayer in the administration of the federal tax system is called for and is long overdue.

Recommendation 1—Only Net Income Taxable

Illustration of the Problem   The big electrical manufacturers were guilty of conspiring to fix prices of electrical equipment. Some of their officers served jail terms. Their customers were entitled to sue for triple damages under the provisions of the Clayton Act. The amounts involved were potentially in the hundreds of millions of dollars. If the corporations could deduct the damage payments, then the actual out-of-pocket cost would be only 50 cents on the dollar.

In 1964, the IRS ruled that the Clayton Act damage payments, attorneys' fees, and other expenses involved were all deductible for federal income tax purposes.

But at the same time as it was allowing the electrical manufacturers to deduct the punitive damages imposed on them by the Clayton Act, the IRS was successfully prosecuting a case against a drapery firm (see chapter 12) in which certain kickback payments were disallowed as deductions and the company had to pay tax deficiencies of almost $100,000 because it was unable to prove that such kickbacks were customary in its industry.

As the courts are quick to recognize, deductions are matters of grace and not anything to which a taxpayer has a right. Yet not to allow those kickbacks as a deduction is to tax not the income of the taxpayer but its capital.

The case of the southern optician (see chapter 12) had to go all the way to the Supreme Court in order for the taxpayer to deduct the kickback payments it made to eye doctors—and the company won its case only by showing that such kickbacks were common practice in the optical industry.

Putting the burden of proof on the taxpayer in a tax case has very practical reasons to support it. The government would be in an impossible position if it had to prove that people were *not* entitled to the deductions they claimed. However, once the taxpayer has proved that he paid the amounts involved, and has proved they were paid in order to produce income, it seems unreasonable to require him also to prove that such payments do not contravene some public policy. Especially is this true when it does not appear that the general public would find such payments sufficiently immoral as to hold them deserving of punishment, even though they may be judged not "nice." If the drapery firm is to be punished for its kickback payments, let it be tried and convicted on that charge and not fined $100,000 by the taxing authorities in a proceeding where the burden of proof is on the accused.

We hold no brief for "improper" business behavior, but we must also admit that if every businessman we know who has engaged in misleading advertising, industrial espionage, payments of some sort to obtain business, or other behavior that someone might view as against the public interest were to be punished, there would be relatively few businessmen left untouched.

Businessmen, and especially small-business men, live in an economic jungle and do what they perceive they must do in order to survive and thrive. This system may not be ideal, but it is our system. If a specific action is wrong, let it be declared wrong by the lawmakers, with appropriate punishment as a crime applied.

Recommended Solution Any expenses incurred for the purpose of producing taxable income should clearly be allowable as deductible business expenses as a matter of right. Only net income should be subject to tax. Otherwise, the income tax has the effect of expropriating capital. The income tax is too convenient a device for compelling compliance with other laws. Double punishment for one crime is normally not legally permissible and it is repugnant to our sense of fair play. Depriving taxpayers of tax deductions for the violation of other laws is exactly the same.

The argument may be advanced that to allow a tax deduction for a payment or penalty charged against an illegal activity, such as an overloading fine paid by a trucker, would be to encourage illegal activities. But this conclusion is justified only if you assume that the right to deduct the expense of producing income is a privilege and that the taxpayer actually should have not only his net income taxed, but also some of his capital taxed. We cannot believe that Congress, in recommending passage of the Sixteenth Amendment, nor the states in ratifying it, consented to tax anything more than net income as that phrase was generally understood. Congress should make the law abundantly clear on this point.

Recommendation 2—Sensible Statutes of Limitations

Illustration of the Problem In order to provide some assurance to taxpayers that they could forget about past years, destroy old records and cancelled checks, for example, Congress provided a basic three-year statute of limitations on tax deficiencies. A six-year statute of limitations exists on criminal prosecution for fraud.

Unknown to most taxpayers, there is no statute of limitations covering civil penalties for fraud. An unusual case illustrating how this can work involves a former federal judge, Reuben D. Silliman. Judge Silliman was seventy-seven years old in 1952 when the government asserted against him a tax deficiency involving the years 1924 and 1926. The deficiency itself amounted to approximately $235,000, but in addition there was a fraud penalty of $117,000 and accrued interest for twenty-eight years at 6 per cent of $380,000—a total of $732,000.

Judge Silliman had been a judge of the Hawaiian Tax Appeal Court, of the Republic of Hawaii, and a judge of the Territory of

Hawaii. In 1905, he moved to New York City and practiced law there until his retirement. He filed tax returns for the years 1924 and 1926. Those returns were audited by what was then called the Bureau of Internal Revenue. After the audit, the Judge cleaned out his files for those years.

His tax problem arose with respect to two persons he represented before the Office of the Alien Property Custodian. A law known as the Winslow Act limited the fee that could be received for such representation to 3 percent of the value of the property recovered. Judge Silliman was unwilling to handle the cases for less than 13 percent. The agreement he made with the clients provided for a fee of 13 percent, if it could legally be paid, and provided that if the maximum fee was 3 percent the client would make a gift to him of the additional 10 percent. The judge claimed he discussed the treatment of this extra 10 percent with an official of the Bureau of Internal Revenue, who told him that since it was a gift it did not have to be reported as income. He also claimed that he did not conceal the receipt of those amounts from the Bureau of Internal Revenue agent who audited his tax returns for 1924 and 1926.

Except for the judge, all the people involved were dead or unavailable by the time he was charged with fraud twenty-eight years after the tax year in question, and he died before the case was completed. All of his supporting records had been destroyed. A criminal case had long since been barred by the statute of limitations, but no statute barred the government from collection of three-quarters of a million dollars.

The Tax Court judge said: "The [taxpayer] places emphasis on the span of years that has elapsed between the occurrence of the events upon which the deficiencies are based and the [government's] determination. We are not unmindful of this fact. It is regrettable that it should occur, but the open statute in case of fraud is the enactment of Congress and it is beyond our power to change it."

Recommended Solution We recommend, as the American Bar Association has already recommended, that the statute of limitations on civil tax fraud be made six years, as it now is in criminal fraud. It is ridiculous to say that the government can reopen cases for years going back to 1913, and with the slightest hint of fraud can require the taxpayer to come forth with evidence showing what his income and deductions were after a long span of time.

The purpose of statutes of limitations is not to protect the guilty from punishment, but to recognize the unfortunate fact that records become lost, memories become blurred, and witnesses die or cannot be located as the years go by. We also recommend that the government should be forced to show reasonable cause for suspicion of fraud before its agents can examine years that are barred by the three-year statute of limitations, and must allow a taxpayer charged with tax fraud complete access to all the evidence the government intends to present against him, at least six months prior to the commencement of trial for fraud. Naturally, proper safeguards would have to be inserted to protect the identity of informers, but the courts have been able to cope with that type of problem in non-tax cases and should not find it insurmountable in tax cases.

Comment There are really two types of tax fraud, criminal and civil.

You go to jail for each offense and/or are fined up to $10,000 for each offense in criminal tax fraud. The government has only six years from the date of the commission of the crime in which to indict you.

It is civil tax fraud that carries no statute of limitations. If any part of a tax deficiency is due to fraud, then the government has forever to proceed against the taxpayer as to the whole deficiency and not just the part due to fraud. A penalty of 50 percent of the whole deficiency is added, plus 6 percent interest.

Thus, when you read that John Jones was fined $10,000 and sentenced to ninety days in jail for evading $213,000 of income taxes, you can be pretty sure that IRS will also be after him for the $213,000, plus $106,500 fraud penalty, plus 6 percent per year interest on the $213,000 from the date it was first due.

Recommendation 3—Reduce the Immunity of Government Officials

Illustration of the Problem A taxpayer named Martin Harrison sued a revenue agent named Horace Henrik, complaining that Henrik, by himself and in conjunction with other IRS personnel, had engaged in a campaign to willfully and maliciously harass him. Harrison charged that the revenue agent had repeatedly audited his records, to the point where he had made it almost impossible for Harrison to conduct his business.

The district court judge involved in the case dismissed the complaint, pointing out that even if the charge were true, and the revenue agent were operating with malice and in bad faith, it would be irrelevant. So long as the revenue agent was operating within the general bounds of his authority, he was completely immune from any suit regardless of how he might be abusing the authority. For whatever consolation it was to Harrison, the judge also said that the court was not attempting to condone that type of behavior, but simply had no power under present law to do anything about it.

Recommended Solution Undoubtedly, government officials need immunity from suit for their official acts. However, the scope of that immunity has become so broad that it is practically a license for abuse. That it has not been extensively abused is a tribute to the excellent people who have served in positions of importance.

However, we cannot rely on "benevolent despots," even though they might provide us with the most efficient government, but must build safeguards into our system's fabric. It should be sufficient protection for government officials if the law provided that, while they could be sued for acts performed in the course of their official duties, it would be a valid defense in such a suit for them to show that they were carrying on the duties of their office in good faith.

The person suing for damages would then have the burden of proving that the acts were not carried out in good faith. If such proof were forthcoming, and if it were of sufficient magnitude to convince a judge or jury, then there would seem to be no particular public detriment in allowing the taxpayer to recover whatever damages he had ssutained.

If the taxpayer who was the victim of the persecution related in Chapter 20 could show that the special agent who persecuted him was not acting in good faith in carrying out the duties of his office, then he should be entitled to some reimbursement for the two and one-half years or more of his life that were disrupted and for the possibly severe and irreparable damage done to his law practice. With government becoming bigger and bigger, and the number of government officials constantly proliferating, there seems to be no reason why they should be clothed with some sort of divine immunity.

Recommendation 4—Right to Appeal Any IRS Action

Illustration of the Problem   On January 10, 1963, just after the Cuban confrontation, the IRS revoked the tax-exempt status of the Fellowship for Reconciliation, a religious pacifist organization that had been tax-exempt since 1926. The basis for the revocation was that the fellowship was engaged in political action.

Specifically, it had opposed the World War II evacuation of Japanese-Americans from the West Coast, had endeavored to make American surplus food available to famine victims in China, and had campaigned against nuclear and other weapons of mass destruction. Peace, said the IRS, is not a religious but a political activity. If the IRS was trying to say that religion is only belief and not action, then it was advocating not religion but hypocrisy. A storm of public protest forced IRS to set aside the ruling. But suppose only a few people, and not a multitude, had complained?

By revoking the tax exemption of such an organization, the IRS can effectively dry up its sources of funds. By treating contributions made to the organizations, even without tax benefit, as items of income subject to tax, it can place further tax burden on the organization. The power to tax is the power to destroy. There is no way even to appeal from such a ruling. Either a contributor must make a contribution that is disallowed and then fight the disallowance, or the organization must file a tax return and pay the tax due and then fight the imposition of the tax. Either of those steps means that years must pass before a final decision is reached.

Recommended Solution   Any taxpayer affected adversely by an actual or threatened IRS action should have the right to obtain a stay of the IRS action by filing a petition with the U.S. Tax Court (see Recommendation 6), and should have a right to a court determination of the correctness of that action.

Recommendation 5—Reimbursement of Cost to Taxpayer

Illustration of the Problem A demonstration of how the government can simply wear down a taxpayer who is without resources is shown in the case (see chapter 7) involving the retired army sergeant who got involved in a tax argument with the government over $204.

If a tax practitioner in Tucson, Arizona, and a prominent Dallas tax attorney had not been willing to represent him free of charge, he would have had to pay professional fees of $5,000 for the help he got in resisting the imposition of the $204 levy. Who in his right mind would pay $5,000 to fight for $204? That's why IRS often wins against taxpayers by default. Yet those taxpayers who can afford to fight do well against the IRS. Of 5,744 cases processed by the Tax Court in one recent year, taxpayers wound up having to pay only 34 percent of the taxes originally assessed against them.

Recommended Solution In any controversy with the government, the taxpayer should be entitled to reimbursement of all his costs, including time lost from work, attorney's fees, accountant's fees, and so on, if he wins his case. Thus, if a tax deficiency were proposed and a taxpayer spent $10,000 succesfully resisting it, he would be entitled to receive that $10,000 back from the government. As it is now, the government incurs no out-of-pocket cost in a controversy and frequently wins cases simply by wearing the taxpayer down. If a taxpayer were partially successful in his suit against the government, he would be entitled to a portion of his costs based on the percentage that the tax finally held not due was of the total amount of tax in controversy.

The amount spent by the government to pay taxpayer claims for those costs should ideally be a separate appropriation item, so that the IRS would have to appear before Congress and justify the expense just as it now must justify its budget. One salutary effect would be a reduction in the IRS practice of proposing as a tax deficiency an amount substantially greater than the Service actually expects to collect.

By providing for the payment of the taxpayer's expenses in a success-ful tax matter, the taxpayer with a meritorious case would be able to obtain both accounting and legal assistance on a contingent fee basis. Thus, no matter how poor he might be, or how little might be involved, the taxpayer who had a valid case would be able to find professional assistance without the necessity for Congress to set up any new bureau-cratic machinery to provide it.

Recommendation 6—Make the Tax Court a Real Tax Court

The confusion as to what is the law in tax matters is compounded by the fact that ninety-odd district courts, the U.S. Court of Claims, and the Tax Court all handle tax cases as trial courts. The decisions of the district courts and the Tax Court are reviewed by eleven courts of appeal. If you live in Florida, your circuit may have a different rule than the one in New York or California. With some cases, you are wise to go to a district court; with others, the Tax Court will give you a better result.

The situation is a delight to some lawyers, with the question of which forum to choose requiring almost endless research and specula-tion. To taxpayers, it is confusing and nightmarish.

We recommend that the Tax Court be made the sole trial court deal-ing with all federal tax matters, with its jurisdiction broadened to include excise taxes, penalties even when unaccompanied by a defi-ciency, taxpayer claims for refund, appeals from IRS rulings on the status of tax-exempt organizations, and appeals from other IRS rulings or refusals to rule on specific proposed transactions. The Tax Court cannot now handle such tax matters.

We further recommend that there be one Court of Tax Appeals to handle appeals from Tax Court decisions.

If the government did not appeal from a Tax Court decision, it would thenceforth have to follow that decision. The decisions of the Court of Tax Appeals, unless appealed to the Supreme Court, would likewise have to be followed.

In such fashion, the process of adjudicating tax liabilities would be simplified and made more certain. In addition, the predictability of planned transactions and the administration of the law would be improved. Bills to that effect have, from time to time, been introduced in Congress and one was before the Senate Judiciary Committee at this writing.

Recommendation 7—Give the Courts Equitable Discretion

Illustration of the Problem A Los Angeles divorcee protested when IRS threatened to seize both her house and her bank account in partial payment of $148,000 of tax liabiilty.

"I never signed those tax returns," she wailed. "My former husband signed my name."

The IRS answered by publishing a notice of sale of the property in the local newspaper.

The ex-wife went to her local U. S. District Court for help. "Can they take my property without at least giving me a chance to prove I don't owe any tax?" she asked.

The IRS argued that it certainly could. It had mailed notices of deficiency and of assessment based on a joint income tax return purportedly signed by her and that was all the law required. The fact that the Los Angeles divorcee had never seen the notices and knew nothing about them was unfortunate, but irrelevant.

The District Court judge sighed and reluctantly did what he saw to be his duty. "It would be intolerable," he said, "to require the IRS to ascertain whether signatures on joint returns were genuine before sending out a notice of deficiency." He concluded by finding in favor of IRS, which meant she faced the loss of virtually all she possessed.

She then asked the U.S. Court of Appeals for help. That court said it was shocked to see that the law could be interpreted to mean that "a taxpayer wife is irrevocably bound by the forgery and duress of her husband and is subject to having all of her property confiscated by the IRS, though she never had any taxable income of her own and never became party to a joint return. Such a harsh result would conflict with the well-established objective of the notice provisions which is fair to the taxpayer in affording him the opportunity to challenge an alleged deficiency in the Tax Court before he has to pay it."

The appeals court said that the IRS right to issue a joint notice of deficiency when a joint return has been filed does not change the requirement of the law that before property can be seized a separate notice of assessment must be mailed to each person liable for the unpaid tax. No separate notice was ever given the divorcee.

The court's decision: "The lien is declared invalid; the judgment of the district court is reversed and the case is remanded for a trial on the merits."

It is important to note, however, that the Los Angeles woman won the case only because the IRS had made a technical mistake.

Another curious and significant case involved the executor of the estate of a dead taxpayer who felt the estate was getting rough treatment from the Internal Revenue Service.

The IRS, in order to tax the estate, invoked a rule that said the deceased should be considered as having owned all the stock in three corporations that actually had been owned by his wife and children. However, IRS denied the estate the benefit of another rule that would have saved taxes, but which required that the dead man must have owned at least 75 percent of the stock of each corporation.

IRS said that when it came to saving taxes, only the stock owned by the dead man, and not the stock owned by his wife and children, could be counted.

The executor argued that IRS was inconsistent—that if the dead man had owned all the stock under one tax rule, he should be treated as having owned all the stock under the other. The courts found otherwise.

The appeals court decision said in part: "Executor of the estate has argued that it would be inconsistent and unjust to treat the deceased as owner of all the stock to produce more tax under one tax provision, and then treat him as not owning all the stock to produce more tax under another tax rule.

"We have, however, examined the legislative history of these and similar provisions of the Code and have concluded that it accords with Congressional purpose and intent. If any inconsistencies exist, they are the product of a body having the power to be not consistent. Whether and to what extent taxes should be laid on ... involves 'consideration of many complex, intricate, and sometimes techically significant factors which Congress, the weaver, evaluates as "like Penelope," it weaves and unweaves the seamy web men call tax law.' If inconsistencies spoil the garment, the change is for Congress, not us."

A church-related Texas rest home filed social security returns and paid social security taxes, but its manager failed to mail to IRS all the necessary forms for electing coverage for the employees. The result was that the government had the money of both the employees and the nursing home, and would neither give it back to them nor grant the employees social security coverage for the amounts that had been paid in. The rest home went to a U.S. District Court to try to get a little justice for its employees. The judge ruled:

> This court does not pretend to be any expert on Social Security matters, but it can perceive of many pitfalls if this matter is to be left in limbo. The failure to credit these employees with earnings might deprive a claimant under the Social Security Act of the necessary amount of quarters needed, or reduce the amount of Social Security benefits to which he is entitled.
>
> So we have here a situation where there is no question that taxes were paid to the government for a specific purpose, part of the taxes being paid by employees whose whereabouts in some cases are unknown. The government has the money but does not want to refund it. Yet there is no way of knowing if the Social Security taxes paid in behalf of an employee will ever be credited to his Social Security account.
>
> We cannot allow the failure to file an apparent perfunctory government form to deprive citizens of benefits under the law when the facts are such that the intent to accomplish what the form would provide is clearly evident, as in this case.

The judge, therefore, ordered that the employees get credit in their social security accounts for the payments that had been made.

The tax people say so often that all they can do is to enforce the law, no matter how unfair it maybe. Why? Why can't our laws provide for the flexibility and fairness that the district court judge—Judge Garza of the Southern District of Texas—meted out in a rest home case?

Recommended Solution The law should be amended to provide that in tax cases the courts shall have the power to interpret the tax statute to prevent the rendering of decisions that would be unjust and inequitable to the taxpayer. The law should further specify that a judge's determination in favor of a taxpayer under this provision shall be final and not subject to appeal.

This power should extend to considerations of the degree of proof required of the taxpayer, and should go so far as to allow the judge actually to set aside an inequitable result although such an inequitable result appears clearly justified under the statute.

For instance, a widow whose house is destroyed by fire should not lose her right to take a casualty loss deduction because the fire destroyed all her records showing the cost and value of her possessions destroyed in the fire. Obviously, she could only imperfectly testify as to those items destroyed, because most of them would have been purchased by her dead husband.

Conclusion

The IRS is no Simon Legree, nor is the United States taxpayer always as pure as the driven snow. But in today's world, the economic rights that undergird our personal liberties are broader than the property rights of the nineteenth century, and these newly important rights must be protected. At the same time, the old system of checks and balances in tax administration seems often to result in the small taxpayer writing all the checks and the IRS accumulating all the balances.

The past quarter of a century has seen no serious reexamination of the basic relationships between taxpayer and government in the administration of the federal system. Review of this relationship indicates that it is basically sound, but also indicates that there is need for specific action in order for it to remain sound in terms of protecting taxpayer rights. We have set forth in this chapter some concrete examples of changes that would cost few or no dollars but which would go a long way toward restoring taxpayer confidence in the fairness of the system.

APPENDICES

OFFERS IN COMPROMISE

Not every taxpayer is right in every tax controversy with the Internal Revenue Service. In fact, the Internal Revenue Service is probably right most of the time. Also, the people at the lower levels in the Internal Revenue Service often have no discretion as to what they can do even though a particular taxpayer is being unfairly treated by the tax law or by the administrative rules.

Much of this book discusses how to handle the situation when you think the Internal Revenue Service may be wrong. But if the Internal Revenue Service is right, if it is, in fact, applying the law as written, this does not necessarily mean you are going to have to pay what it says you owe. This is where the offer in compromise comes into play. The offer in compromise procedure can only be utilized after the IRS has determined the deficiency and you, the taxpayer, have agreed that you owe it.

A taxpayer normally receives three notices requesting payment before the IRS collection people move to seize assets and file liens and levies. If there is doubt as to the liability for the tax, or doubt as to collectibility, or if actual hardship would result from immediate payment, the taxpayer should contact the Collection Division of the Internal Revenue Service immediately upon receiving the first notice requesting payment.

He can often work out an acceptable solution to his financial and tax problems with a minimum of frustration and inconvenience for himself. Many of the problems between taxpayers and IRS in the collection area result from a lack of communication between the taxpayer and the Internal Revenue Service, although many others also result from the failure of the taxpayer to face realistically the requirements of the tax statutes and regulations.

Compromises

Compromises will be entered into only if there is doubt on the part of the IRS as to the liability for the tax or the collectibility. When the amount involved is under $500, the district director has complete discretion as to acceptance or rejection. If the amount involved is $500 or more but less than $100,000, the regional counsel's office must concur in acceptance of the offer. If the amount involved is $100,000 or more, then the national office must concur in acceptance of the offer.

Offers in compromise are submitted on Form 656. If the offer is based on inability to pay, the Form 656 should be accompanied by a financial statement on Form 433. Before filing a formal offer on Form 656, it is usually desirable to discuss the amount that might be acceptable with the collection personnel involved.

If the offer in compromise is rejected by the collection division, a district conference can be obtained. A written request for such a conference is necessary, and a written protest is required if the amount for any return or taxable period exceeds $2,500. If agreement is not reached at the district conference, then Appellate Division consideration of the offer can be obtained by so requesting in writing, and submitting a written protest if the amount for any return or taxable period exceeds $2,500.

When an offer is based upon inability to pay, the facts of the matter are investigated by the Collection Division. If the offer is based on doubt as to liability, then the investigation is made by a revenue agent.

"Where liability has been established by a valid judgment or is certain, and there is no doubt as to the collectibility of the amount due, mutual concessions are not possible, and there is no basis for a compromise." Op. A. G.6, CB Dec. 1934, p. 442.

Deferred Payments

Even though there may be no doubt as to the liability of a taxpayer and the amount may be collectible from the taxpayer in the sense that seizure and sale of the taxpayer's property could conceivably satisfy all or a substantial part of the amount due, the taxpayer can often work out a plan for liquidation of his liability on a deferred basis. Collection Division personnel have a high degree of discretion as to what they will accept in arriving at plans for deferred payment. Some of the basic factors that they consider in reaching a decision include:

1. What is the past performance of the taxpayer? Does he *now*

properly prepay his taxes through estimated tax declarations and payments of trust fund amounts (payroll taxes, excise taxes) to federal depositories? If the taxpayer is a "chronic offender" or a "repeater," the attitude of the IRS is apt to be unsympathetic unless the taxpayer can show he has "reformed."

2. What is required of the Service to protect the revenue?

a. Other creditors may threaten or may take action and may not permit a possible resolution of the problem.

b. The taxpayer may not be realistically facing the payment problem. The IRS is not sympathetic to simply seeking time rather than seeking the solution. Does the financial record of the taxpayer indicate he can perform as per his desired plan?

c. What the taxpayer may term "hardship" the IRS may call merely" inconvenience." Document the fact that actual physical or emotional damage could result to the taxpayer or his family.

The procedure is similar to that of an offer in compromise. Again, discussions should be had with the collection people before submitting a Form 656, and, again, appeal can be made to a district conference and to the Appellate Division. It should be noted that a commonly used form in connection with deferred payments is Form 2159, which is an agreement for the liquidation of federal tax liabilities through payroll deductions.

Excess Earnings Agreements

A type of compromise settlement that has aspects of a deferred payment agreement involves the taxpayer who presently is unable to pay but has contingent assets or is in an occupation in which his income could rise dramatically in the future. In such a situation, the tax liability may be compromised, but a collateral agreement may be obtained providing that if the taxpayer's income exceeds a certain amount, then a certain percentage of that income must be paid to the IRS.

Similarly, in a normal deferred payment agreement, it may be provided that the payment schedule shall be proportioned to the size of income. Thus, a taxpayer who is currently earning $100 a week may be obligated to pay $10 a week to the IRS. However, he may also be obligated to pay IRS 20 percent of any amounts he may earn in excess of $100 per week, 30 percent of any amounts in excess of $200 per week, and 50 percent of any amounts in excess of $300 per week.

Conclusion

While IRS collection people are bill collectors and are accustomed to dealing with individuals who may employ a variety of devices to avoid paying their debts, this does not mean that most collection problems cannot be worked out if a realistic approach is taken and every attempt made to establish and maintain communication with the responsible IRS personnel.

PROCEDURES FOR APPEAL

ROLE OF THE APPELLATE DIVISION

There are two levels of administrative appeal within the Internal Revenue Service. The first, which is used most frequently, is at the district level where discussions of disputed issues may be had through the district conference procedure. If agreement cannot be reached at the district conference level or if the issue or issues are not susceptible of district conference settlement, a second level—the appellate conference—is available to taxpayers.

Each of the seven regions has from four to seven Appellate Branch Offices, a total of forty, located in major cities throughout the United States. Each branch office is headed by a chief who is under the direct management of the assistant regional commissioner (appellate) for that region. Thus, the appellate conference is on a regional level removed from the district and provides the opportunity for a completely new, fresh review of the tax controversy.

Authority for the settlement of tax cases in the Appellate Division flows from the commissioner through the regional commissioners to the chiefs, associate chiefs, and assistant chiefs at the branch level. The national office provides functional direction but has no delegated authority to enter into the technical discussions, to make decisions, or to settle any tax cases that are under the jurisdiction of the branch offices.

Appellate's mission is to resolve tax controversies without litigation on a basis that is fair, and impartial, both to the government and taxpayers. This mission is accomplished through a program of considering appeals, conducting hearings, and negotiating settlements in "nondocketed" cases where the taxpayer has protested the findings of the district director and also "docketed" cases where the taxpayer has petitioned the Tax Court of the United States for review. In rare instances conferences may be held in the ninety-day period during which a taxpayer may file a petition with the Tax Court following issuance of a statutory notice of deficiency.

The vast majority of conferences are held in the local Appellate Branch Office at times and dates reasonably convenient to taxpayers and the representative. However, if a sufficient number of cases make it economically sound, the conferee will travel to another city to hold conferences. In Arizona, for instance, the Appellate Branch Office is located in Phoenix but "circuit-riding" trips are made to Tucson to hold conferences in that city. An early conference is offered at the branch office, with the option to await the next "circuit-riding" trip if the taxpayer prefers.

Appellate Authority

Appellate settlement authority is broad but still subject to some limitations. Appellate has jurisdiction for determination of liability for income, estate, gift, and employment taxes, and offers in compromise covering these areas. Appellate also has similar jurisdiction over most excise taxes but does not determine the liability for those involving alcohol, tobacco, narcotics, firearms, and wagering taxes.

When a taxpayer properly requests it, Appellate will assume jurisdiction and determine the liability for all taxes mentioned. The "protest" may follow a district director's preliminary notice of tax deficiency after an agent's examination, or claim disallowance, or a rejection of an offer in compromise. In a "nondocketed" case the conference is conducted by an appellate conferee who has been assigned the total responsibility of considering the case, negotiating settlements, and preparing a statement recommending to the chief, Appellate Branch Office, or other appellate supervisor having proper authority, the action to be taken. When a case is docketed in the Tax Court, following issuance of a statutory notice of deficiency either at the district or appellate level, jurisdiction continues in Appellate in conjunction with regional counsel until the case becomes a session case. The regional counsel attorney assigned to the case attends and participates in settlement conferences on docketed cases. He and the appellate conferee agree on any settlement or action they recommend for concurrent approval of the appropriate supervisors in the Appellate Branch Office and the local Regional Counsel Office. If a settlement is agreed upon, a stipulation of settlement and decision document is filed with the Tax Court for entry of its decision. If no agreement is reached, the case is sent to regional counsel for preparation for trial.

A case changes from presession status to session status at the first moment of the opening day of the trial, pretrial, or report session of the court. Regional counsel assumes sole jurisdiction over docketed cases in session status.

Appellate Procedures

A written request is generally required before Appellate will accept jurisdiction of a case. *Internal Revenue Publication No. 5, Instructions—Unagreed Income, Estate, Gift, Employment and Excise Tax Cases* explains the overall appeal rights and how to prepare the required protest. This instruction sheet is enclosed with virtually all preliminary notices sent to taxpayers by the district director transmitting the agent's report inviting a district conference, or correspondence notifying the taxpayer of the district director's conclusions in cases where a protest has not previously been filed. It is also available upon request from all district offices.

The original and one copy of all protests should be filed with the district director and must contain:

(1) Name and address of taxpayer (the residence address of individuals; the address of the principal office or place of business of corporations).

(2) The date and symbols on the letter which transmitted the proposed adjustments or findings covered in the protest.

(3) The taxable year(s) involved.

(4) A statement that you desire a district conference.

(5) If a district conference is not desired, a statement that you desire consideration of your case by the Appellate Division of the Regional Commissioner's Office.

(6) An itemized schedule of the adjustments or findings to which you take exception.

(7) A statement of the facts upon which you rely concerning each contested issue where the facts are in dispute. Such statement and all evidence submitted, except that of a supplementary or incidental character, must be declared true under penalties of perjury. This requirement may be satisfied by adding to the protest the following statement signed by the taxpayer (by an authorized officer in the case of a corporation): "Under the penalties of perjury, I declare that the statement of facts presented in this protest and in any accompanying schedules and statements has been examined by me and to the best of my knowledge and belief is true, correct, and complete."

(8) A statement outlining the law or other authority upon which you rely (generally, this statement is not required in offer-in-compromise cases), and

(9) If the protest is prepared or filed by an attorney or agent, it should contain, in addition to the declaration required in (7) above, a statement signed by such attorney or agent indicating:

(a) Whether he prepared the protest.

(b) Whether he knows of his own knowledge that the information contained therein is true.

The protest must be filed within thirty days from the date of the district director's letter transmitting the agent's report if addressed to a taxpayer in the United States or within sixty days if addressed to a person outside the United States. However, the district director may grant extensions of time for filing a protest when, for appropriate reasons, a timely request is made by the taxpayer or by the authorized representative for the taxpayer.

All protests are reviewed in the district office to make sure they are adequate and complete, and also to see if the dispute might possibly be resolved without sending the case on to Appellate. The district conference staff will, in cases in which they consider the issue or issues to be susceptible of district conference settlement, contact the taxpayer or his representative and ask that they discuss the disputed tax issues.

No written protest is required in cases where the proposed tax deficiency is $2,500 or less, if the taxpayer otherwise asks for an appellate conference, and has taken advantage of the district conference procedure.

Appellate conference procedures require that: on nondocketed cases, an attorney or certified public accountant must be present, or have on file, a written declaration that he is currently qualified as an attorney or certified public accountant and is authorized to represent the taxpayer. *Instructions for Forms 2848 and 2848-D* contains information relating to these requirements and the forms may be used for this purpose.

If the taxpayer files a petition with the Tax Court, his case then comes to Appellate without further request or protest.

Type of Proof Required

In conducting conferences, an appellate conferee has a quasi-judicial duty to determine the correct tax liability with strict impartiality between the taxpayer and the government. A conferee is not an examining officer and is not expected to gather or verify additional facts in a case. Facts that are set forth in the taxpayer's protest and are declared under penalties of perjury to be correct, true, and complete are, of course, given careful consideration. The revenue agent's report is assumed to set forth the facts of a situation accurately, and unless contradicted by the taxpayer, the factual statements in the report would be accepted.

Any information that has a bearing upon development of the issue, such as third party records, affidavits that might have been obtained, expert's analysis or reports, letters that show contemporary intent of the parties, and other relevant material and information, will be considered by the conferee and evaluated according to the weight the conferee feels they should be given.

A conferee will, when appropriate, write or telephone a taxpayer or his authorized representative prior to an initial conference if it appears that additional data may be required in order to more adequately prepare for the conference. Also, to avoid surprises at the conference, if a conferee intends to discuss court cases, rulings, or other precedent having a material bearing on the issue and not previously mentioned in district reports or the taxpayer's protest, he will ask the taxpayer or representative to review these matters so they can be knowledgeably discussed at their meeting. Additionally, the taxpayer or representative may, prior to the initial conference, contact the conferee and obtain clarification of any item needed in order to more adequately prepare for the conference.

Role of the Appellate Conferee

The appellate conferee considers the technical questions referred to Appellate and endeavors to resolve the controversy.

In most cases the conferee and the taxpayer will be successful in finding a mutually satisfactory basis of disposition. The issues will sometimes be conceded in full by one party or the other, and sometimes resolved on an intermediate basis. In recognition of the difference between abstract theory and practical administration, when substantial uncertainties exist either in law, in fact, or both, the conferee will give serious consideration to an offer of settlement that fairly reflects the relative merits of the opposing views in the light of the hazards that would prevail if the case was litigated. However, he may not base the settlement of any case upon nuisance value to either party. He is not expected to settle all cases, since even reasonable men may differ in their opinions. However, if a settlement is not reached, he must clearly and fully explain the reason for his position and the further procedural rights open to the taxpayer.

The conferee should ordinarily not concede a strictly legal issue if such concession would be inconsistent with the regulations or a revenue ruling and the issue has not been clearly resolved by the courts. He may, however, settle such an issue by giving due recognition to the strengths and weaknesses of the government's position and the consequent hazards of litigation.

A conferee himself, under the commissioner's delegation orders, does not have authority to make the final decision in a case. Full settlement authority extends only to the Appellate Branch Office chiefs, associate chiefs, or assistant chiefs. Authority which extends to the assistant chief is limited to those cases in which the amount in controversy is $50,000 or less. Accordingly, a conferee submits his findings and recommendations to his immediate supervisor in the form of a report called a Supporting Statement. If the chief, associate chief, or assistant chief, as the case may be, concurs in the conferee's recommendation, the case will be closed on that basis and the taxpayer will be so notified. If the recommendation is to issue a statutory notice or defend a case before the Tax Court, the supervisor must likewise agree.

Appellate supervisory officials will hold conferences with a taxpayer or his representative upon request if an agreement reached with a conferee is turned down by a supervisor as not acceptable.

Policy Regarding Settlement Offers and Counterproposals

If the taxpayer makes a proposal of settlement that the conferee does not consider acceptable, and yet it is apparent that the taxpayer is trying in good faith to reach an agreed disposition of the case on a fair basis, the conferee is expected to give his own evaluation to enable the taxpayer to understand clearly the kind of settlement the conferee would recommend for acceptance.

Theoretically, if the taxpayer's representative and the conferee each fully, frankly, and honestly presents his position and the basis for such position, each party should be aware of the basis on which the other will settle. However, if the negotiations are to culminate in a settlement, the position of each party should ordinarily be converted into a specific disposition of each issue. The conferee should encourage a prompt offer in settlement and should be prepared to make a counteroffer (where the taxpayer's offer is unacceptable) and proceed with the disposition of the case.

Settlement negotiations are not a bargaining process but one of evaluating what a court might decide in a case on the basis of provable facts, effective testimony, interpretation of the law and regulation, and precedent case law.

Settlement Philosophy

The majority of issues coming to Appellate cannot be resolved by set rules or precise settlement by mathematical computations. Correct tax liability as sought by Appellate means an amount (not necessarily a precise amount) that fairly and impartially reflects the merits of the case in light of the facts, law, IRS position, and hazards of litigation involved. Questions of judgment and opinion enter into most issues, and as to some of them reasonable and honest men may hold views that vary widely. Debatable issues, such as reasonable compensation for services, the value of unlisted stock, worthlessness of a debt, and dozens of similar questions, present areas for negotiated settlement. Doubts as to various issues are to be weighed and balanced against each other. In many cases mutual concessions must be made. Final result should be one that will reflect a fair overall disposition of the entire case. Such negotiations frequently involve some give and take on both sides. However, IRS says the conferee's approach should never be one of mere bargaining or trading, but rather an attitude reflecting reasonable appraisal of the merits of the issues by both parties. There must be an ability to see both sides of the questions presented and a willingness to adopt a judicial attitude seeking only an impartial solution.

The settlement approach in docketed cases is the same as in non-docketed cases. Taxpayers can expect the same evaluation of the case at either stage. Except for intervening developments that justify reevaluation, a proposal for settlement that is unacceptable in nondocketed status remains unacceptable when the case is docketed. After all, the taxpayer is still negotiating with the same conferée.

Litigating Hazards

Considering and giving effect to "litigating hazards" is one of the basically distinguishable features of Appellate settlement authority. What, then, do we mean by this term? Litigating hazards include all the factors that come into play creating uncertainties as to the outcome of trial.

When a new law or regulation has not been tested, there may be doubt as to legal interpretations and conclusions a court will reach. There can also be doubt as to the conclusions of fact that the court may make based upon testimony of witnesses and other evidence presented.

Application of a section of law may turn upon establishing facts through witnesses, third party records, and other evidence and testimony that may or may not be readily available or capable of being brought into the record. Credibility of prospective witnesses and the competency of expert witnesses who may reach widely differing conclusions are also factors to consider.

It is the responsibility of the appellate conferee to analyze all the various factors and facts of the case and, applying his experience, evaluate the probability of the outcome in presenting the merits of an issue to the court.

Nuisance Value Settlements

Nuisance value settlements are strictly prohibited by IRS. A nuisance value settlement is a token flat sum, or a percentage concession by either the government or the taxpayer, that is unrelated to the merits of the case and is made primarily to avoid the inconvenience of cost of trial. The amount involved is usually insignificant in absolute amount and in relation to the total amount in issue and is frequently equated with litigating costs, professional fees, or expense in further developing the case.

However, all minor concessions by the taxpayers or the government are not necessarily in the nuisance category. For instance, where each issue in the case is settled on its merits, the settlement does not fall in the nuisance category even if the concession is small, since the tax liability determined by this method is correct.

New Issues Raised by Appellate Division

Appellate conferees are instructed not to raise new issues casually, indiscriminately, promiscuously, or haphazardly, and never, under any circumstances, to raise or mention them for bargaining purposes.

A new issue in a nondocketed case is any possible adjustment to or change in the taxpayer's tax return or the district report of examination, or conference report, that is not in contest when the case is received by Appellate and is raised or discussed by either the conferee or the taxpayer.

A new issue in a docketed case is any possible adjustment to or change in an item affecting taxpayer's tax liability that is not included in the statutory notice of deficiency or included in the notice but not petitioned and is raised or discussed after the petition is filed.

As a matter of policy a previously agreed issue will not be reopened nor will a new issue be raised by an appellate conferee to the taxpayer's detriment unless grounds for such action are substantial (strong, possessing real merit) and the potential effect on tax liability is material (having real importance and great consequence).

Although strict criteria govern the raising of new issues, there will be circumstances when a new issue should be raised, such as change in the law, recent decision of courts, recent change in IRS position, clear error or omissions in prior handling of the case, newly discovered facts or evidence, and requirement for discussion of unusual or substantial items in cases reported to the Joint Committee on Internal Revenue Taxation.

In most instances minor errors that would increase the tax will not be corrected; however, corrections of errors will always be made if they are to the taxpayer's benefit. Restrictions on raising new issues apply as a matter of policy only to those raised by the government to the detriment of the taxpayer. The appellate conferee will always give full, fair, and impartial consideration to a new issue raised by the taxpayer himself and will give effect to any adjustment regardless of how material it might be if it is to the taxpayer's benefit.

Possible Requests for Technical Information

The Office of Assistant Commissioner (Technical) is in general responsible for the issuance of rulings and establishing the position of the IRS. However, a ruling will not be issued by that office to a taxpayer or a taxpayer's representative with respect to an issue in a case under consideration by an Appellate Branch Office.

The Appellate Branch Office has the duty and responsibility to make an independent and final determination in each case properly referred to it by a District Director or by the Director of International Operations, notwithstanding the prior action in the case. Accordingly, the Appellate Branch Office is not bound to follow published revenue rulings nor prior ruling or advice from the Office of the Assistant Commissioner (Technical) that is adverse to the taxpayer.

An appellate conferee is never precluded from exercising his own judgment respecting the merits of an issue. However, conferees occasionally do request technical information from the national office when they feel that in the interest of good administration such action is necessary before a final determination of the issue is made.

Binding Effect of the Form 870-AD

The Appellate Division has developed special types of agreements for use only in nondocketed cases where mutual concessions are made for settlement. The agreements are intended to reflect a degree of finality closely equivalent to that obtained by settlement of a docketed case by stipulation.

The form most commonly used is the Form 870-AD, Offer of Waiver of Restrictions on Assessment and Collection of Deficiency in Tax and Acceptance of Overassessment. This is designed for use in cases involving income, profits, or gift taxes. For estate tax cases settled upon the basis of mutual concession, Form 890-AD may be used. A form incorporating similar provisions for use in excise and employment tax cases is Form 2504-AD.

All of these forms become effective as a waiver of restrictions on the date of acceptance on behalf of the commissioner—not as of the date executed by the taxpayer. When so accepted, the form is considered as binding upon both parties and as accomplishing a final disposition of the case in the absence of fraud, malfeasance, concealment or misrepresentation of material facts, or an important mistake in mathematical calculation. Form 870-AD permits reopening of a case to correct excessive tentative allowances and for claims with respect to deductions for carrybacks, except where the carrybacks formed a part of a settlement in which finality was intended. When other unusual features are present in a case, the agreement form is modified and specific reservations or other conditions added to the form.

Form 870-AD is considered a mutually advantageous agreement. There is need, of course, to put an end to the argument—especially so when a debatable issue or issues are settled with both sides sharing in the give and take. When agreement is finally reached after mutual concession, the case should normally be considered forever closed as to those issues in the absence of such exceptions, as fraud, malfeasance, and the like. It is this finality that is intended through the use of the Form 870-AD.

When finality is not necessary or justified in view of lack of mutual concessions, as, for example, when a strictly factual issue is resolved, a regular Form 870 agreement is used in the same way as if the case were closed at the district level. Cases closed without finality may be reopened by a taxpayer by appropriate means, such as filing a timely claim for refund. However, Appellate will not initiate reopening of such a case unless the prior disposition involved fraud, malfeasance, concealment or misrepresentation of material facts, or an important mistake in mathematical calculation, or such other circumstances as would indicate that failure to take such action would be a serious administrative omission, and then only with the approval of the director of the Appellate Division.

Under certain unusual circumstances favorable to the taxpayer, such as retroactive legislation, a case closed with an 870-AD by the Appellate Division on the basis of mutual concessions may be reopened upon written application from the taxpayer, subject, however, to the approval of the director of Appellate.

Trial Status Order

Early consideration and disposition of docketed cases is the purpose and reason for Revenue Procedure 60-18 (1960-2 C.B. 988). Under this procedure, The Tax Court issues a Trial Status Order to petitioner's counsel and regional counsel approximately six months before a proposed Tax Court calendar. The Order requires both the petitioner and respondent to report, about three months before the calendar date, the status of such docketed cases. After review of these reports, the Tax Court issues a Trial Calendar.

The time between issuance of the Trial Status Order and the originally scheduled date of issuance of the calendar is referred to as the "T.S.O." period. It is the intent of Revenue Procedure 60-18 that all settlement negotiations be completed during this period. At the conclusion of this three-month period, all unsettled cases appearing on the T.S.O. are ordinarily returned by Appellate to regional counsel for preparation for trial.

During the three-month period before the date selected for the Trial Calendar, regional counsel's attorneys hold stipulation-of-facts conferences and otherwise prepare for trial. Further settlement conferences are not held during this period unless the petitioner submits a new proposal of settlement substantially equal to the IRS evaluation, new material evidence is developed, or there has been a change in the precedent case law. (Adapted from an informal procedure release issued by the Arizona District, IRS, and the Arizona Society of CPA's.)

TAX COURT OF THE UNITED STATES
WASHINGTON, D.C.

Outline of Procedure for the Handling of
Small Tax Cases (Effective January 1, 1969)

Definition. Any case filed with the court involving a tax deficiency in the aggregate amount of $1,000 or less for all years (exclusive of additions to tax) will be placed in the small tax case category.

Identification. These cases will be assigned a small tax case docket number in which the identifying element will be the letters "SC" at the end of such number.

Petition Form. A simple printed form petition with instructions for completing and filing the petition with the Court will be supplied to taxpayers upon request to the Clerk of the Court. The forms and instructions may be obtained at the Clerk's Office, Room 2415, 1111 Constitution Avenue, N.W., Washington, D.C., or by mail upon request addressed to the Clerk of the Court, Tax Court of the United States, Box 70, Washington, D.C. 20044.

Imperfect Petitions. Where the taxpayer has not made use of the printed form petition and he files with the court a defective petition, the

Clerk of the Court will so advise him in writing and supply him with a set of the form petitions to be completed and filed as a proper amended petition. Failure to file such an amended petition and to pay the filing fee within a reasonable time (30 days) may result in dismissal of the case by the Court for failure to prosecute.

Service and Pleadings. After the Court has a properly petitioned small tax case docketed, service of a copy of the petition will be made in the usual way upon counsel for the Commissioner of Internal Revenue (respondent). At the same time a printed form of notice will be sent to petitioner and to respondent stating that the petition has been docketed as a small tax case petition and describing briefly the small tax case procedure. It is expected that respondent will confine his motions against small tax case petitions to jurisdictional questions and that he will find it possible in these cases to file his answer in less than the 60 days allowed under the Court's general rules.

Upon the filing of the answer, the case will be treated as fully at issue, with no reply being required of petitioner (who may, of course, file a reply if he so desires). All affirmative allegations in the answer will be deemed denied.

Removal From Small Tax Case Category. After notice to the parties that a case has been designated by the Court as a small tax case, should either party desire to remove the case from the small tax case category and have it put in the regular category of Tax Court cases, he may file a motion for that purpose, setting forth his reasons. If the parties join in such a motion, or if it be endorsed "No Objection" by the party other than the movant, the Court will normally grant the motion, the "SC" identification will be deleted from the docket number, and the case will thereafter follow the usual and regular procedures in Tax Court cases. Any unilateral, nonagreed motions will be considered and acted upon by the Court in its discretion, with or without hearing.

Trial Calendar Assignment. No trial status order will be issued in a small tax case. When a small tax case is at issue, it will be placed on the next trial calendar regularly or specially scheduled for the city designated for trial which will permit reasonable notice to the parties. During the year 1969, the Court plans to schedule special sessions for small tax cases in each of the Fall, Winter, and Spring Terms in New York, Chicago, Los Angeles, and Washington, D.C. In cities where the Court normally conducts its regular session with less frequency than it does in the larger cities, if there should appear a need to hear small tax cases sooner, the Court may schedule a session to be conducted by a Judge who would be in a relatively nearby city conducting another session.

Informal Trial Procedure. At the trial of small tax cases, particularly where the taxpayer is not represented by counsel, the Court will conduct the hearing as informally as may be permitted by law. A transcript of the testimony and trial proceedings will be made. Where feasible, the trial Judge will dispense entirely with the requirement for filing briefs, or he may request only the filing of informal memorandum briefs. In the event that briefs or memorandum briefs are to be filed, the trial Judge ordinarily will require that such briefs be submitted within a relatively short period of time, so that the case may de decided promptly. The Court will make every effort to decide these cases as promptly as possible in accordance with present requirements of law.

Legal Aid. Taxpayers in these cases frequently lack counsel or competent legal advice. The Court will encourage local bar associations to develop arrangements with legal aid groups to make available several tax lawyers for consultation with *pro se* taxpayers, should such assistance or advice be desired.

Procedure Subject to Change. This procedure may be changed or suspended by the Court at any time it becomes apparent to the Court that it is unnecessary, undesirable, unworkable, or for other reasons determined by the Court.

Instructions to Taxpayers for Preparing the Tax Court Form Petition in Small Tax Cases

The form petition is made available by this Court for the optional use of the taxpayer-petitioner. If the form does not adequately serve the taxpayer's use, he should draw up his own petition; it is recommended that he follow the general format of the petition. The petition need not be limited to only the two pages of the form, but be sure that the last page of the petition contains the required verification.

If the notice of deficiency from the Commissioner of Internal Revenue has been addressed to both husband and wife, and if both want to join in filing a petition based on the notice of deficiency, then the names of both should be placed in the blank space at the top of the petition form.

Both husband and wife are not required to join in a single petition. Each may file his or her separate petition. However, where one spouse does not join in or file a separate petition within the 90-day period, immediate assessment may be made against that spouse by the Commissioner.

1. Under the first numbered paragraph of the petition there should be shown the date of the notice of deficiency which was received from the Commissioner of Internal Revenue. A copy of the notice of deficiency should be attached to the original and each copy of the petition; photocopies may be used.

2. The second numbered paragraph of the petition should show the address of the office of the Director of Internal Revenue where the tax return for the period involved was filed.

3. Under the procedures prescribed for the classification and processing of petitions as "small tax cases," the tax deficiency in dispute may not total more than $1,000 for all years, exclusive of additions to tax. This limitation, however, should not be interpreted as prohibiting a taxpayer from filing his petition under the "small tax case" procedure just because the notice of deficiency asserts a total tax deficiency greater than $1,000, unless the taxpayer wishes to contest more than $1,000, in which event the "small tax case" procedure cannot be used. If the tax deficiency in dispute is $1,000 or less, the petition will be filed under the "small tax case" procedure. It is important to remember that any addition to tax, such as penalties, need not be considered in determining whether the tax deficiency in dispute comes within the $1,000 limitation.

4. In the paragraph numbered 4, where the assignments of error are made, petitioner is required to make only simple, short, direct statements regarding those adjustments to his taxable income made by the Commissioner of Internal Revenue in the notice of deficiency which

petitioner deems to be wrong. A petitioner may agree that some of the adjustments are correct, and, if so, no mention need be made of those adjustments in the petition. Where an adjustment is thought to be in error, the assignment of error may be stated in terms such as the following:

    a. The Commissioner erred in disallowing a dependency deduction.

    b. The Commissioner erred in disallowing as a deduction charitable contributions in the amount of $_____.

You will note that the form petition provides for only three assignments of error (a, b, and c). This is not intended to limit a petitioner but rather to serve as a guide from which the petition may be prepared. If other errors are to be assigned, they should be identified in the same manner, such as d, e, f, g, etc. In like manner, this same identification should follow under paragraph 5.

5. In the paragraph numbered 5, the facts upon which the petitioner relies to sustain his assignments of error should be set forth briefly. For example, a statement of facts might read somewhat as follows:

    a. Petitioner's son is 15 years of age. During the taxable year he resided with petitioner's former wife. Petitioner provided over one-half of his son's support.

The petition must be signed by both husband and wife if both are joining in filing the petition, and the verification of their petition must be accomplished by both before an official authorized to administer oaths. A notary public is such an official.

If the petitioner is represented by an attorney, the attorney may sign the petition in lieu of him; however, the petitioner (or petitioners) must sign the verification under oath. Under the Court's Rules, petitioner's counsel may not also serve to administer the oath required for the verification by petition.

An original and four copies of the petition are required to be filed with the Court. A filing fee of $10.00 is required to be sent with the petition. Checks or money orders should be made payable to the order of the Treasurer of the United States. The petition should be sent to the Tax Court of the United States, P. O. Box 70, Washington, D.C. 20044.

To be certain that your petition will be timely filed, take it to a post office and have the envelopes in which it is mailed, properly addressed as above, stamped with a postmark in which the date is legible. The postmark might be critically important in establishing timely filing within the 90-day period.

NOTE: Federal law requires that the petition must be filed within 90 days after the notice of deficiency is mailed. This means that the petition must either be received by the Court in Washington within the 90-day period, or the envelope in which it is mailed to the Court must bear a clearly legible postmark bearing a date not more than 90 days after the date the notice of deficiency was mailed. This requirement is jurisdictional and the Court has no authority to extend that time.

APPENDIX C

TAX COURT OF THE UNITED STATES

WASHINGTON

Petitioner(s),	)))
v.	) Docket No.
COMMISSIONER OF INTERNAL REVENUE,	))
Respondent.	)

PETITION

1. Petitioner(s) request(s) the Court to redetermine the tax deficiency(ies) for the year(s) _____, asserted in the notice from the Commissioner of Internal Revenue dated _____, copy of which is attached.

2. Petitioner(s) tax return(s) for the year(s) here involved was (were) filed with the Director of Internal Revenue, _____ (city and

_____.

state)

3. Petitioner(s) dispute(s) $_____ of the asserted tax deficiency(ies).

4. The Commissioner made the following errors in asserting this (these) tax deficiency(ies):

a. _____
_____
_____.

b. _____
_____
_____.

c. _____
_____
_____.

5. Petitioner(s) assert(s) the following facts to support the assignment(s) of error(s) set out in paragraph 4:

a. _____

_____

_____.

b. _____

_____

_____.

c. _____

_____

_____.

_____
Signature of Petitioner (Husband)   Present Address

_____
Signature of Petitioner (Wife)   Present Address

_____
Signature and address of counsel, if retained by petitioner(s)

VERIFICATION

State of _____ County of _____

_____ being duly sworn, say(s) that he (they) is (are) the petitioner(s) in this case; that he (they) has (have) read the petition, or had the same read to him (them), and is (are) familiar with the statements contained herein, and that those statements are true.

_____
Petitioner (Husband)

_____
Petitioner (Wife)

Subscribed and sworn to before me this _____ day of _____, 19__.

(Seal)

_____
Notary (or other official)

Index

Index